Business Object Design and Implementation III

OOPSLA'99 Workshop Proceedings

Springer
London
Berlin
Heidelberg
New York
Barcelona
Hong Kong
Milan
Paris
Santa Clara
Singapore
Tokyo

D. Patel, J. Sutherland and J. Miller (Eds)

Business Object Design and Implementation III

OOPSLA '99 Workshop Proceedings
2 November 1999, Denver, Colorado, USA

Springer

D. Patel
School of Computing, Information Systems and Mathematics, South Bank University, 103 Borough Road, London SE1 0AA

J. Sutherland
IDX Systems Corporation, 116 Huntingdon Avenue, Boston MA 02116, USA

J. Miller
Electronic Data Systems, 5500 Wayzata Blvd., Ste 200, Golden Valley MN 55416, USA

ISBN 1-85233-217-4 Springer-Verlag London Berlin Heidelberg

British Library Cataloguing in Publication Data
Business object design and implementation III : OOPSLA 99
Workshop proceedings
1.Business - Computer programme - Congresses
2.Object-oriented databases - Congresses 3.Object-oriented programming (Computer science) - Congresses
I.Patel, D. (Dilip), 1957- II.Sutherland, Jeffrey V.
III.Miller, J. (Joaquin)
658'05'511
ISBN 1852332174

Library of Congress Cataloging-in-Publication Data
A catalog record for this book is available from the Library of Congress

Printed in Great Britain

Typesetting: Camera ready by contributors
Printed and bound by the Athenæum press ltd., Gateshead, Tyne & Wear
34/3830-543210 Printed on acid-free paper SPIN 10744193

Preface

The NCITS Accredited Standards Committee H7 Object Information Management, now part of NCITS T3 Open Distributed Processing, and the Object Management Group Business Object Domain Task Force (BODTF) jointly sponsored the Fifth Annual OOPSLA Workshop on Business Object Component Design and Implementation.

The focus of the workshop was on design and implementation of business object component frameworks and architectures. Key aspects discussed included:

- What is a comprehensive definition of a business object component?
- Are the four layers (user, workspace, enterprise, resource) presented at the OOPSLA'98 workshop the right way to layer a business object component system?
- How is a business object component implemented across these layers? What are the associated artefacts? Are there different object models representing the same business object component in different layers?
- What are the dependencies between business object components? How can they be plug and play given these dependencies? How can they be flexible and adaptive? How do they participate in workflow systems?
- How will the emergence of a web-based distributed object-computing infrastructure based on XML, influence business object component architectures? In particular, is the W3C WebBroker proposal appropriate for distributed business object component computing?

The aim of the workshop was to:

- Enhance the pattern literature on the specification, design, and implementation of interoperable, plug and play, distributed business object components.
- Clarify the design and implementation of component based systems, including systems in which workflow patterns and the REA accounting model are basic building blocks for production business systems.
- Contribute to emerging architectures for Intranet/Internet/Extranet applications, particularly those applications that integrate business object components, object and relational databases, and XML.
- Pursue issues developed in previous years workshop stimulated by papers on heterogeneous distributed workflow systems. Specify business object component solutions to mobile agents, process engines, and systems that exhibit emergent behaviour. Cross-fertilise business object design concepts with experience from the field of complex adaptive systems.
- Provide explicit experience reports on business object component systems developed and in production.

The papers included in this proceedings address some of the above issues and the workshop provides a forum for practitioners, researchers and academics to share and explore developments in this area.

Contents

An Interoperability Approach for CCISs based on Business Objects and WorkFlows

Zakaria Maamar

Interoperability Research Group
Information System Technology Section
Defence Research Establishment Valcartier
2459 Pie-XI Blvd North, Val-Bélair QC, G3J 1X5, Canada
zakaria.maamar@drev.dnd.ca

Abstract. *The paper introduces the concepts of Business Objects (BOs) and WorkFlow (WFs) for the design and development of interoperable environments. Interoperability is a process that allows cooperative interactions between several systems. These systems are distributed across networks and present incompatibilities at different levels (material, software, and terminology). Our research is applied to the IC2IS project that aims at developing an interoperable environment for Command & Control Information Systems (CCISs). The use of a single CCIS seems "easy". However, the operation becomes much complex when several CCISs, generally distributed and heterogeneous, are required. Therefore, we intend to set up BOs to support the interoperability of these CCISs. Moreover, given the complexity of managing such CCISs, we suggest specifying the operating mode of these BOs, using WFs.*

Keywords. *Interoperability, Business Objects, WorkFlows, CCIS.*

1 Introduction

The rapid development of information and communication technologies results in the availability of several types of systems that are usually used *independently* and operated in *isolation* from each other. Integrating distributed and heterogeneous systems in order to answer users' needs is a complex operation. Therefore, it becomes urgent to propose an interoperable environment that will free users from these constraints. Interoperability is a process that allows cooperative interactions between several systems.

The main motivation behind the development of an interoperable environment for distributed and heterogeneous systems is to facilitate the exchange of information and services. However, there exist only few design approaches that orient designers in the development of such an environment. Furthermore, it becomes urgent to assist users in satisfying their needs. Currently, a user has to locate adequate systems, adapt his behavior to their interfaces, and finally, understand their functional and structural characteristics. In this paper, as a possible solution, we suggest to involve several specialized components, called Business *Objects* (BOs) [Eeles and Sims, 1998], that will perform these operations on users' behalf. Moreover, given the complexity of managing distributed and heterogeneous systems, we suggest to specify the operating mode of these BOs, using *WorkFlows* (WFs) [Georgakopoulos et al., 1995]. WFs have the following broad advantages: streamlining processes, improving coordination across an organization, eliminating unnecessary and redundant work, and minimizing delays in the retrieval of information.

Our research on BOs and WFs is applied to the IC2IS (IC2IS stands for *Interoperable Command & Control Information Systems*) project, in which we aim at developing an interoperable environment for *Command & Control Information Systems* (CCISs). CCISs are the skeleton of many military computer systems. For instance, a CCIS can be used for gathering information, processing this information with some criterion, and producing the necessary actions to be taken directly by the CCIS or by the commander. A CCIS is based on three components [Malerud et al.]: a *structure*, *tasks*, and *functions*. The CCIS structure represents an assembly of facilities, arranged to meet the CCIS's objectives. To reach these objectives, the CCIS's functions are initiated in order to carry out the needed tasks. These tasks require the facilities of the structure, for instance the technical equipment and computing time. While the exploitation of only one CCIS seems obvious, it is a very complex operation to work concurrently with several CCISs in order to satisfy a user's needs. Therefore, the objective of the IC2IS environment is to provide users with services that will free them from worrying about the characteristics of the interconnected CCISs.

Motivating Example

The Canadian Armed Forces (CAF) are being called upon increasingly to ensure a safe environment for the protection of refugees, to deliver food and medical supplies, and to provide essential services in countries where civil society has collapsed. Such operations constitute a *humanitarian* scenario for the CAF that have to cooperate with non-government organizations as well as with armed forces of other countries. Each participant in such a scenario has its own systems and uses its own standards. This raises the need for an interoperable environment.

The paper is organized as follows. Section presents an overview of the IC2IS project. Section 2 proposes guidelines to deal with interoperability issues. Section 3 describes the architectural and functional characteristics of the IC2IS environment. Finally, Section summarizes the main points brought out by our study.

2 Guidelines for Interoperability Issues

In order to develop an interoperable environment, we have to deal with the following issues: users' needs, distribution, and information disparity. In the IC2IS project, we considered the following research domains to overcome these issues.

1. Business Objects for users' needs issue: a BO "*is the representation of a thing active in the business domain, including at least its business name and definition, attributes, behavior, relationships, and constraints*" (The Object Management Group, Business Object Management Special Interest Group). According to the Business Object Management Architecture (BOMA) [BOMA], a BO describes and models something that belongs to an organization and hence, has a meaning in the business world. Using BOs allow managers and users to understand each other, by using familiar concepts and creating a common model for interactions.
2. WorkFlows for users' needs issue: a WF is "*the automation of a business process, in whole or part, during which documents, information or tasks are passed from one participant to another for action, according to a set of procedural rules*" (The Workflow Management Coalition). WFs are used in coordinating and streamlining business processes and hence, identifying "who is responsible of doing what". To handle these operations, WorkFlow Management Systems (WFMSs) allow to design WFs, to manage their instantiation and controlled execution, and to define the integration of distributed and heterogeneous

applications within these WFs. BOs are part of WFs; they carry out their business processes [Baker, 1996].

3. *Distributed Object Computing for distribution issue*: in the OMG's perspective, objects can be distributed across a network and hence, collaborate together to perform common operations. In that context, we can rely on OMG's *Common Object Request Broker Architecture* (CORBA) protocol [Watson, 1996]. OMG's objective is to allow applications to use distributed objects and invoke their services without any consideration to these objects' location in the network. In order to associate distributed objects to common operations, *enchainment suites* for the description of these operations are defined [Orfali et al., 1996]. *Enchainment suites can be thought as WFs.*
4. *Mobile code for distribution issue*: with the increasing use of communication means, the mobile code technology has attracted a lot of attention for its flexibility and efficiency [Chess et al., 1994]. This technology is considered as a new alternative to the traditional client-server mode. A mobile code can efficiently access the needed resources, since it moves to their network location rather than transforming remotely multiple requests and responses, sometimes across a low-bandwidth connection.
5. *Ontology for information disparity issue*: to ensure the interoperability across systems, we must resolve potential *knowledge disparities* that might occur between these systems. Indeed, each system is part of an organization that has its own standards. To enable these systems to interoperate efficiently, an ontology must be built in order to harmonize the terminology used in the representation of the exchanged knowledge [Jones et al., 1998].

To illustrate the several concepts discussed above, i.e. BOs, WFs, Distributed Object Computing, Mobility, and Ontology, we describe their use in the particular case of the IC2IS environment.

3 Presentation of the IC2IS Environment

In the following sub-sections, we describe the IC2IS environment in terms of architecture, types of BOs, operating-mode, and ontology.

3.1 IC2IS's Architecture

Before elaborating the IC2IS architecture, several elements have been considered. For instance, *maintain* the autonomy and independence of the different CCISs; *reduce* the informational disparities of the interconnected CCISs; *evaluate* the communication channels performance, particularly in low-bandwidth situations; and *help* users satisfy their needs without worrying about the individual characteristics of the different CCISs. Based on these considerations, we propose architecture for the IC2IS environment (Figure 1).

At the basis of the IC2IS architecture, three types of BOs are required: a *BO-CCIS* to identify a CCIS, a *BO-User* to identify a user, and a *BO-Supervisor* to monitor the interactions that occur between BO-CCISs and BO-Users. In the IC2IS environment, BO-CCISs and BO-Users have the capacity to involve dynamically several BOs during the performance of their operations, whenever required.

Three modules constitute the backbone of the IC2IS architecture. The first module, called *services provider*, contains CCISs with their corresponding BO-CCISs. The second module, called *services consumer*, contains users with their corresponding BO-Users[1]. Finally, the third module, called *meeting infrastructure*, allows BO-Users and BO-CCISs to meet and collaborate in a common workplace. The BO-Supervisor manages the meeting infrastructure. In this infrastructure, BO-CCISs and BO-Users have respectively *capabilities to advertise* and *needs to satisfy*.

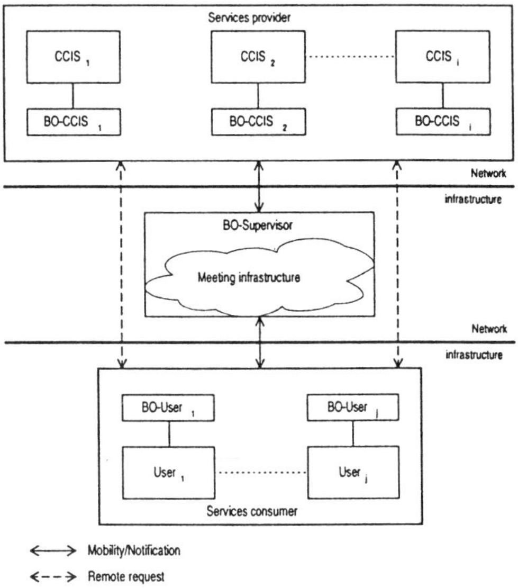

Figure 1 Architecture of the IC2IS environment

In Figure 1, several types of interactions occur between the IC2IS environment's components. BO-CCISs and BO-Users may interact *locally*[2] in the meeting infrastructure, or *remotely* using traditional communication mechanisms (e.g. Remote Procedure Calling or Messaging). BO-CCISs and BO-Users also interact with the BO-Supervisor before entering the meeting infrastructure. To enter this infrastructure, BO-CCISs and BO-Users have to migrate.

3.2 IC2IS's BOs

As stated in [Herzum and Sims, 1998], a business component starts as a single concept that maps directly to the business domain and emerges at the end as a set of software components that evolves as the business changes. Based on these statements and the requirements of the IC2IS environment, three types of BOs exist: BO-CCIS, BO-User, and BO-Supervisor. In what follows, we detail the BO-CCIS, in terms of responsibilities, reference model, and life cycle, and describe briefly the other types of BOs.

A BO-CCIS acts on the behalf of a CCIS in order to maintain its *autonomy* and *independence* towards the IC2IS environment (Figure 2). To achieve this operation, the BO-CCIS

[1] Services provider and services consumer modules provide parallels with some aspects of a large-decentralized organization.

[2] BO-CCISs and BO-Users can also interact locally, but in the services provider module. Therefore, BO-CCISs migrate to this module and meet BO-Users.

encapsulates its CCIS and advertises, through its *services* (a service corresponds to a problem solving activity that involves one or several functions of a CCIS), the *functions* its CCIS performs. In the IC2IS environment, a BO-CCIS has the ability to *create an agent*[3] and *send* this agent to the meeting infrastructure, i.e. mobility operation. Moreover, a BO-CCIS is characterized by a *business card* that is used once the agent of this BO-CCIS negotiates with other BO-Users' agents in the meeting infrastructure. The BO-CCIS's business card contains the following elements: an identifier, contact information, a list of offered services, and a security level to access the meeting infrastructure.

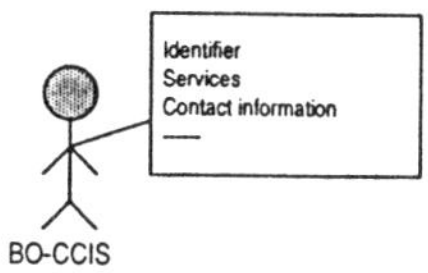

Figure 2 Overview of a BO-CCIS

The BO-CCIS reference model contains four components that are[4] encapsulated in a *communication* layer (Figure 3): *Design of Services*, *Execution of Services*, *Monitoring*, and *Mobility*.

1. The Design of Services Component is used in the description of the operations that are needed to achieve a service. The execution chronology of these operations as well as their required resources are also part of this description. The resources correspond to the CCISs' functions. Each service that is designed by the administrator of the IC2IS environment is saved in a *Bank of Services*. Moreover, this service is specified using the concepts of the *CCIS-oriented Ontology* (cf. Section 3.4).

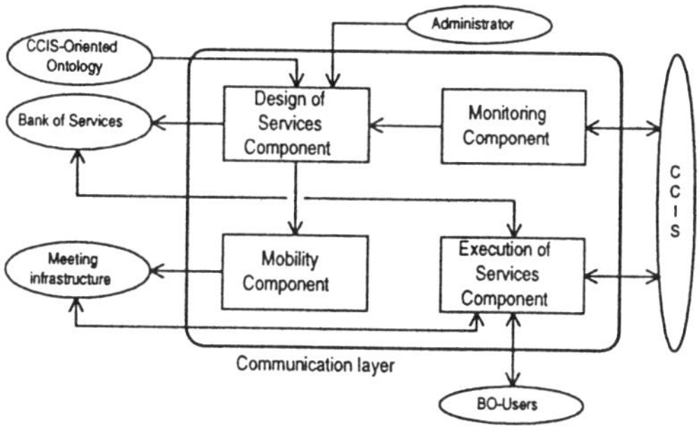

Figure 3 BO-CCIS reference model

2. The Execution of Services Component is used in the realization of a service that is obtained from the Bank of Services. To reach this objective, the Execution of Services component invokes the CCIS's functions.
3. The Monitoring Component is used in the detection of the modifications that occur at the CCIS level, for example by adding a new function. The purpose of the monitoring is to notify the Design of Services component about these modifications and hence, to adapt the services that exist in the Bank of Services. Moreover, the agent of the BO-CCIS that

[3] An agent acts for a BO in the meeting infrastructure.
[4] The proposed components of the BOs can be mapped to the four layers, i.e. user, workspace, enterprise, and resource, that constitute the structural model of a business component, as defined in [Herzum and Sims, 1998].

evolves in the meeting infrastructure, has to be notified about these modifications, through the Mobility component.

4. The Mobility Component is used in the creation of the BO-CCIS agent and the migration of this agent to the meeting infrastructure. The agent of a BO-CCIS has two components: *identification* to access the meeting infrastructure and *negotiation* to collaborate with other BO-Users' agents.

In the IC2IS environment, the behavior of a BO is defined by a *life cycle*. Four concepts are used in a life cycle: step, passing to another step, operations[5] of a step, and interactions between steps. Figure 4 illustrates the BO-CCIS life cycle. It consists of three steps: *Setting-up*, *Operating*, and *Monitoring*. The purpose of the setting-up step is to create and enhance the BO-CCIS with appropriate mechanisms. These mechanisms allow the BO-CCIS to understand the capabilities of its CCIS and to define the services this BO-CCIS will offer. The purpose of the operating step is to create an agent of the BO-CCIS and to perform the offered services of this BO-CCIS. Finally, the purpose of the monitoring step is to detect the updates that may occur at the CCIS level. When two distributed BOs interact, i.e. BO-CCISs and BO-Users, it is, in fact, the operations of their BOs life- cycles that exchange messages through a communication middleware, like CORBA.

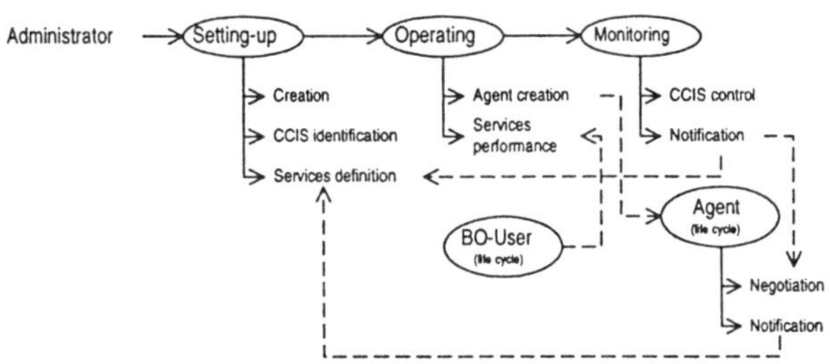

Figure 4 BO-CCIS life cycle

A BO-User acts on the behalf of its user (Figure 5). In fact, it satisfies the users' *needs* using BO-CCISs' *services*. A BO-User has the ability to *create an agent*, *send* it to the meeting infrastructure, i.e. mobility operation, and *build* realization *scenarios* for users' needs. In the IC2IS environment, scenarios are called WFs. Furthermore, a BO-User manages a *profile* on its user that contains his needs and interests. A BO-User is also characterized by a *business card*. For a sake of simplicity, the BO-User's business-card integrates the user profile and contains the following elements: an identifier, contact information, user's needs and interests, an authorization level, and a security level to access the meeting infrastructure.

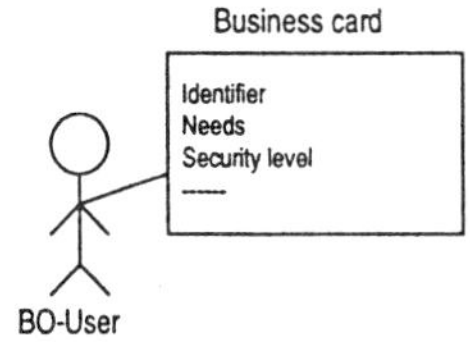

Figure 5 Overview of a BO-User

[5] In the life cycle of a BO, the operations that constitute a step are the methods to *implement* by a programming language. Therefore, the life cycle can be used as a specification means for the implementation level.

A BO-Supervisor *manages* the meeting infrastructure, *sets up* a security policy to monitor the access of BO-CCIS's and BO-User's agents to this infrastructure, and *installs* BO-CCIS's and BO-User's agents, to resume their operations, as soon as they arrive to this infrastructure.

3.3 IC2IS's Operating Mode

Based on the structural characteristics of the IC2IS environment (cf. Section 3.1), we defined five stages for the operating mode of this architecture: *initialization*, *meeting*, *post-meeting*, *operating*, and *maintenance* (Figure 6). Each stage can be considered as a *use-case* that provides results to the external world as well as to other stages. In what follows, we detail the IC2IS's stages according to the operations to perform.

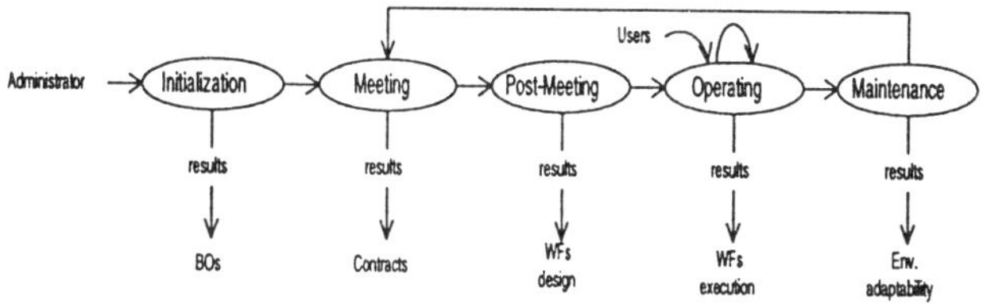

Figure 6 Stages of the IC2IS environment operating-mode

Initialization Stage

The Initialization stage consists of the following operations:

- BO-CCISs are associated to their CCISs. The purpose of this operation is to understand the functional and structural characteristics of the CCISs and to constitute the services provider module.
- BO-Users are associated to their users. The purpose of this operation is to build the users' profile and to constitute the services consumer module.
- The BO-Supervisor initializes the meeting infrastructure and initiates the *security policy*.

Before entering the next stage, i.e~meeting, BO-CCISs and BO-Users create agents and transfer them to the meeting infrastructure (Figure 7.a).

Meeting Stage

Once BO-CCIS's and BO-User's agents arrive to the meeting infrastructure (Figure 7.b), they are checked and installed by the BO-Supervisor. Next, the agents resume their operations and exchange information according to their capabilities and needs. BO-CCIS's agents offer their business cards to BO-User's agents. And, based on their users' profile, BO-User's agents pick-up the pertinent cards and establish *collaboration agreements* with BO-CCIS's agents[6]. Agreements result in the definition of *contracts*. Each agent of a BO-CCIS has to ensure that its BO-CCIS has sufficient capacity to provide a service before this agent commits itself to

[6] Other coordination strategies exist, particularly in the Distributed Artificial Intelligence (DAI) field. For instance, the *Contract Net* strategy where several components, known by agents, have the capacity to coordinate their activities, through *contracts*, to perform specific operations [Davis and Smith, 1983]. One of these components, acting as a *manager*, advertises a contract to the other components. These components receive and evaluate the advertisement, and those with appropriate resources, workload, and capabilities reply to the manager with *bids* that indicate their ability to perform the advertised contract. The manager evaluates the bids it has received and awards the contract to the component, called *contractor*, that returned the winning bid. Finally, manager and contractor interact during the contract performance.

providing that service to an agent of a BO-User. At the end of the meeting, BO-CCIS's and BO-User's agents notify their respective BOs about the agreed contracts (Figure 7.c).

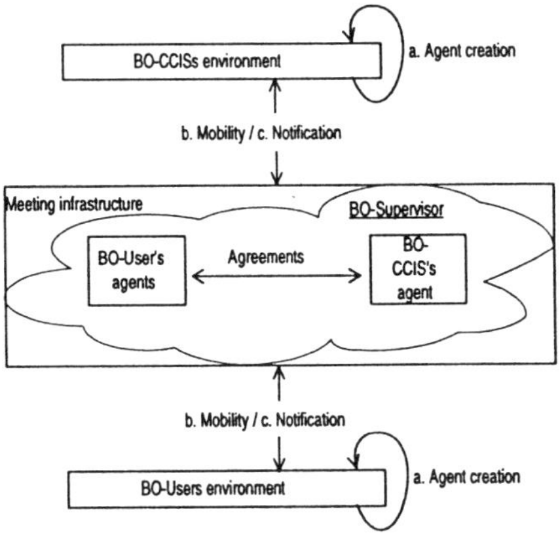

Figure 7 BO-CCIS's and BO-User's agents at the meeting infrastructure

Although the meeting operation between the agents of the BO-CCISs and BO-Users seems obvious, it is, in fact, complex. These agents have different origins and may not understand each other (cf. Section 3.4). This complexity raises the need to define a means, for instance a common language, to describe the several BOs' capabilities and needs in a standard manner.

Post-Meeting Stage

Using the contracts that are signed between BO-CCISs and BO-Users, a BO-User designs the WFs that are required to satisfy its user's needs. WFs require BO-CCISs' services that are advertized in these BO-CCISs' business card. To define a WF in the IC2IS environment, the following statements are made:

- A BO-User involves different objects in the performance of its operations, whenever required. Therefore, *BO-Realizations*[7] are requested by the BO-User from a *factory* of BO-Realizations (Figure 8). BO-Realizations evolve under the supervision of BO-Users.
- A BO-User generates WFs using the following concepts: *goals*, *processes*, *resources*, and *organization* [BOMA].
  - Goals are the objectives of a BO-User that acts on the behalf of its user.
  - Processes represent the activities to perform by a BO-User. Processes are delegated to the BO-Realizations.
  - Resources represent the CCISs' functions that are available through the BO-CCIS's services.
  - An organization represents the facility structure and its use policy.
- A BO-Realization corresponds to each a WF process. It is possible that all of the processes could be associated to a single BO-Realization. However, each process is assigned to a different BO-Realization in order to take advantage of the benefits of distributed problem solving.
- The BO-Realizations interact together according to the *dependence constraints* that exist between processes and their activities

---

[7] A BO-Realization is another type of a BO that is introduced in order to meet the requirements of the IC2IS environment.

In the IC2IS environment, a BO-User designs a WF using the goal decomposition approach [Moulin and Brassard, 1996]. Each WF is associated to a *global goal* that is decomposed into a set of sub-goals, until each sub-goal is defined by a process (Figure 8). Decomposition allows the nesting of goals with goals. The BO-User assigns each process to a BO-Realization that collaborates remotely with one or several BO-CCISs to perform this process. A process defines the sequence of primary activities to be executed as well as their precedence constraints. Moreover, each activity produces outputs, which will be used as inputs by other activities. Therefore, activities have to be executed in controlled and ordered way.

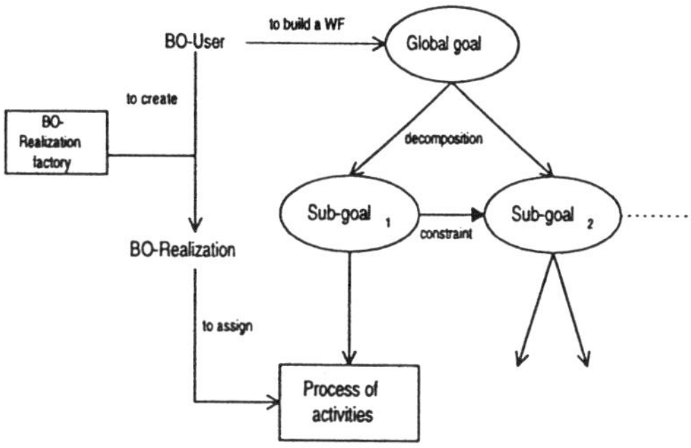

Figure 8 Process generation approach

Operating Stage

Once the several WFs have been defined by the BO-User in terms of goals, processes, resources, and organizations, the user invokes the WFs whenever required. When a WF is initiated, the BO-User manages the execution of this WF's processes by delegating their logical execution to the BO-Realizations and ensuring that each BO-Realization performs in a timely and efficient way within the constraints of the agreed contracts. A logical execution, is a knowledge about WF processes, WF activities, WFs participants, as well as their relationships, that is used to make appropriate decisions about routing, triggering, and monitoring work. Figure 9 summarizes the process performance approach. To achieve a process, a BO-Realization interacts remotely with the BO-CCISs. During the process performance, the BO-User may interact with the user by displaying results or asking for details requested by BO-Realizations.

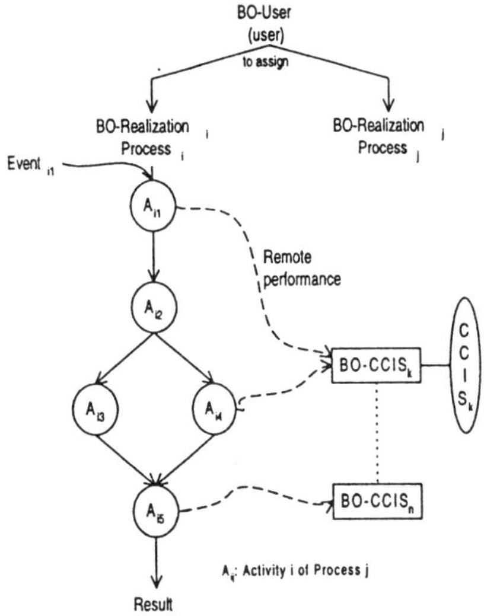

Figure 9 Process performance approach

In the current performance approach (Figure 9), different BO-Realizations interact remotely with different BO-CCISs. Another alternative that we are working on is to *enhance* BO-Realizations with mobility mechanisms. Each process of activities is supported by a BO-Realization that migrates to the CCISs in order to meet their BO-CCISs [Cai et al., 1996]. While travelling, a BO-Realization carries process-specific code and data. BO-Realizations can also run in parallel, increasing the performance of the IC2IS environment.

Figure 10 illustrates an example of a mobile BO-Realization. Numbers in this figure indicate the chronology order of operations processing. The logical execution of Process-1 mentions that Activity-11 requires the functions of CCIS-1, Activity-12 requires the functions of CCIS-3, and finally, Activity-13 requires the functions of CCIS-2. Once BO-Realization-1 has received this logical execution, it moves to CCIS-1 (1) and interacts with its corresponding BO-CCIS to perform Activity-11 (2). Next, it moves to CCIS-3 (3) in order to perform Activity-12 (4). Finally, it moves to CCIS-2 (5) in order to perform Activity-13 (6).

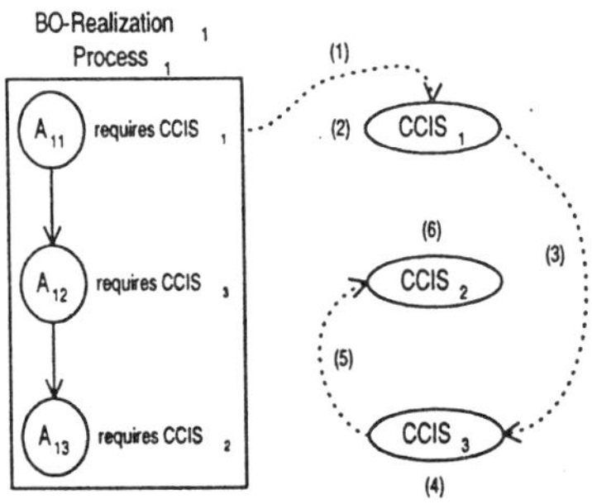

Figure 10 Example of a mobile BO-Realization

We believe that the mobility approach suits the situations that are characterized by low-bandwidth communication-channels. Therefore, instead of interacting remotely, and hence overloading the network, a BO-Realization migrates to the CCIS and performs its operations locally. The mobility approach is interesting, but several aspects have to be taken into account, such as the security issue and the definition of a route that optimizes the moves of an object.

Maintenance Stage

The IC2IS environment is an *open* system. Indeed, the IC2IS environment can register a new CCIS, a CCIS can leave the IC2IS environment,~etc. Therefore, the purpose of the maintenance stage is to consider the situations that have an impact on the architecture of the IC2IS environment as well as its operating mode. Four situations have been enumerated. In this paper, we briefly present two of them.

- It happens that a CCIS adapts its structural or functional characteristics, for example by adding a new function to its capabilities. Therefore, the BO-CCIS of this CCIS has to be informed in order to update its list of services. Moreover, this BO-CCIS has to inform its agent about the modifications. As a result, the different contracts that have been signed and the WFs that have been designed may have to be reviewed.
- It happens that a BO-User is no longer interested in a certain service of a certain BO-CCIS. Therefore, this BO-User has to inform this BO-CCIS and review the different WFs that it has designed previously.

3.4 IC2IS's Ontological Disparities

One of the main issues to address in the design of an interoperable environment, is the *ontology* issue. We consider ontology as a *means* to represent and exchange information that are understood by all the participants of the interoperable environment. These participants may already have their own ontology, but it is important to *commit* together to a common ontology. In addition to this commitment, participants that exchange information have to be added with the following elements [Gruber and Olsen, 1994]: a common representation format, a communication protocol, and a specification of the communication content. This specification, known by ontology, is a set of classes, relationships, instances, functions, and axioms [Gruber and Olsen, 1994]. Ontology ensures that information received by a participant can be interpreted in the same way as the sending participant intends it.

By establishing a common ontology for the application domain, we offer a common terminological basis for the various interconnected systems, hence reducing for users the risks of getting inconsistent information. For the CCISs, ontological disparities exist at different levels. First, being generally developed in an independent way, CCISs present disparities in the vocabulary used to describe their information (different ontologies), which makes it difficult for users to use several CCISs simultaneously. Moreover, a user has to express his needs according to his own vocabulary and to his own comprehension. In the IC2IS environment, BOs cooperate in order to solve the problems resulting from *ontological disparities*.

4 Conclusion

In this paper, we described the major characteristics of the IC2IS project that aims at applying BOs and WFs to the design of an interoperable environment for CCISs. In this environment, BOs are able to fulfill services offered to users and specified by WFs. BOs and WFs-based interoperable-environment have a number of key advantages: BOs are a key to the standardization and hence, to the re-use in other similar application domains. And, WFs summarize the management of an interoperable environment, by isolating the control structure of this environment's functionalities from their data structure.

The IC2IS project is still an on going research. Currently, several issues related to the implementation of the IC2IS environment are under investigation: How to implement the IC2IS's BOs? How to allow the agents of the IC2IS's BOs to move? How to specify the behavior of the IC2IS's BOs? And, how to allow the IC2IS's BOs to initiate the CCIS's functions?

The IC2IS environment is a set of independently developed and deployed BOs that are accessible at run time by other BOs. BOs collaborate according to WFs in order to deliver the desired functionnalities.

References

M. Baker. Workflow meets business objects. In the proceedings of OOPSLA'96 Workshop, Business Object Design and Implementation II: Business Objects as Distributed Application Components - the enterprise solution? , 1996.

BOMA. Business Object Management Group. http://www.sesh.com/Guide/BusinessObjects.html.

T. Cai, P. Gloor, and S. Nog. Dartflow: A workflow management system on the web using transportable agents. Technical report, PCS-TR96-283, Department of Computer Science, Dartmouth College, Hanover, NH 03755, 1996.

D. Chess, G. Harrison, and A. Kershenbaum. Mobile agents: Are they a good idea? Technical report, IBM Research Division, RC 19887, 1994.

R. Davis and R.G. Smith. Negotiation as a metaphor for distributed problem solving. *Artificial Intelligence*, 20:63--109, 1983.

P. Eeles and O. Sims. *Building Business Objects*. John Wiley, 1998.

D. Georgakopoulos, M. Hornick, and A. Sheth. An overview of workflow management: From process modeling to workflow automation infrastructure. *Distributed and Parallel Database*, 3:119-153, 1995.

T.R. Gruber and G.R. Olsen. An ontology for engineering mathematics. In J. Doyle, P. Torasso, and E. Sandewall, editors, *the proceedings of Fourth International Conference on Principles of Knowledge Representation and Reasoning*. Morgan Kaufmann, 1994.

P. Herzum and O. Sims. The business component approach. In *the proceedings of OOPSLA'98 Workshop, Business Object Design and Implementation IV: From Business Objects to Complex Adaptive System*, Vancouver, Canada, 1998.

D. Jones, T. Bench-Capon, and P. Visser. Methodologies for ontology development. In *the proceedings of IT&KNOWS - Information Technology and Knowledge Systems, 15th IFIP World Computer Congress*. Vienna (Austria) and Budapest (Bulgaria), 1998.

S. Malerud, Feet E.H., and U. Thorsen. A method for analysing command and control systems. Norwegian Defence Research Establishment (FFI) N-220 Kjeller, Norway.

B. Moulin and M. Brassard. A scenario-based design method and an environment for the development of multiagent systems. In *First Australian Workshop on Distributed Artificial Intelligence*, n. 1087, pages 216-231. D. Lukose, Zhang C. (edts.), Lecture Notes in Artificial Intelligence, Springer-Verlag, 1996.

R. Orfali, D. Harkey, and J. Edwards. *The Essential Distributed Objects Survival Guide*. John Wiley & Sons, 1996.

A. Watson. The omg after corba~2. *Object Magazine, SIGS Publication*, pages 58-60, March 1996.

Bridging Legacy and Business Components with Parameterizable Business Objects: The *BALES* Methodology

Willem-Jan van den Heuvel and Michael Papazoglou
InfoLab, Tilburg University
5000 LE Tilburg
The Netherlands
E-mail: wjheuvel@kub.nl, mikep@kub.nl

ABSTRACT. *This paper describes the BALES methodology (binding Business object to Legacy Systems) methodology that aims at linking (off-the-shelf) business components to legacy system components on the basis of their interface definitions. This methodology results in business object interfaces, which are parameterized in legacy and/or business (ERP)-components. The BALES methodology is supported by an integrated toolset to automatically generate interface definitions on the basis of forward or reverse engineered (reference) models and deduce potential parameters of the business object.*

KEY WORDS: legacy systems, business object, business change, enterprise architecture

1. Introduction

Legacy componentization as well as ERP package/component integration are increasingly important issues as many companies consider to implement ERP systems to improve the organization's efficiency and ability to cope with business change (wilkes, 99). Business object technology is generally being perceived as the required solution since this technology enables organizations to build configurable business information systems that are based on heterogeneous building blocks which are described in terms of the services they offer without concerning the actual implementation (language). One additional benefit of business object technology is the ability to proavticely react on business change as interfaces can be changed without affecting the underlying implementation. Many technologies, such as wrapping and database/application gateways are nowadays available to support this philosophy. However, a cookbook that can be followed to build configurable business objects in terms of legacy and business components from analysis down to implementation (wrapping) is lacking. In this paper, we propose a methodology, called *BALES* (binding Business Applications to LEgacy Systems), that addresses several of these issues.
This paper is organized as follows. In the next section, we will sketch the *BALES* methodology. The *BALES* methodology is supported by a tool (COMBINE) which is presented in section 3. In the remainder of the paper, we present some conclusions and future research.

2. The *BALES* Methodology

The *BALES* methodology, that still is under development, aims at building parameterizable business objects in terms of legacy components and/or business application components. Legacy components encapsulate legacy data as well as functionality. Both the services of business objects as well as the legacy components are described by their interface (contract). To achieve this, we make use of an adapted version of an interface representation language, called the Component Definition Language (CDL) that has been developed by the Business Object Domain Task Force (BODTF) of the Object Management Group (OMG) (access, 97).
The core of *BALES* essentially comprises three phases: forward engineering, reverse engineering and linking (see figure 1). Before we start explaining these phases, we will take a closer look at a general architecture that we use throughout the methodology to structure the forward engineered as well as reverse engineered / reference models.

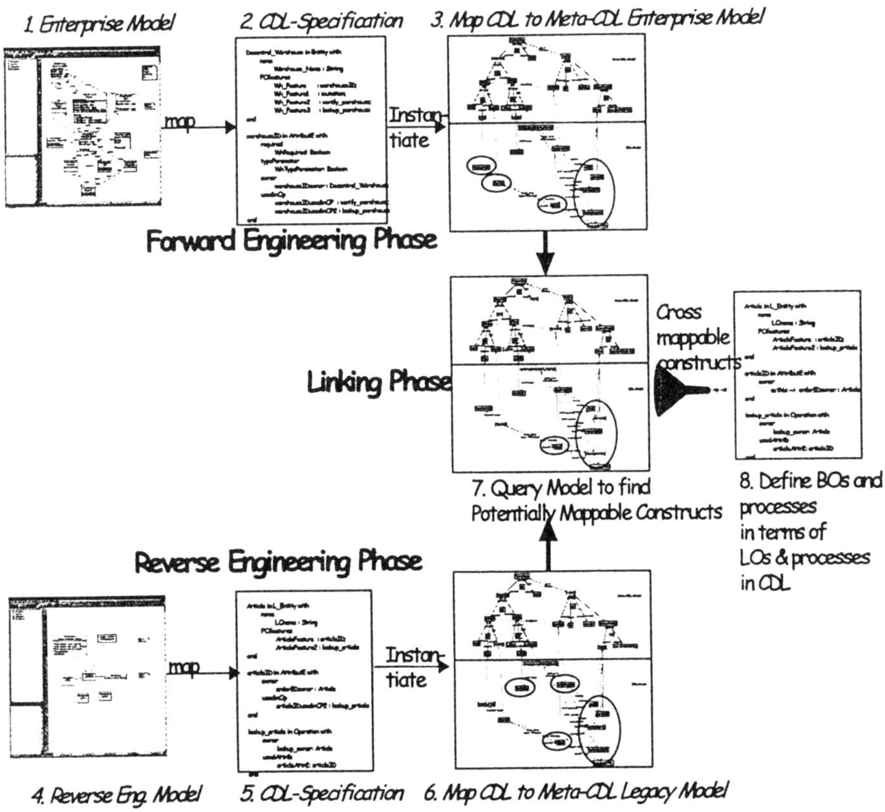

Figure 1: The BALES method

2.1 The Enterprise Architecture

Business objects are the key building block for building and maintaining adaptable business information systems as they can be grouped in coherent components to support business processes and workflows. Business (entity) objects encapsulate business data as well as policies. The dynamic, coordination processes in the business domain on the other hand, are stored in business process objects. Business process objects are a kind of controller objects that define business tasks performed by the actors in the domain and use business entities as a kind of data containers to store and retrieve the required business data (herzum,98). The flow of work in a corporation is defined in terms of a sequence of tasks that are triggered by business events. This planning and control cycle is implemented by workflow objects. Workflow objects control the sequencing of business tasks that collectively implement a value chain, and might be supported by a variety of workflow products. In case the flow of work transcends the corporation to other cooperating firms, e.g. a production planning process might start an order entry process in another organization, workflow objects can be used to glue the supporting ISs together, and avoid islands of automation.

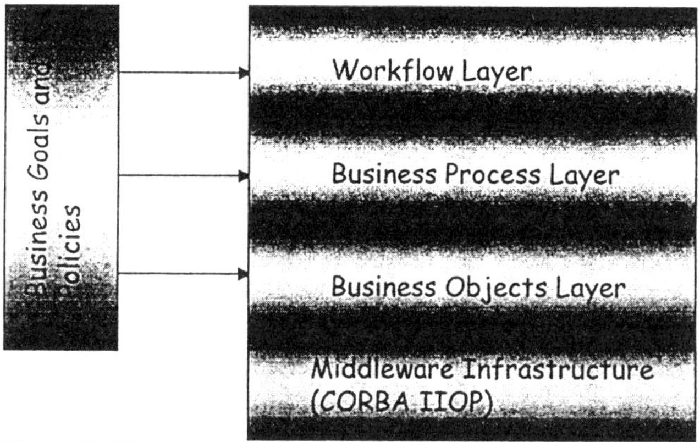

Figure 2: The enterprise architecture

Business objects, processes and workflows are organized by the enterprise architecture (see figure 2). Architectures have proven to be useful to structure system components to enhance future adaption as well as extension, and foster reuse (bäumer, 97). The enterprise architecture is used during the forward as well as reverse engineering phase of the *BALES* lifecycle. It has been influenced by the architecture as developed by Rob Prins (prins,96), as well as other architectures that have been described by (sims,94), (eeles, 98) (schmid, 98) and (jacobson, 97). The framework is inherently object-oriented: higher level objects (e.g., business process objects) can make use of lower-level components (business objects).

The highest two levels of this framework provide the core business processes and workflow applications that can be easily combined and extended to offer cross-organizational business solutions. At the next layer, business objects are defined as basic building blocks to encapsulate business data. Business policies can be attached to all top three level layers in order to define enterprise specific constraints on doing business[1]. The layers of the enterprise framework can be predefined within a specific vertical industry, or across such industries (common business objects).

2.2 Forward engineering Phase

During the forward engineering step of *BALES*, the enterprise model is created (see step 1 in figure 1), transformed into interface descriptions (step 2) and finally linked to a canonical, meta-model in order to compare it afterwards with the reverse engineering model of the legacy system or some reference models of a certain business application, e.g., SAP Reference Models (step 3).

The enterprise model reveals the business activities, tasks, recourses, actors, constraints and goals. The *BALES* methodology uses a dialect of UML, that we have called *BALES*-UML, which is inspired by the Boca-UML as defined by Data Access (access, 99), to represent the enterprise model in terms of the layered architecture that we described in the above. We have extended the Boca-UML with business specific concepts (e.g., business policies) and legacy constructs (e.g., legacy objects and processes) to make it suitable for our purposes. The main advantage of the *BALES*-UML enterprise modeling language is that there is a close fit to textual interface descriptions that can be easily queried, compared and linked.

To illustrate the *BALES* mapping methodology a simplified example is drawn from the domain of maintenance and overhaul of aircrafts (see figure 3). The upper part of this figure shows the enterprise model of this domain, in terms of business objects, processes, workflows and policies. As can be seen in this figure, the `Request_Part` workflow controls three business processes: `Request`, `Prognosis` and `Issue`. The `Request_part` workflow is initiated by a `Maintenance_Engineer` who is authorized to request parts that he needs to service a fighter-plane from a decentral warehouse. The `Request` process monitors the maintenance engineer's process, and stores it in an order list. The `Request` process utilizes the `Part` and `Warehouse` business entities in order to perform this operation. After this task is completed, the control is sent back to the `Request_Part` workflow. The workflow now either initiates a `Prognosis` process, or directly issues the part to the maintenance engineer on the basis of the quantity/price of the requested part. If the quantity/price remains under a certain level, the workflow starts the `Issue` process. The `Issue` process registers the administrative consequences of dispatching the part and updates the part inventory record by means of the `Part-Stock` object. In case the quantity/price ratio is exceeds a predefined limit, the workflow triggers the `Prognosis` process before it issues the part. The `Prognosis` process uses information from part and warehouse to run a `prognosis` on the basis of availability and consumption history in order to adequately cope with future demand.

The next step in the *BALES* process is the translation of the enterprise model into a *BALES*-CDL interface definition. CDL is a declarative interface definition language, that can be used to represent collections of business objects, their structural relationships, constraints and temporal dependencies. The *BALES* CDL extends the standard CDL in the following three ways: *BALES*-CDL adds constructs to support the *BALES*-specific enterprise model constructs, the dialect extends CDL to represent legacy processes (/ERP

---

[1] An elaborated description of business policies can be found in (papazoglou99a) and (papazoglou99b).

processes) and objects and lastly the *BALES*-CDL encompasses mechanisms to parameterize business objects. For a detailed description of CDL as developed by Data Access we refer to: (access,97), (access,99). The *BALES*-CDL variant has been described in: [heuvel99], [papazoglou99]. In figure 4, we represented the CDL code for the business process `Prognosis` as found in the enterprise model.

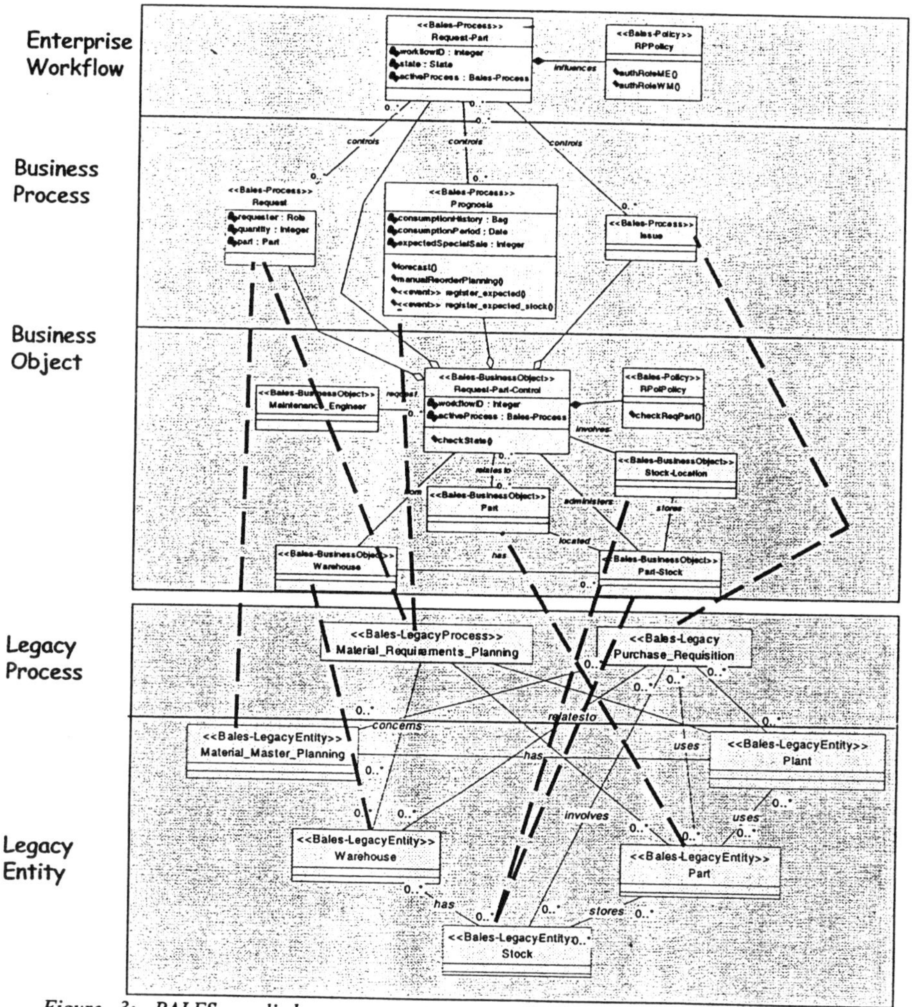

Figure 3: BALES applied to area of maintenance and overhaul of Defense

```
Business_process Prognosis {
    attribute consumptionHistory, consumptionPeriod,
    expectedSpecialSale,
    totalExpectedConsQuantityinPeriod;
    relationship boRPC  IsPartOf  Request_Part_Control inverse bpP ;
    relationship wflR  Many 0..* Request_art_Workflow inverse bpP ;
    attribute String consumptionHistory;
    attribute Date consumptionPeriod;
    attribute Integer expectedSpecialSale;
    attribute Integer totalExpectedConsQualityinPeriod;
    Void forecast (in Integer partID, in Integer stockID, in
    Integer warehouseID, in Date consumptionPeriod,
    in String  consumptionHistory);
    Void manualReoderPlanning (in Integer partID, in Integer stockID,
    in Integer warehouseID);
    signal register_expected ();
    signal register_expected_stock ();
}; // End: Prognosis
```

Figure 4: Excerpt of BALES-CDL definition of the Enterprise Model

After we have transformed the enterprise model to the corresponding *BALES*-CDL representation, the business object/process and workflow defintions are linked to a canonical, metamodel. The metamodel is an abstraction of both the forward and reverse engineered model, and exactly describes how both model types relate to each other. The *BALES*-Metamodel has been represented by means of Telos. Telos is a formal knowledge representation language designed to build and query (meta)models (mylopoulos, 92). We refer to (heuvel99) for an in depth description of the metamodel.

2.3 Reverse Engineering Phase

The reverse engineered model shows the functionality of the legacy systems in terms of legacy objects and processes (step 4 in figure 1). The wrapped legacy component `Material_Requirements_Planning` (MRP) encapsulates business logic and data to plan parts and assemblies that are required during the maintenance process. The `Purchase_Requisition` process is used to purchase the required parts as determined in the MRP legacy process.
Again, we translate the model to CDL in order to be able to link it to the *BALES* Metamodel (see step 5 and 6).

```
Legacy_process Material_Requirements_Planning {
        signal register_expected ();
        signal start_long_term_planning ();
        signal start_stat_analysis ();
        Void forcastDetModel (in Integer partID, in Integer stockID, in
        Integer warehouseID, in Integer consumptionPeriod, in Integer
        consumptionHistory);
        Void planProduct (in Integer partID, in Integer stockID, in
        Integer warehouseID);
    }; // End: Material_Requirements_Planning
```

Figure 5: CDL description of the legacy process object MRP

2.4 Linking Phase

During the linking phase the (features of) business objects, processes and workflows are being mapped to legacy objects and processes on the one hand, and reference models on the other hand. The first activity (step 7) of this phase comprises enumerating potentially mappable items by querying the enterprise model and legacy/reference models that are linked to the metamodel. In figure 6, we present an example of a query that is used to infer mappable operations with parameters

```
QueryClass OpWithSameParameters isA Operation with
  retrieved_attribute
    owner : LOType
  parameter
    proto_op : Operation
  constraint
    con:
      $ ( forall a/parameter (this usedParam a) ==>
      ( proto_op usedParam a))
    and
      ( forall b/parameter (proto_op usedParam b) ==>
      ( this usedParam b)) $
end
```

Figure 6: A Telos Query to infer linkable operations

This query determines those operations which are owned by (attached to) a legacy object, and have the same signature (`usedParam`) as the operation `proto_op`, signifying a prototypical operation. In other words, this query looks for operations with the same interface in all models that are linked to the metamodel (in this case both the enterprise model and the reverse engineered model).

A call `OpWithSameAttributes[forecast/proto_op]` of this query may yield the following result, which indicates a match between the BO operation `forecast` and the legacy operation `forecastDetModel`, see figure 7.

```
forecastDetModel in OpWithSameParameters[forecast/proto_op] with
  owner
    fmdet_owner : Material_Requirements_Planning
end
```

Figure 7: Result of Telos Query in figure 6

The answers obtained by this type of queries are first checked against some simple static type-safety criteria that basically comprise co-/contravariance checks to garantuee minimal conformance, and are also validated by an analyst to resolve semantic mismatches at the operational level. After successful validation, the interfaces of the `forecast` and `forecastDetModel` can be linked. For reasons of simplicity, we assume that there are no name differences at the business and legacy object level.

The evaluated results of the queries are used to actually parameterize the business objects to their legacy/business component counterparts. In the following, we give an example of the parameterized business process object `Prognosis`.

```
Business_process Prognosis {
    attribute consumptionHistory, consumptionPeriod,
    expectedSpecialSale,
    totalExpectedConsQuantityinPeriod;
    relationship boRPC IsPartOf Request_Part_Control inverse bpP ;
    relationship wflR Many 0..* Request_art_Workflow inverse bpP ;
    attribute String consumptionHistory;
    attribute Date consumptionPeriod;
    attribute Integer expectedSpecialSale;
    attribute Integer totalExpectedConsQualityinPeriod;
    // Mapping of forecasting method to legacy process component MRP
    Void forecast (Warehouse.Material_Requirements_Planning.
     forecastDetModel(in partID, in stockID, in warehouseID, in
     consumptionPeriod, in consumptionHistory);
    );
    Void manualReoderPlanning (in Integer partID, in Integer stockID,
    in Integer warehouseID);
    signal register_expected ();
    signal register_expected_stock ();

}; // End: Prognosis
```

Figure 8: Paramerized business process object Prognosis

As can be seen in this figure, the business process operation prognosis is linked to the legacy operation `forecastDetModel` that is attached to the legacy process `Material_Requirements_Planning`.

Although the example we presented in this paragraph is rather simplistic (f.e., we did not take semantic mismatches into or account, and focused at a rather simple mapping), it illustrates how the *BALES* methodology can be applied to real-world cases.

The parameterized business objects can easily be retrofitted to proactively react to changing business requirements by changing their parameters, ergo, pointers to legacy or ERP components (papazoglou,99).

3. The Tool

The *BALES* methodology is supported by a tool, called COMBINE (which stands for: COmponent BINding Engine). COMBINE supports all phases of the *BALES* methodology ranging from the construction of the enterprise and legacy system model to the actual mapping process.

Figure 9 illustrates the architecture of COMBINE. As can be seen in the figure, this hybrid toolset comprises the following components.

- Modeling Tool: Rational Rose

The modeling tool is used during all three main phases of the *BALES* method. We have chosen Rational Rose to support the enterprise and legacy system modeling (step 1 and 4 of figure 1), but in principle any other tool with the same functionality could be used here.

The modeling tool supports the *BALES* CDL UML notation and semantics, so that the analist can easily define *BALES* enterprise models. Moreover, the analyst can automatically generate a CDL description of the legacy, reference and/or enterprise model. The converter that provides this functionality is added as a special plug-in to Rational Rose. During the reverse engineering phase, Rational Rose can be used to visualize the wrapper/CDL specifications of the software components. Finally, the modeling tool can be used to graphically represent the parameterized business objects and processes that result from the last step in the *BALES* methodology.

♦ Converters

The *BALES*-tool encompasses four types of converters to support both the forward and backward engineering phases. We have used JavaCup (a java-based YACC implementation) to generate the "meta-compiler" (the compiler that generates the CDL metamodel in terms of Telos) as well as the "compiler" (the compiler that links CDL to the CDL metamodel, ergo that translates CDL in Telos CDL metamodel representations). Again, any other YACC-like compiler with the same functionality could be introduced. We will discuss each compiler as indicated in figure 9 in the following:

- UML-to-CDL Compilers

  The UML to CDL converter transforms a textual UML model representation into CDL (between step 1-2, and 4-5 of figure 1). For the moment, we have used a plug-in to Rational Rose, which has been developed by Data Access, to implement our experimental prototype.

  This converter will be adapted to cope with the *BALES* CDL-dialect and support the reverse engineering phase in the near future.

- CDL-to-CDL-Metamodel Compilers.

  This category of compilers (labeled "metacompiler" in figure 9) automatically generates that part of the canonical, meta-CDL-model (stated in Telos) that is required to instantiate the CDL-enterprise/ legacy model definitions.

- CDL-to-Telos Compilers.

  After the meta-compilers have generated the meta-CDL-model, the CDL-to-Telos compilers can be executed in order to link (instantiate) the enterprise/legacy model to the canonical model.

- BNF-to-YACC Compiler.

  This last type of compilers is used to generate the required (CDL) specification file that defines the production rules (these rules comprise the grammar rules and the actions) of the language that serve as input for Yacc (in our case a JAVA implementation of YACC called JavaCup). This compiler can perpetuate changes in the *BALES* CDL automatically down to the other converters, thereby providing enormous flexibility. The transformation rules between BNF and the Yacc-input file as well as the compiler itself are still under research scrutiny.

♦ ConceptBase: Deductive Database Management System

Both the forward as well as the reverse engineered (meta) model definitions are stored in an advanced deductive database management system, called ConceptBase, that has been designed to store, retrieve and deduce Telos statements. The querying mechanism of

ConceptBase is used to: deduce potential linkable items between the enterprise and the legacy/ERP model, and check the type-safety of the potentially mappable items.

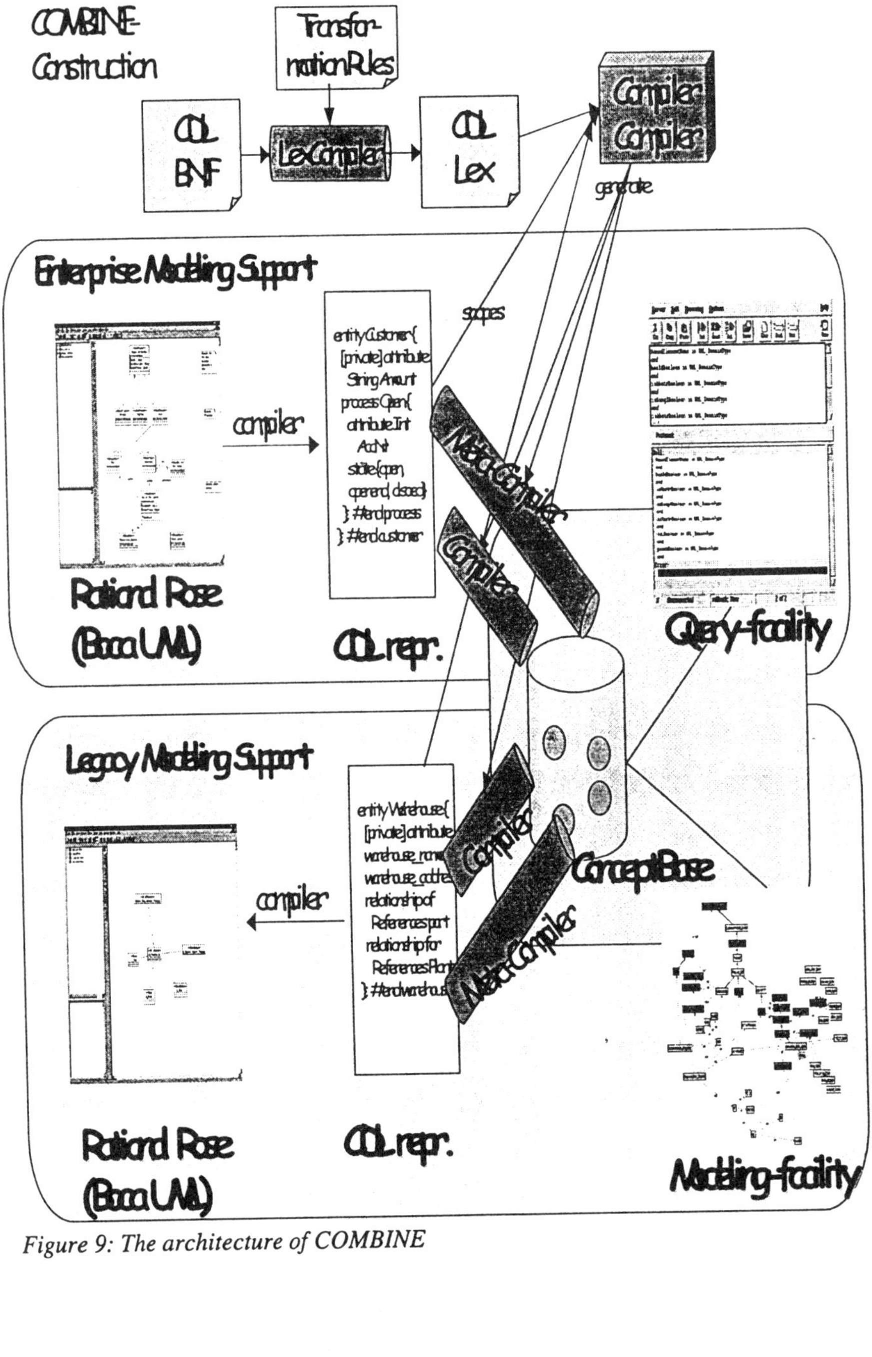

Figure 9: The architecture of COMBINE

5. Future research and conclusions

In this paper, we have described the *BALES* methodology that can be used to construct paramerizable business objects that might be used to seamlessly glue business and legacy objects together in terms of their interface definitions. Though the case we described in this article shows how part of the business object implementation can be implemented by some *legacy* component(s), the methodology is equally applicable for *business* components, e.g., SAP business objects.

The *BALES* methodology propagates building under architecture, called the Enterprise Architecture, in order to structure the business domain as well as the legacy/ERP systems and enhance future reuse. In case of business change, the parameters of the business objects can easily be adapted to proactively deal with the changed business processes (papazoglou99a).

In the last part of this paper, we sketched the global architecture of a tool we are constructing right now that can be used to support/automate all phases of the *BALES* roadmap.

In the near future, we intend to extend the BALES-CDL Metamodel with SAP BAPI definitions, improve the static type checking mechanism (to adequately deal with co- and contra-variance), and elaborate the business policy mechanism. Moreover, we plan to validate the BALES method and improve the functionality of COMBINE on the basis of a case study.

References

(access, 97) Data Access Technologies, "Business Object Architecture ({BOA}) Proposal", BOM/97-11-09, OMG Business Object Domain Task Force, 1997.

(access, 99) Data Access Technologies, "Boca Specification, version 1.3", http://www.dataaccess.com/dat/Download/standards%20info/standards_and_specifications_dow.htm

(bäumer, 97) Dirk Bäumer et al. "Framework Development for Large Systems: Experiences with successful large-scale industrial banking projects", Communications of the ACM, 40(10): 52-59, 1997

(eeles, 98) Peter Eeles and Oliver Sims, "Building Business Objects", John Wiley & Sons, New York, 1999

(heuvel, 99) W.J. van den Heuvel, M.P. Papazoglou and M. Jeusfeld, "Connecting Business Objects to Legacy Systems", Proceedings of the CAiSE Conference, Springer, 1999

(herzum, 98) Peter Herzum and Olliver Sims, "The Business Component Approach", in: Proceedings of the Business Object Workshop IV, Springer, 1998

(jacobson,97) Ivar Jacobson, "Software Reuse", Addison Wesley Lognman, Harlow, England, 1997

(mylopoulos, 92) John Mylopoulos, "Conceptual Modeling and Telos", in P.~Loucopoulos and R.Zicari, editors, Conceptual Modeling, Databases and Case: an Integrated View on Information Systems Development, J. Wiley, New York, 1992 (papazoglou,99) M.P. Papazoglou and W.J. van den Heuvel, "Leveraging Legacy Assets", to appear in M. Papazoglou, S. Spaccapietra, Z. Tari, editors, Advances in Object-Oriented Modeling, MIT-Press, 1999

(papazoglou, 99a) M.P. Papazoglou and W.J. van den Heuvel, "Configurable Business Objects for Building Evolving Enterprise Models and Applications", in: "Business Process Management: Models, Techniques, and Empirical Studies", W. van der Aalst, J. Desel and A. Oberweis (editors), Stringer-Verlag, to appear: 1999

(papazoglou, 99b) M.P. Papazoglou and W.J. van den Heuvel, "From Business Processes to Cooperate Information Systems", in: Intelligent Information Agents, Klusch (editor), Springer, 1999

(prins,96) Robert Prins, "Developing Business Objects: A Framework Drive Approach", Mc-Graw-Hill Companies, London, 1996

(schmid, 98) Hans Albrecht Schmid, "A Business Object Framework Architecture", Proceedings of the Business Object Workshop IV, Springer, 1998

(sims,94) Oliver Sims, "Business Objects: Delivering Cooperating Objects for Client/Server", McGraw-Hill Book Company, London, 1994

(sutherland, 98) Jeff Sutherland, "Business Object Component Architectures: A Target Application Area for Complex Adaptive Systems", in: Proceedings of the Business Object Workshop IV, Springer, 1998

(wilkes,99) Lawrence Wilkes, "Legacy Componentization and Wrapping", Component Strategies, SIGS Publications, 1(8): 50-57, 1999

A Recursive Common Business Object System Model

William Z Wu, Information System Researcher

BE, Information System Engineering, in 1983; LL.M, Intellectual Property Law, in 1989;

Address: 4/10 Marriott Street, ST Kilda East, VIC 3183, Melbourne, Australia

E-mail: wuwilliam@yahoo.com or j.lin@pgrad.unimelb.edu.au

William Z Wu

Abstract: This paper, through a Copyright Information project, presents a Common Business Object Model which may be further included in a Common Object System Model. The object system is independent from its implementation. It is recursive, reflecting the complexity of the real business object relationship in a relatively simple and easily understandable manner.

The primary focus of this paper is not just on a single corporation concept model, but on the overall object system to address issues such as reusability, interoperability and extensibility in a systematic way. The Common Object System Model also has many ramifications relevant to natural language process, common knowledge representation, legal rule enforcement, component technology as well as business object architecture.

Key Words: Business Object Architecture, Object System Model, Natural Language and Object Oriented Analysis and Design, Corporate Information System.

1 Introduction

1.1 Background

OO technology, programming languages, UML, COM and CORBA have provided us with advanced data access and representation tools, distributing architectures and methodology. However, little progress has been made on general data modelling theory itself. It is one of the major factors that restricts the potential development of advanced information technology and its sophisticated application in business domain.

Since general data modelling theory requires the combination of knowledge and expertise in both IT and business domain, obviously it will be difficult for IT professionals alone to address this problem and joint efforts must be made by business experts as well as IT experts. In the past, high level abstractions failed to be reached due to the lack of in-depth understanding of OOP paradigm by business experts, and vice versa. We notice that although OO technology is a very useful methodology for knowledge representation, communication and process, which has already been widely used in the field of Information Technology, however, it has not received active response in other fields.

We can encapsulate legal rules, one of the essential types of business rules in business object, which may be called Legal Business Object. Based on this belief, a Copyright Information Project is currently under development by the author. The initial purpose is to encapsulate copyright law rules in Work Object, but later it has resulted in the creation of a Common Business Object System Model. We sunk into the work of building a base

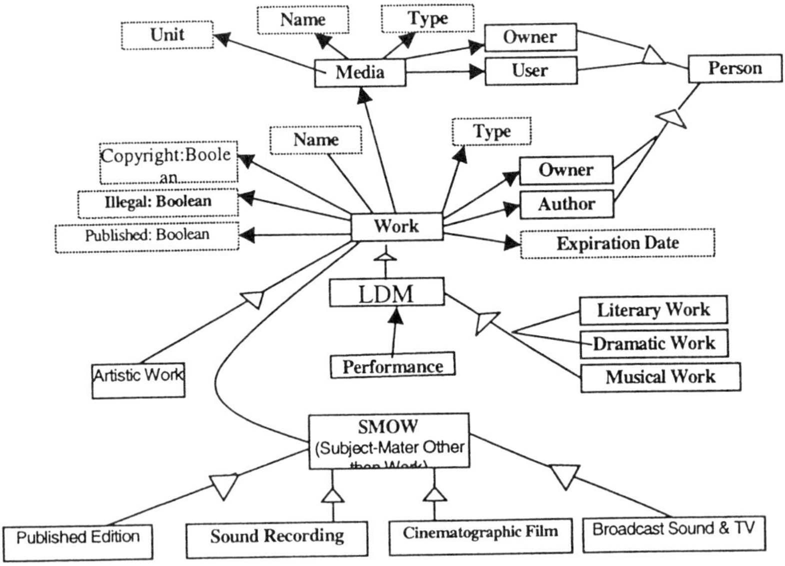

Figure 1

object, Entity, and many interesting issues are identified. Further abstraction has been made and resulted in a Common Object System Model.

This development process represents a consistent process of abstraction just like the development of many other projects. We also try to give a more complete blue print of information system engineering, including natural language process, legal rule enforcement, knowledge representation, application design and implementation.

1.2 The Initial Copyright Object Model

An initial copyright object model was built and illustrated in an Object System Model (OSM) diagram as shown in Figure 1.[1]

This copyright OSM diagram is a common style of many business models, but it is far from being optimised. The complexity and inherent characteristics of work object system could not be well addressed by this model. Further abstraction is needed.

---

[1] Symbols used in the OSM diagrams of this paper are:

Specialisation/ Generalisation — Relationship

1.3 The Recursive Common Business Object System Model

A work created by an author is typically protected by copyright, a proprietary right, and is used by a user, one person or more persons. The copyright, just like other kinds of Intellectual Property rights, such as patents and trademarks, is an intangible property. The generation, protection and exploitation of such intangible property maybe different in many aspects with tangible property. However, as a kind of property, Intellectual property also possesses some common features with the tangible property.

The Common Business Object System Model (hereinafter is referred to as CBOSM) framework, as shown in Figure 2, intends to reflect the inherent relationship between Asset, Intellectual Property object and other business objects. In the next section, a more detailed description about this CBOSM will be given.

1.4 Copyright Object Model Extending the CBOSM

Derived from the Intellectual Property object in the CBOSM, the Copyright Object System Model may be as simple as the framework shown in Figure 3. Actually, almost all other business objects may be derived from the CBOSM. The following part of this paper will analyse some basic features of the CBOSM.

2 Natures of the Common Business Object System Model

In the CBOSM, the focus has been placed on Asset object instead of Work or Intellectual property. Three abstract concept objects, Entity, Legal Business Object and Business Process Object, and more importantly recursive architecture are introduced.

2.1 Entity Object

Every thing is an Entity, sharing the same attributes: ID, Name and Description (or

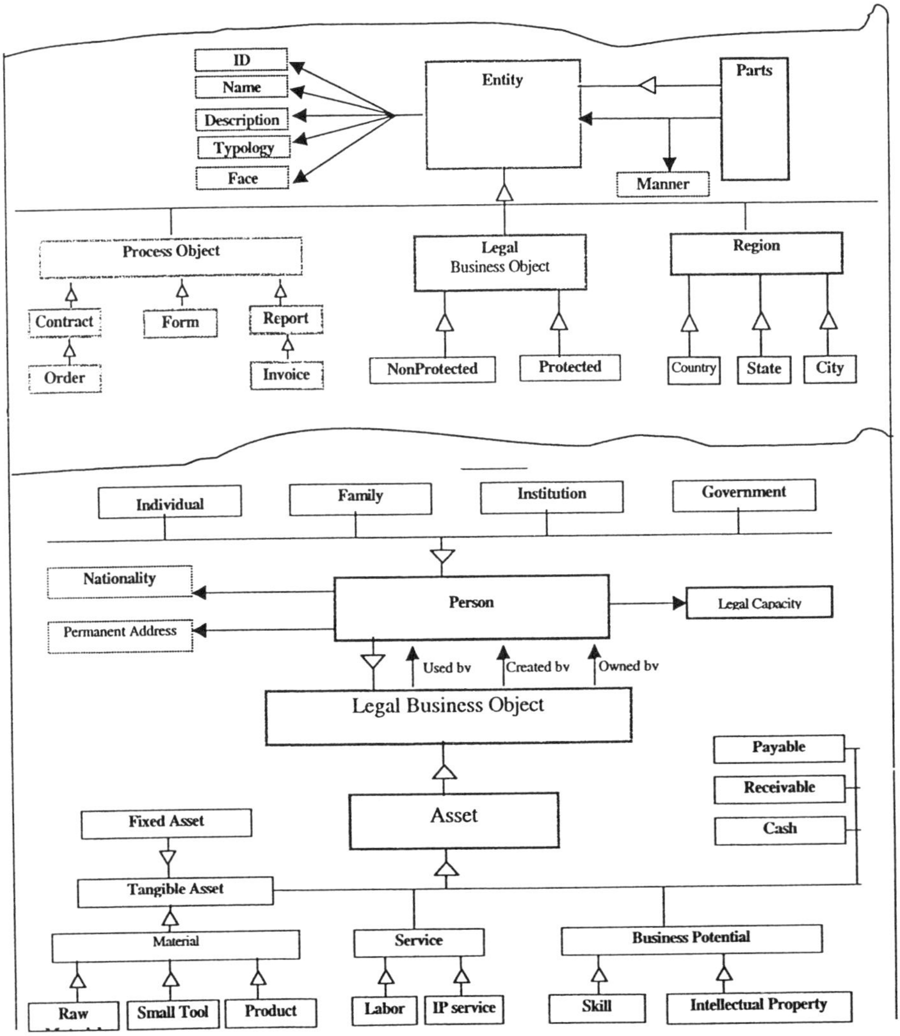

Figure 2

Definition). We also give every Entity a Face attribute and Typology attribute. The Face enables us to have a visual sense on each entity, which may be a picture or audio / video animation. Typology, the class type of an object, represents each object's position in the Common Business Object System Model.

2.2 Part Object

The Part object is an abstract relationship object representing the recursive relationship between entities. Any Entity is consisted of other entities. For example, a person as a legal

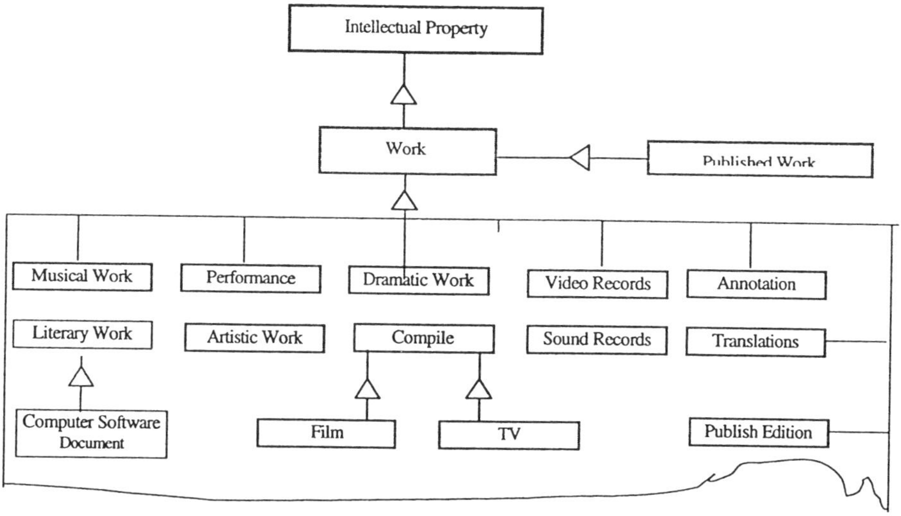

Figure 3.

body may be an individual or an institute; it also may be a group of persons yet remaining to be a new instance of person, another legal body. An Asset is always composed by other assets, including tangible assets and intangible assets.

The Part object is a set of entities that is also one of the attributes of other entity. This attribute is inherited by all the descendants of the base object, Entity, so it makes the CBOSM recursive. This kind of architecture reflects the complexity of the business object relationship and also gives this model a clear outline.

2.3 Legal Business Object

General legal rules may be encapsulated in this base object, the ancestor of all business objects, such as Person and Asset. It is the central place to process some basic legal attributes or natures, such as whether an object is governed by a particular legal system.

2.4 Person Objects and Rights (Legal Body Model)

A person is a legal body, which may be an individual, institute, family and even a government organisation, who has rights----methods in terms of OO methodology----to act on other Legal Business Objects, which includes other persons and the person object itself. Assets are always owned or used by persons.

When a method is enabled, it means that the person has the right to do something. A method will be disabled when the owner does not have the correspondent right. A right also may be granted or disabled by an agreement between two legal bodies.

2.5 Asset objects and classification (Asset Model)

Assets and their classification are crucial in corporate information systems. This part of the model falls into the accounting theory and related legal rules. Here we introduce a Service Object and a Business Potential Object. By doing so, the classification of assets becomes clearer and easier to operate in consideration that the Intellectual Property is also one part of the Asset Object Model and its value should also be interchangeable with other types of assets.

A Service is not only cost to the user of the service but also the user's asset that is intangible and its value will be add to its container, tangible asset. Tangible assets is in a value added process in the goods' manufacture and distribution system while services are continuously created and its value is added into its container by persons in the economic system.

Furthermore, the Account Receivable and Account Payable are treated as typical types of assets, in their natural way, but they have a wider meaning.

2.6 Business Process Object

A Process Object is actually a Form. A Form is widely used in the business workflow by business people as well as software developers, in software development. The use of computer makes our business process be automatic. This object has many descendants, such as Report, Invoice, Contract and Order. They provide means for different entities, including entities in the real world and their counterparts in cyberspace, to act on each other.

2.7 Space and Time Dimensions

The Space is also an entity inheriting the recursive architecture. A region may be a country, state, city, etc.; One region may be divided into smaller regions.

Time can not be seen in this General Model. It seems to be a problem. But we have made this model a real time model by adding time dimension fields in relationship tables when implementing this model via relative database tables to reflect the status of an entity and their dynamic relationship.

2.8 Multiple Implications of the Relationships, Owned By, Used By and Created By

For different entities, the relationships, eg. *owned by, used by* and *created by,* have different meanings, but share the same structure.

For example, for an individual, the creator of the individual is obviously his/her parent, while his/her owner may be a guardian of the individual who legally represents him/her. The creator of a work is its author. Copyright in a work may be assigned and owned by other persons other than the author of that work.

By updating the 'owned by' and 'used by' relationship, we may implement the 'Give/Take pattern' proposed by accounting research. (see [REAAM])

2.9 Commonality of the CBOSM

We assume this model is common to all other domain specific applications although further proof is needed. Our belief is that the CBOSM reflects the underlying principle of legal jurisprudence and accounting theory. All objects are classified according to some categories as in jurisprudence.

In particular, we may derive from the Service object of the CBOSM and create different types of service, such as insurance, hospital, tourist and banking system objects, etc.

2.10 Implementation of the CBOSM

Because of the CBOSM, databases, whether in a local DBMS or a remote server, share the same conceptual schema. That means, workflow may vary in different corporate environments, in different business stages or in different industries, but they share the same data model architecture. To the most, they are a set of physical data storage or a view. Interoperability, reusability and portability are the natural consequence of using the CBOSM.

Nevertheless, the CBOSM, OO technologies, distributed architectures and DBMS must comprehensively work together. OO programming language is the first option to build the business object because this model is inherently object oriented. In a distributed environment, DCOM or CORBA should be taken into account.

It is desirable to implement this CBOSM via RDBMS or ODBMS. This is because SQL is still a very effective tool to satisfy our purpose and table is still the best way to store attributes of entities and relationship. More importantly, DBMS provides us with the interoperability from the bottom layer to top layer in a multi tiered architecture environment.

We may see from the CBOSM that the aggregation technology has become a vital technology to implement a comprehensive Object System Model. While we still can not find a sophisticated solution by using commercially available OO products, Enterprise Java Bean (EJB) gives us very deep impression. The Entity beans of the EJB are persistent objects and represent an object view of data stored in permanent storage, relative database. (See [SJVA]).

Other technologies or theories such as the Complexity Adaptive System (cas) and Agent system may also be introduced in this process.

3 Further Abstraction—A Common Object System Model

The introduction of an abstract object, Entity, and the recursive architecture have significantly simplified the CBOSM yet still reflecting the inherent complexity of the Business object relationships. However, this model has not yet reflected the relationships between Entity and other software-developer-oriented objects, which are unfamiliar to the business world. Where is the bridge that may link the two separated worlds systematically? We are also aware that there are some other concepts objects relevant to business object that may not be properly included in this model.

A further step is obviously necessary to be taken. The framework as shown in Figure 4

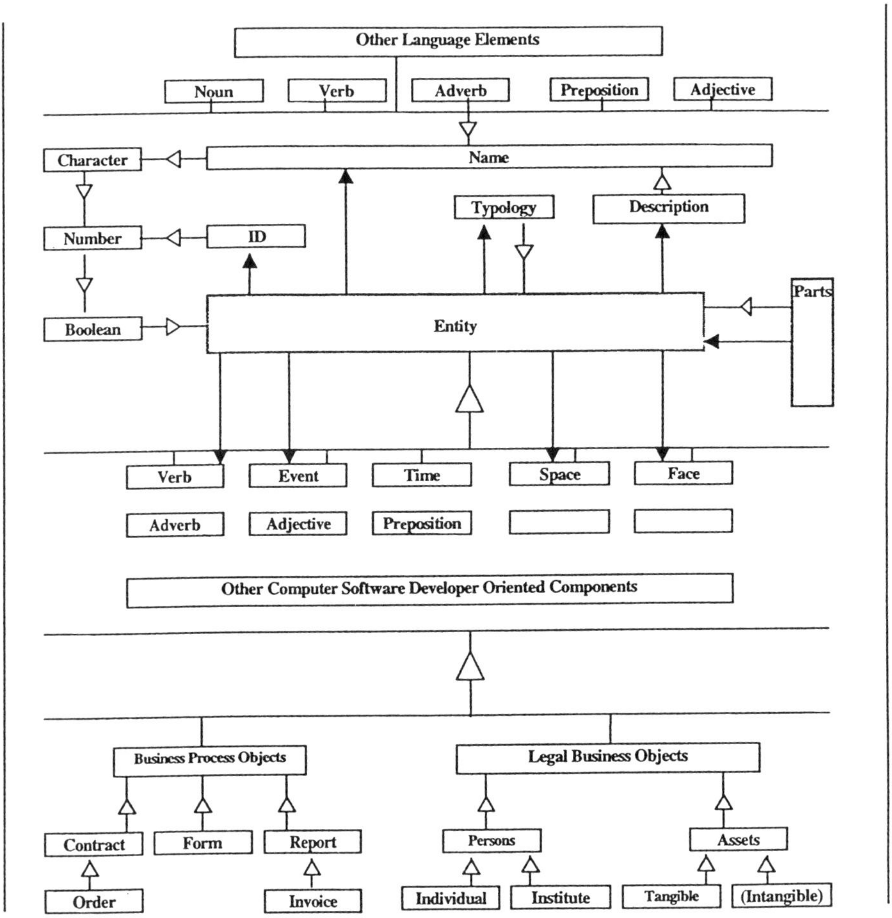

Figure 4

provides a Common Object System Model (COSM) and we give the following brief explanation at the current stage.

3.1 Everything is an Entity (Object)

Is the entity recursive model that has been introduced in the CBOSM only fits the CBOSM? The negative answer is evident. One thing is always composed by other things.

This is a basic law of nature. In other words, the entity object should be situated on the top of a object system model. It is the ancestor of the object family. Furthermore, the recursive architecture should be reflected throughout the COSM.

In particular, Typology object is also a descendant of the Entity. Typology's typology is typology. This nature is important because it enables users to expand a system by creating new objects at run time instead at design time. The model may be further improved or adjusted depending on the actual need of a user.

We are pleased to see that in some OO programming languages, there is a container component as one of the base components. A container itself is a component yet still contains other components. They work together and form a new different component. This functionality is not provided inadvertently. An Entity object is a container and should be the ancestor of all other objects in the cyberspace. The container component will make simple implementation of CBOSM and recursive architecture a reality.

3.2 Object System versus Natural Language

A natural language, such as English, is per se object oriented. For every natural language element, there are at least a string object and a concept object in the COSM. The string object gives a name to each object in the COSM. The root object, Entity, provides a way for them to be linked together. The interchangeability between XML and Java Bean is another aspect of the same nature of the COSM. (See [JBEAN])

Now we have been able to develop many classes or components that mirror their counterparts in natural language, such as noun, verb, adverb, adjective, preposition, etc. Actually, a natural language is not the highest level of abstraction. All characters of Natural languages may be finally represented by 0 and 1. As we develop more and more components that mirror their counterparts in a nature languages and the real world, OO programming language may be expected to be a more comprehensive and useful language. Then business object and business rule, that are now largely represented by natural language, may be well represented and processed in OO programming language.

3.3 Object System versus Legal Rules

As the Business Object is a natural extension of OO programming language component hierarchy and mirrors their counterparts in real world, they are governed by legal rules as well as programming language syntax. In terms of OO technology, legal rules are constraints. They are essential business rules. The Accounting Model, which used to be believed to be common to other business object, could also be derived from a common component: Legal Business Object.

Encapsulating of legal rules is necessary and possible. We see that a large amount of workload of lawyers are referencing and citation of statutes and cases. Legal rules are documented just like programming language code. Lawmakers are actually doing their jobs to create business object systems and their interoperation constraints. However, they use natural language that makes the object system so complicated that only specialists could understand. What if we use a new OO programming language to make the legal object model alive? We will have relieved the burden of legal professionals as well as businessmen. This will surely dramatically change our social system structure when every business object in the real world has a counterpart in the cyberspace. We can not imagine there will be a day when legal professionals have to become familiar with OO technology.

3.4 Implication to RDBMS implementation and OO technology

According to this Object General Model, database schemas may be designed. There is just one Entity table while all other tables are pure relationship tables. The Entity table provides the central place to identify and classify entities. It also provides a place to link each language element to its counterpart in the object system. In this sense, the table is still a relationship table.

From software-developer-oriented components to the Legal Business Object is a consistent evolving process. Both are needed to be involved in a systematic analysis, design and implementation. We may see that there is a highest level abstraction that leads to every thing may finally be represented by Boolean object: 0 and 1, the 'root' of the computer technology.

3.5 Implication to Domains Specific Professions

Business Objects are natural extension of the component hierarchy of OO programming language and blur the boundary between IT knowledge and other domain specific knowledge. OO technology as a general methodology may help people think more systematically and clearly. Sometimes, by using OO technology, high level abstraction may be more easily obtained than by using a natural language.

Business Object model should be built up jointly by business experts as well as IT experts and legal professional will play a vital role to the future work as the Legal Business object located in the up stream of the business object hierarchy. The Legal Business Object and its descendants will be constrained by legal rules can dramatically release the burdens of legal professionals. However, this process can be accelerated if legal professionals introduce OO technologies, such as UML and Common Business Object System Model, into their jobs.

3.6 Some Further Requirements to OO Programming Language

Globally Unique ID (GUID) is the most common way to identify a class or a component in an OO programming language. When a new class is created, it must be registered so a computer will 'know' it. However, what if we are trying to find a class that has not been registered in computer system? We just receive an error message and the computer stops compiling or executing a program. This makes computer accurate, reliable and at the same time, a 'dead machine'!

We need a way to let computer do things by analogy. When processing an instance of class that is new to a computer system, the most closely relevant class may be used. The closest relatives of the new class may be determined by information on its position in the COSM, or some other specific attributes.

Analogy is not accurate, but we use it often in reality world and it usually works. If we just want to sell a piece of painting, which is an instance of Work, it still works if we treat it as a normal asset. If we did not have a Work object registered in a computer, it does not matter, we may use Asset object class to process the data. Sure the user should be reminded when a computer using analogy to solve problems. After all, we need more intelligent way to initiate an object's instance, taking, to the most extent, advantages of polymorphism and inheritance.

We also need more dynamic ways to create new descendants of a class by end users, at run time, instead of by a developer, at design time. The COSM is an open model. New typology may be added to the model at run time. This needs to be supported by OO programming language. We will also be able to use analogy to create new object class.

Another option is to make IDE open to end-users. A sophisticated business object system will dramatically reduce the need to hard code. Mouse plus GUI is enough. It also enables a user to code in a language that is close to a natural language. End users create their own applications by drag and drop Business Components from component palette, assign some simple properties' value then compile it and got what they want.

In short, Analogy, dynamic deriving mechanism of object class and opening IDE to end users may be good ways to make an OOP system a learning system that adapts by its users as needed. Architects provide houses which can be further decorated by the user of the house. Software engineering also can work in a similar manner.

3.7 A Brief Comparison against REA Accounting Model

The CBOSM and COSM is designed entirely in a natural way, reflecting the underlying principles of jurisprudence, accounting theory as well as object oriented technology. This characteristic determines that the model will share many aspects with other models already existed. Among those is REA Accounting Model (REAAM) which has been widely accepted as the base concept model of many corporate information systems. (See [REAAM])

The CBOSM (contained in the COSM) and REAAM share the following aspects:

1) They reflect the underlying principles of accounting theory while trying to avoid using those accounting procedures, such as double entry book keeping, that are not necessary for computerised information system, so to make the system acceptable to both accountant and non-accountant.

2) They use some terms that reflect the natures of objects, such as entity, person, aggregation, generation, resource, event and asset.

The COSM (which contains CBOSM) and REAAM have at least the following differences:

1) COSM focuses more wider areas than a single accounting or corporate information system through a higher level of abstraction to systematically reflect the overall object system applying underlying principle of OO technology, jurisprudence, accounting theory and even linguistics. We treat accounting system only a set of legal rules in a legal system. A corporate model is only a set of the COSM. In other word corporate information system may be only a set of entire information system of the society.

2) Account Payable and Account Receivable are also specific assets in their natural way and have wider meanings.

3) Explicitly includes the Business Potential object in the Asset Model.

4) Introduce Contract object as a more general object than Order while avoiding to form a fixed work flow pattern or activity pattern.

5) Add attributes, owner, user, creator and different methods to reflect stock flows from one person to another person.

4 Summary

>From a Copyright Information Project to a Common Object System Model (COSM), it represents a continuous process of abstraction, sharing many ramifications with other application system. In the past, we usually are not able to do so because of time limitations, system boundaries and difficulties for comprehensive high level abstraction.

By introducing this CBOSM and COSM, although we may not in this short paper give a detailed description about them and give comparisons against other existing models, we are trying to make a more clearer view about the future software system engineering.

4.1 Entity and Recursive Hierarchy

In an OO programming language component hierarchy, there should be a root abstract concept object, Entity, which is a container object, to make the COSM recursive, reflecting the complexity of relationships between different entities yet in a simple manner.

4.2 Natural Language and Its Counterparts in OOP

Each component of a natural language, such as character, word, sentence and paragraph, has two counterparts in OOP. One is string a set of characters; the other is concept object. In the COSM, Entity's attributes provide a way to link them together, table Entity is essentially a relationship table instead of a pure entity table. While a word processing system provides us a way to process language as string object, OOP will hopefully provide us a way to process concept object, as more concept components are developed by IT professionals. Then an OOP language will be more analogous to a natural language.

4.3 Legal Business Object and Business Process Object

The Legal Business Object (LBO) provides us a way to encapsulate legal rules into Business Object with other business rules. LBO is a descendent of Entity while Entity is the ancestor of all other objects. By encapsulating legal rules into business object, it will largely reduce the burden of professionals to learn legal rules, at the same time, it will provide another way to enforce law which has many ramifications we may not anticipate. LBO provides a foundation for IT professionals to develop other domain specific business application based on the Legal Body Model and the Asset Model.

While Business object represents entities in business, Business Process Object help us to change and report entity status and relationships. It represents forms, contracts, reports, invoice and orders in business workflow. It also encapsulates legal rules, eg. Contract law.

They are different from their counterparts in the real world because they can do jobs automatically according to relevant business rules.

4.4 Legal Body Model and Asset Model

Derived from the Legal Business Object, the Legal body Model(Person) and Asset Model(Asset) are built up in their natural ways applying the underlying principles of jurisprudence and accounting. Correspondent to Human Resource System and Accounting System, they may be the base concept models of a corporate information system.

4.5 Further requirement to OO Programming Language

To develop more quickly, IT industry should follow a more systematic path. The IT professionals will also focus more on business object analysis as well design and implementation. By systematically analyse business object hierarchy, more end-user-oriented OO component can be developed. The end-user-oriented OO components make sense to businessmen and can be easily used by them. By introducing more flexible mechanism, eg. Analogy, dynamic instance and deriving of new type of object and opening IDE to end user, information application system will be able to learn and evolve by the end users as needed. We can expect the day when information system may be as sophisticated as Microsoft Office desktop system or they integrated together.

4.6 Implication to domain specific professionals

Joint effort should be made by professionals from different industries. We argue again that more effort should be made to take full advantage of the fruit of legal science----legal professionals unconscientiously have an object system model of the society in their mind or underlying theories.

OO technology in turn will also provide an effective tool to help legal professionals, accountants or linguists changing the way to learn, analyse and work.

5 References

1. [ALI] Pamela N. Gray, *Artificial Legal Intelligence,* PUBLISHED Aldershot: Brookfield, USA: Dartmouth, c1997.
2. [BDDG] Steve Teixeira & Xavier Pacheco, *Borland Delphi4 Developer's Guide*, PUBLISHED Sams Publishing, 1998.
3. [BOAS] Cory Casanave, *Business Object Architectures and Standards*, Patel, D., Sutherland, J., Miller, J. (Eds), *Business Object Design and Implementation: OOPSLA'96—98 Workshop Proceedings.* Springs, 1998 / http://jeffsutherland.org/oopsla98.
4. [DDKS] Giovanni Guida and Carlo Tasso, *Design And Development Of Knowledge-Based Systems: From Life Cycle To Methodology,* PUBLISHED Wiley, 1994.
5. [ERMC] William D. May. *Edges Of Reality: Mind Vs. Computer*, PUBLISHED New York: Insight Books, c1996.

6. [ISFB] Suran Goonatilake and Philip Treleaven, *Intelligent Systems for Finance and Business*, PUBLISHED New York: Wiley, c1995.

7. [ITAG] Munindar P. Singh, Arand Rao, Michael J. Wooldridge (eds.), *Intelligent Agents IV: Agent Theories, Architectures, And Languages:* 4th International Workshop, ATAL'97, Providence, Rhode Island, USA, July 1997: proceedings (4th: 1997: Providence, R.I.) PUBLISHED New York: Springer, 1998.

8. [JBEAN] Mark Johnson, JavaBeans, Part 1, XML JavaBeans, http://www.javaworld.com/jw-02-1999/jw-beans.html.

9. [MART] Magnus Boman, Walter Van de Velde, (eds.), *Multi-Agent Rationality:* 8th European Workshop on Modelling Autonomous Agents in a Multi-Agent World, MAAMAW'97, Ronneby, Sweden, May 13-16, 1997 proceedings, European Workshop on Modelling Autonomous Agents in a Multi-Agent World (8th: 1997: Ronneby, Sweden), PUBLISHED Berlin; New York: Springer-Verlag, 1997.

10. [MSVC] Microsoft Corporation, *Microsoft Visual C++ Language Reference*, PUBLISHED Redmond, WA: Microsoft Press, 1997.

11. [MVJS] John A, *Microsoft Visual J++ Sourcebook*, PUBLISHED New York: Wiley Computer Pub., c1997.

12. [OODB] Embley, David W. *Object Database Development: Concepts and Principles*. PUBLISHED, Mass. : Addison-Wesley, c1998.

13. [OSDI] Bernard P. Zeigler, *Objects And Systems: Principled Design With Implementations In C++ And Java*, PUBLISHED New York: Springer, c1997.

14. [PLES] James Popple, *A Pragmatic Legal Expert System*, PUBLISHED Aldershot; Brookfield, USA : Dartmouth, c1996.

15. [REAAM] William E. McCarthy, *The REA Accounting Model: A Generalized Framework for Accounting Systems in a Shared Data Environment*, PUBLISHED The Accounting Review Vol. LVII, No. 3 July 1982.

16. [SJVA] Anil Hemrajani, *The State of Java Middleware*, Part 2: Enterprise Java Beans, http://www.javaworld.com/javaworld/jw-04-1999/jw-04-middleware.html

The Emergence of a Business Object Component Architecture[1]

Jeff Sutherland

SVP Engineering and Product Development
Chair, OOPSLA'95-'99 Business Object Component Workshops

IDX Systems Corporation
116 Huntington Avenue
Boston, MA 02116
E-mail: jeff.sutherland@computer.org

ABSTRACT: Object technology, a necessary but not sufficient condition for software reuse, requires an infrastructure that supports plug compatible Business Object Components for fast and flexible delivery of new or enhanced products to the marketplace. The Object Management Group (OMG) Business Object Domain Task Force (BODTF) has been the initial focal point for standardization of a Business Object Component Architecture (BOCA).[2] Priming this effort required joint work of the OMG BODTF, the Accredited Standards Committee X3H7 Object Information Management[3], and their joint sponsorship of the OOPSLA Business Object Component Design and Implementation for the years 1995-99.

This paper serves as a retrospective on some of the conceptual issues driving BOCA standardization and the global effort to build a unified set of life cycle standards for component based systems. Initial tools are available that will generate BOCA applications from an annotated UML design document. Generating complete systems from design will radically accelerate implementation of business processes in software.

1 Background

1.1 X3H7 Object Information Management

The International Standards Organization (ISO) is extending the international standard Reference Model for Open Distributed Processing (RM-ODP[4]) to incorporate enterprise modeling. RM-ODP compliance is a requirement for OMG standards submissions, and is the primary linkage between the ISO and the OMG.

X3H7 (now part of NCITS Technical Committee T3: Open Distributed Processing) is the U.S. technical committee for this international work item and is tasked with the following:

- Refine the RM-ODP enterprise language, explicating the relationship of an enterprise specification of a system to other RM-ODP viewpoint specifications of that system to enable the RM-ODP to be used for specification of object-based application architectures.

- Ensure that the enterprise language together with other RM-ODP viewpoint languages is suitable for the specification of a concrete application architecture to fill a specific business need.
- Measure success with a demonstration of the use of the RM-ODP viewpoint languages to specify a concrete application architecture.

1.2 OMG Business Object Domain Task Force (BODTF)

With a membership of over 800 software vendors, software developers, and end users, the OMG goal is to establish CORBA as standard middleware through its worldwide standards specifications: CORBA/IIOP, Object Services, Internet Facilities and Domain[5] Interface specifications. Established in 1989, OMG's mission is to promote the theory and practice of object technology for the development of distributed computing systems. The goal is to provide a common architectural framework for object oriented applications based on widely available interface specifications.

The Object Management Group has chartered the BODTF to facilitate and promote:

- the use of OMG distributed object technology for business systems,
- commonality among vertical domain task force standards,
- simplicity in building, using, and deploying business objects - for application developers,
- interoperability between independently developed business objects,
- the adoption and use of common business object and application component standards, and
- to issue requests, evaluate responses and propose for adoption by the OMG, specifications for objects, frameworks, services and architectures applicable to a wide range of businesses.

1.3 OOPSLA Workshop on Business Object Component Design and Implementation[6]

OOPSLA (Object-Oriented Programming, Systems, Languages, and Applications) has been the leading object technology conference for more than a decade. There are a wide variety of participant-driven workshops, tutorials, invited speakers, panels, debates, and technical papers capturing the latest in both research and in development experiences.

The OOPSLA Workshop on Business Object Component Design and Implementation is jointly sponsored by X3H7 and the OMG BODTF for the purpose of soliciting technical position papers relevant to the design and implementation of business object component systems.

The goals of the OOPSLA Workshop on Business Object Component Design and Implementation are to:

- Enhance the pattern literature on the specification, design, and implementation of interoperable, plug and play, distributed Business Object Components.
- Clarify the design and implementation of component systems, particularly systems in which workflow patterns and the REA accounting model[7] are basic building blocks for business applications.
- Contribute to emerging architectures for Intranet/Internet/Extranet applications, particularly those applications that integrate business object components, web servers, object and relational databases, and XML technologies.
- Pursue issues developed in previous workshops stimulated by papers on heterogeneous distributed workflow systems. Specify business object solutions to mobile agents, process engines, and systems that exhibit emergent behavior. Cross-fertilize business object design concepts with experience from the field of complex adaptive systems.
- Provide explicit experience reports on business object component systems developed and in production.

2 Why Business Object Component-Based Development?

For many years, members of X3H7 and the OMG BODTF have been intensely aware that the global market has become a highly competitive environment moving at an accelerating rate of change. Gradual improvements in productivity and enhancements in quality are no longer enough to maintain market leadership. Time to market of new products and rapid evolution of old products and applications are key success factors. This awareness led these groups to join forces in 1995 to initiate a radical change in software development environments, a change that would take years to specify and decades to implement.

Accelerating product evolution requires reinventing the processes that bring products to market and eliminating processes that do not add value. Since modern corporations have embedded many rules and procedures for product delivery in computer systems, the software applications that run the business must undergo significant change. To gain the strategic advantages of speed and flexibility, corporations must remodel their business processes, then rapidly translate that model into software implementations. The rapid adoption of the Internet since 1995 has accelerated the pace of software evolution and pushed it in the direction of global, distributed object computing, the target environment for BOCA.

Business Process Reengineering (BPR) sets the stage for continuous evolution of business processes to meet rapidly evolving business requirements. Implementation of software systems that support BPR requires Business Object Components that can both simulate corporate procedures and translate smoothly into software objects. Well-designed Business Object Component implementations can be easily modified as the business changes. In particular, if software implementation can be generated from design, change becomes easy, rather than difficult or impossible.

Reorganization of business processes is most effective when:

- there is a well understood model of the existing business,
- an evaluation of alternative future models against the current business,
- a model-driven approach is used to realign the business strategy, processes, and technology.

A multi-layered, object-oriented blueprint of the enterprise can drive the refocusing, realignment, and reorganization of the business.[8] Current attempts to implement this process under the rubric of business process reengineering (BPR) have been largely ineffective due to difficulties in changing monolithic organizations, processes, and information systems.

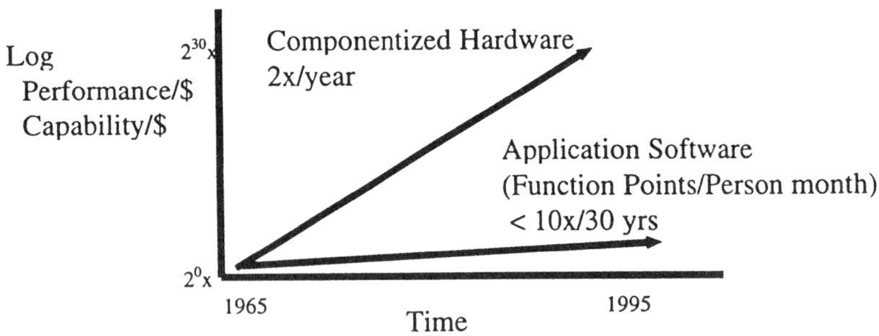

Figure 1: Hardware Price/Performance vs. Software Price Performance[9]

Figure 1 demonstrates that enhancing the productivity and performance of integrated circuits (IC) has led to exponential growth in computing power over the past thirty years, while software development productivity has increased only one order of magnitude. Hardware performance gains have been driven by "the observation made in 1965 by Gordon Moore, co-founder of Intel, that the number of transistors per square inch on integrated circuits had doubled every year since the integrated circuit was invented. Moore predicted that this trend would continue for the foreseeable future. In subsequent years, the pace slowed down a bit, but data density has doubled approximately every 18 months, and this is the current definition of Moore's Law. Most experts, including Moore himself, expect Moore's Law to hold for at least another two decades."[10]

Moravec[11] has more recently observed that information handling capacity in computers has been growing about ten million times faster than it did in nervous systems during our evolution. The power doubled every two years in the 1950s, 1960s and 1970s, doubled every 18 months in the 1980s (Moore's Law), and is doubling each year in the 1990s.

Custom chip development, which is largely software based, has followed Moore's Law due to the heavy capital investment in tools and technology common in the IC chip industry. However, this has not led to comparable gains in business application software development, largely due to the lack of automated software construction from design artifacts and failure to achieve large scale reuse of software components in business applications.

Developing an understanding of the reasons for rapid advancements in custom chip development clarifies the direction that application software development must take to achieve comparable results. The software productivity problem is a core issue for the X3H7 and the OMG BODTF as they assess how to maximize the impact of software standards development on the worldwide business community.

2.1 X3H7 Contributions

Document X3H7-93-23, Objectives and Operations[12], provided guidelines for work of the X3H7 during the period 1993-96.

- Develop liaisons with groups working on object oriented standards and review their progress.
- Complete the X3H7 Object Model Features Matrix document[13] that defines in some detail the characteristics of object models being proposed by different groups.
- Develop an X3H7 reference document based on the Features Matrix to present to targeted groups working on object model standards.
- Based on importance of each liaison group and the timing of each group in the standards development process, present formal proposals to these groups to facilitate harmonization of object model standards and enhance interoperability of distributed object systems.
- Develop scenarios of problems arising in the interaction of object systems to clearly illustrate the technical issues involved in distributed object interoperability.

The majority of members of X3H7 are also members of the OMG and committed to seeing relevant standards implemented by industry bodies. Under the editorship of Frank Manola, the X3H7 Object Model Features Matrix developed an analysis of issues involved in harmonizing object models. This showed that competing object models provided not only different structures, but often different semantics underlying the concepts that supported these structures.

Interoperability of object models requires understanding the structure and semantics of commonly used object-oriented frameworks and the interfaces between these development frameworks. Object models must interoperate within widely used frameworks and the number of frameworks should be few. An X3H7 consensus was reached in 1994 that 80% of new object-oriented development would be done in three application languages (Smalltalk, OO COBOL, and C++). These applications would communicate through a Business Object Request Broker to four external environments – X3H2 SQL standard databases, ODMG standard object databases, Microsoft's COM environment, and the OMG CORBA environment. Figure 2 illustrates the views of X3H7 at that time, updated to reflect the impact of the Web.

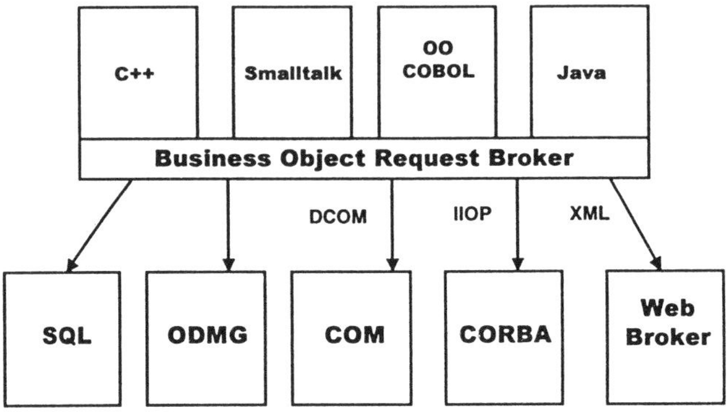

Figure 2. ANSI X3H7 Standardization Targets. 24 Sep 1994[14], updated 16 Feb 1999

The widespread adoption of the Internet since 1995 has accentuated the need for interoperable, distributed object standards and added Java to the list of widely used development languages. One of Java's primary benefits is enhancing interoperability of distributed systems, a primary objective of X3H7. In 1998, a World Wide Web Consortium (W3C) proposal for a WebBroker combined with an evolving set of standards for an XML distributed object computing infrastructure added a fifth environment requiring interoperability.[15]

Even before the rapid growth of the Internet, there was a consensus that application developers should be shielded from the detailed of these implementation environments. They should be able to use Object-Oriented Analysis and Design (OOAD) tools to build an application in a standard notation. OOAD tools should be able to import legacy models from CASE tools. The application model and all of its artifacts should be stored and versioned in an object repository and the runtime application binary objects should be generated from the repository to conform to standard component interface specifications. Request broker technologies should provide automated mapping between development frameworks. Figure 3 shows the X3H7 conceptual view of this problem.

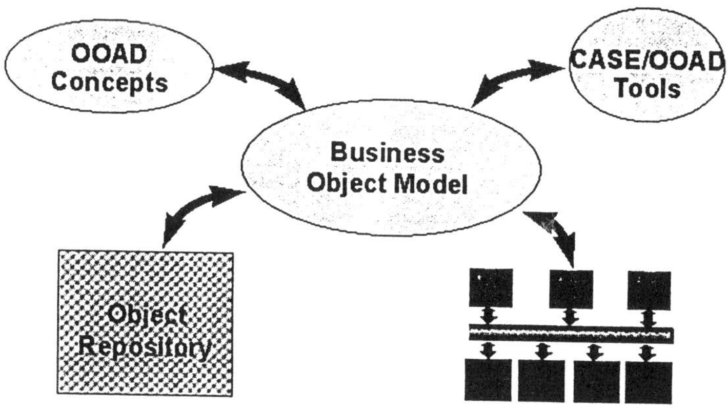

Figure 3. ANSI X3H7 Standardization Targets. 24 Sep 1994.

X3H7 members participating in OMG and other standards bodies began driving the agenda of object model harmonization in multiple organizations. They were key contributors to ISO standard RM-ODP, the distributed processing reference model that OMG technologies must conform with in accordance with agreements between ISO and OMG. They also agreed to co-sponsor, with the OMG BODTF, a Business Object Component Design and Implementation Workshop at the 1995 Conference on Object-oriented Programming, Systems, Languages, and Applications (OOPSLA), in order to draw research contributions into the drive for common Business Object Component standards.

2.2 OMG BODTF Contributions

In 1994, Sutherland[16] presented his findings on key issues in building life cycle object-oriented development environments for business objects to standards organizations, including the OMG Business Object Management Special Interest Group (BOMSIG, now BODTF). Simultaneously, Cory Casanave, 1995 Chair of the OMG BODTF, edited a BOMSIG Business Application Architecture White Paper[17] and later OMG Common Facilities RFP4: Business Object Facility and Common Business Objects.[18]

2.3 Business Objects as Reusable Components

Objects are not enough to gain the benefits possible with object technology. Only plug compatible, larger grained components can achieve a productivity breakthrough. Early adopters of object technology asserted that packaging software in object classes would allow software to obtain the benefits of Moore's Law seen in IC chip fabrication[19] and some projects have achieved major productivity benefits. For example, a Maintenance Management System at General Motors originally written in PL/I was rewritten under EDS contract in Smalltalk and achieved a 14:1 increase in productivity of design, coding, and testing. Detailed analysis of this project showed 92% fewer lines of code, 93% fewer staff months of effort, 82% less development time, 92% less memory needed to run, and no performance degradation.[20]

While there are many isolated projects that used object technology to achieve dramatic productivity gains during the past decade, this success has not translated into broad improvements across the software industry. In 1995, META Group reported that, "despite the promise of reusable objects, most IT organizations have realized a scant 10%-30% productivity improvement from object technology (OT)."[21] Failure to achieve larger productivity gains was attributed to:

- Data-centric, task-oriented application development.
- Methodologies and cultures that do not promote reusability.
- Few linkages between BPR-defined business processes and IT support initiatives.

Business Objects are designed to support a clearly defined relationship between BPR-defined business processes and software implementation of these components. Using an object-oriented development methodology yields quick time to market and object-oriented design allows for rapid evolution of Business Objects in response to market conditions. The bottom line is that object technology is a necessary, but not sufficient condition for large returns on investment. It must be combined with focus on delivering Business Object Components that enable fast and flexible delivery of new or enhanced products in the marketplace.

3 The Need for a Business Object Component Architecture

As business models are renewed, software architectures must be transformed. A Business Object Component Architecture (BOCA) is an effective solution for dynamic automation of a rapidly evolving business environment.

Dynamic change requires reuse of chunks of business functionality. A BOCA must support reusable, plug-compatible business components. Historically, the two primary strategies used for implementing client/server systems to support reengineering of business processes where visual 4th Generation Languages and classical object technology. While both of these approaches are better than COBOL, neither of them can effectively implement plug and play Business Object Components, nor do they allow systems to rapidly evolve with changing business requirements.

What is needed is a component standard that can be implemented with object technology. These components need to plug and play into standard frameworks. The concept of a BOCA incorporates objects, components, and frameworks along with the essential tools and infrastructure to allow autogeneration of full blown distributed object systems from design artifacts. Furthermore, these systems can be dynamically updated by changing the design and regenerating code, allowing synchronization of software systems with the constantly changing business processes seen in most enterprises.

3.1 Building Business Object Components

A group of objects is the ideal unit of reuse. These groups of objects should behave as a higher-level business process and have a clearly specified business language interface.

Business Object Components are encapsulated with a protocol that allows efficient communication with other objects on the network. Work on the concept of Ensembles[22] has shown that there is a minimal design specification for a plug compatible component.[23]

Consider a typical client/server application like an order entry system. This system takes a Purchase Order as input and produces a validated order as output. The internals of this component should be a black box to the external world. The resulting order is input for another subsystem or, alternatively, an exception condition is raised if the Purchase Order is not valid for processing (see Figure 4).

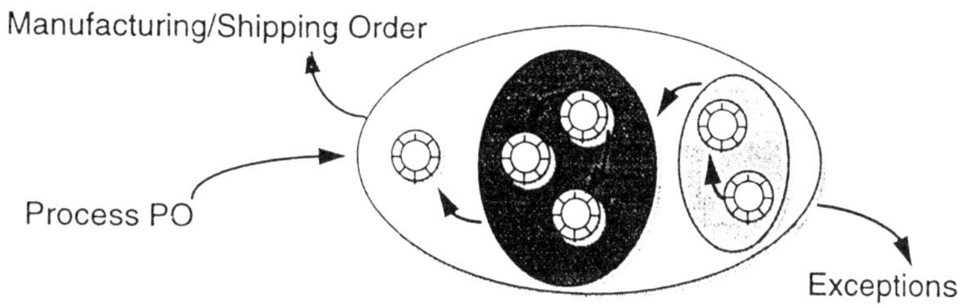

Figure 4. An Order Entry Business Object

To support plug-compatible reuse, a business component needs encapsulation in the following ways. The external world must not know anything about component internals, and the internals must not know anything about external components, other than allowing interested objects to register for notification of specific events or exception conditions.

The internals of a business component are made of other encapsulated business components. For example, when a Purchase Order passes through the membrane of the Order Entry business object, an internal component must see it, validate it, look up customer information, inventory availability and catalogue pricing, and build an order that is consistent with business rules and procedures. Each of these tasks is accomplished by embedded components, many of them communicating with external data sources.

External databases must be encapsulated as business objects components or reuse will not be easily achieved. There must be a resource tier with a database access component that causes values from any kind of database to materialize as objects inside the business component. Whether object-oriented, relational, or other database access is required, a set of class libraries designed to automate this interface will result in a major savings in development resources.[24]

An Order Entry business object will typically have multiple user interfaces. A clerk may be taking the order over the phone, entering purchase information, validating customer records and credit data, and reviewing an order for consistency and customer acceptance. Other users may require different presentation screens. User interfaces are difficult and time consuming to build at the code level. Today, much of this process can be automated. They should be encapsulated as separate objects that communicate by message passing to the Order Entry component..

A simple Order Entry client/server component has at least four large-grained components, one or more presentation objects, a workspace component that manages context during the creation of a transaction, and an enterprise component that models transaction state, and a database access component that shields the application developer from database access languages, database internals, and network communications (see Figure 5).

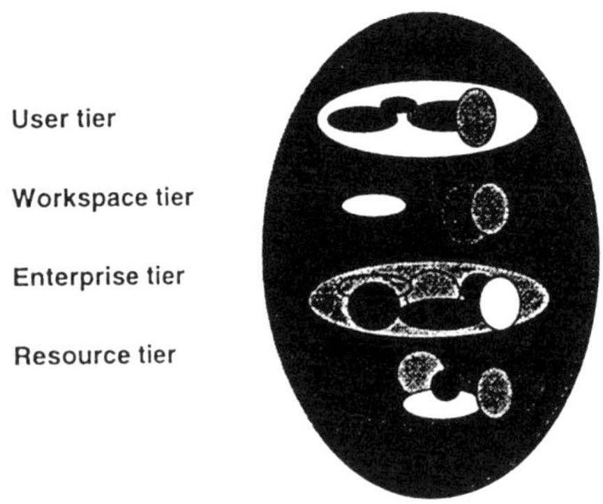

Figure 5. Business Object Component

Herzum[25] defines a business object component as follows:

A business component represents the software implementation of an autonomous business concept or business process. It consists of all the software artifacts necessary to express, implement and deploy a given business concept as an autonomous, reusable element of a larger information system.

Business component programmers focus their efforts on the software implementation of a concept which is a composition of software artifacts, including distributed components.

Szyperski[26] takes a complementary approach:

A software component is a unit of composition with contractually specified interfaces and explicit context dependencies only. A software component is deployed independently and is subject to composition by third parties.

The first definition focuses on the concept of a component within an enterprise system. The second surfaces the key issues for components used across enterprise systems.

3.2 Distributing Business Object Components

System evolution will invariably distribute these Business Object Components to maximize network performance and processor utilization, and to ensure proper control, integrity, and security of information. With the widespread adoption of standards-based Internet technologies, distributed object systems have become the norm. Business reengineering implies implementing a distributed environment where components encapsulating business functionality can be migrated to nodes on the network that allow maximum flexibility, scalability, and maintainability of a Business Object Component system.

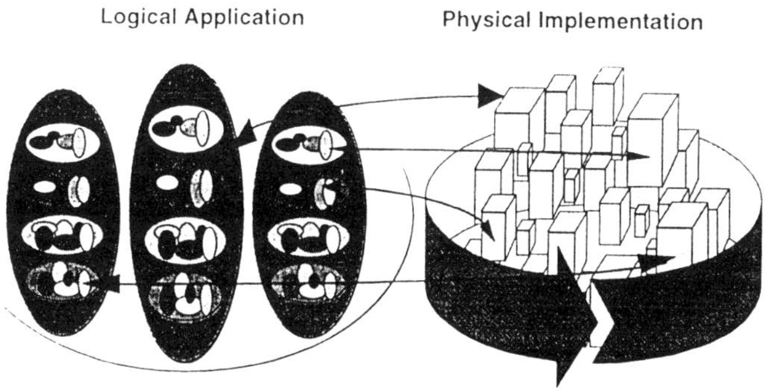

Figure 6. Application Business Object with Nested, Tiered Components

Business objects made up of nested components allow distribution of these components across a network. Figure 6 shows the logical application as a coherent set of nested client/server components. Deployment of this large-grained object may include distributing subcomponents across multiple heterogeneous computing resources in dispersed locations. Thus, an application designed on one processor is scattered across a network at run time.

Developers of business information systems have taken advantage of building applications with OLE components. At Object World in San Francisco, Allied Signal won the Computerworld Award for best object-oriented application of 1995.[27] They reengineered the Supply Management Business Process that took 52 steps to purchase a single part, so it now requires only three steps to complete the same transaction. The old process required seven people and took nine weeks to produce an approved purchase order. The new Supply Management Specialist Tool (SMST) allows one person to complete the same process in nine minutes for established suppliers with long-term agreements in place. In the case of new suppliers, where a Request For Quote (RFQ) is required, the process takes nine days. Table 1 summarizes these benefits.

	Before	**After**	**Improvement**
Process Steps	52	3	17.3
Staff	7	1	7
Time	9 weeks	9 min	2400

Table 1: Reengineering a Purchase Order Component

In this example, cycle time of the process is reduced 2400:1 for established suppliers, and 5:1 for new suppliers. Cost reduction is operational staff is 7:1. The impact of improvement in business efficiency leading to greater customer satisfaction and resulting market share is far larger than reduced costs in operations overhead or development time. It is the prime objective for use of Business Object Component design tools to assure success of Business Process Reengineering practice.

Despite isolated success stories, Brodie[28] reported in 1995, after a survey of 201 distributed object computing (DOC) applications worldwide, that this technology was not and would not be ready for prime time until vendors could deliver standards based Business Object Component frameworks.

"For the moment, DOC is in its infancy and does not meet industrial-strength requirements or the claims of its proponents… There are even very recent claims that a major breakthrough has occurred and that a DOC renaissance is upon us.[29] Based on our experience, GTE has decided to halt the design, development, and deployment of DOC technology and applications. In part this relates to our recognition of the problems described... In part, it also relates to our pursuit of commercial off the shelf (COTS) applications for which the vendors are largely responsible for the issues raised. Following a significant study of and investment in DOC technologies and methodologies, we have concluded that the benefits do not currently warrant the costs to overcome the challenges described... The claims for increased productivity, re-use, and lowered costs cannot be achieved with other than very highly skilled staff who must work with immature technology and methods. We will continue to investigate the area and observe its progress and will be prepared to take full advantage of the technology when DOC is more mature. I look forward to a highly competitive market for the DOC infrastructure and highly competitive products."

Progress has been made towards addressing Brodies' concerns since 1995. After the turn of the millenium, BOCA standards and Web technologies will resolve these problems and make distributed object computing easily accessible to the average developer. Significant events leading up to this capability are outlined below.

4 The Challenge of Achieving Moore's Law for Software

Working with Capers Jones at Software Productivity Research, Sutherland did an analysis in 1993 using a database of thousands of projects on productivity of language environments.[30,31] This study showed that 4GL environments were twice as productive in the real world as COBOL environments in a full life-cycle analysis.

Smalltalk had the capability of doubling the productivity of a 4GL environment, but only if 80% reuse was achieved. Since the average amount of reuse by Smalltalkers in the study was only 20% (not much better than C programmers at 15%) special tools needed to be used to enable this level of productivity.

In Figure 7 below, OOAD+ is an example of a tool that guarantees 80% reuse largely through automation, enables roundtrip engineering from design to code and back, is tightly integrated with user interface tools that allow nonprogrammers to develop user interfaces, and generates runtime components from design. Achieving these objectives, consistent with the X3H7 design targets noted previously in Figure 3, doubles the productivity of a Smalltalk environment.

The ORB bar in Figure 7 refers to an OOAD+ environment that automates the mapping between application objects and relation database storage of these objects. Sutherland observed that in multiple projects in heterogeneous business environments, hand coding object/relational mapping absorbed more than 30% of development resources.

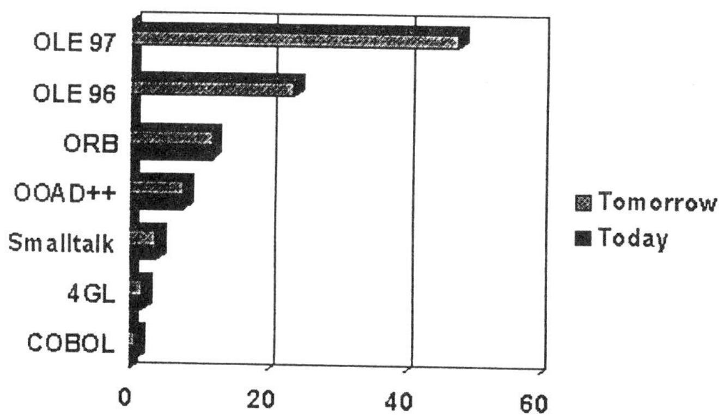

Figure 7: Moore's Law for Software

Sutherland estimated that by 1996, it would be possible to buy 50% of an application as off-the-shelf components, effectively doubling productivity. By 1997, early adopters would be buying 50% of the application as external components and reusing internally generated components for another 25% of the application, effectively doubling productivity on an annual basis, and beginning to achieve Moore's Law for Software. Brad Cox's vision of software as IC chips could be realized in such a component environment.

Successes in achieving these goals have occurred on a isolated basis. At OOPSLA'98, Zincke[32] gave an experience report showing a production system that was developed at the rate of 7.52 function points per person-day, an order of magnitude faster than industry average. Widespread achievement of these results has been limited by redeployment of software tools for Internet applications, effectively forcing the industry to repeat the lessons of the last two decades of Smalltalk innovation, and the lack of standard component environments in which to build domain-based object-oriented frameworks.

4.1 OMG BOMSIG Business Application Architecture and Common Facilities RFP-4

By mid-1995, BOMSIG has completed its second revision of a Business Application Architecture,[33] noting that "with a system comprised of a set of cooperative business objects, the outmoded concept of monolithic applications becomes unnecessary. Instead, your information system is comprised of semi-autonomous but cooperative business objects that can be more easily adapted and changed. This type of component assembly and reuse has been recognized as a better way to build information systems."

The consensus notion of a Business Application Architecture had evolved to what is now the standard three-tier architecture with Business Objects in the middle tier. A distinction began to be drawn between Business Objects as entities and Business Objects as processes (see Figure 8).

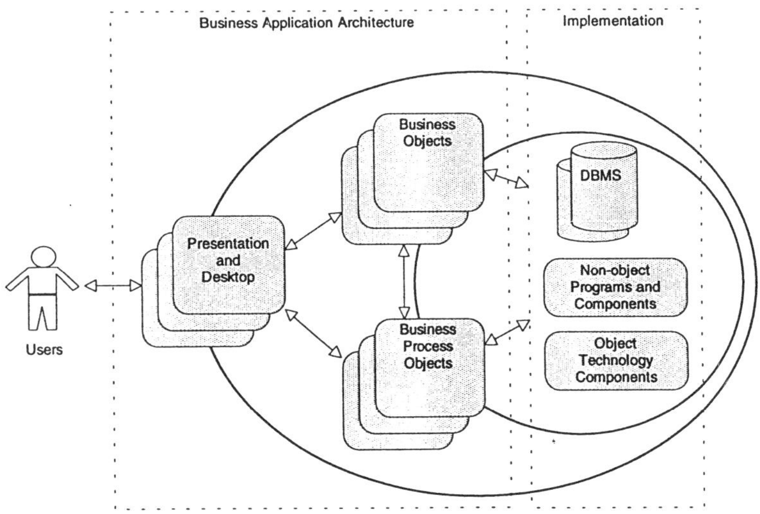

Figure 8. Business Application Architecture Revision 2. OMG 95-04-01

Towards the end of 1995, the Business Application Architecture concepts had evolved into the issuance of OMG Common Facilities RFP-4: Common Business Object and Component

Interoperability Facility (later known as the Business Object Facility (BOF)). The thrust of the RFP was to begin to build a layer on top of the OMG CORBA infrastructure to enable a plug-and-play environment. Figure 9 became the central view of the problem:

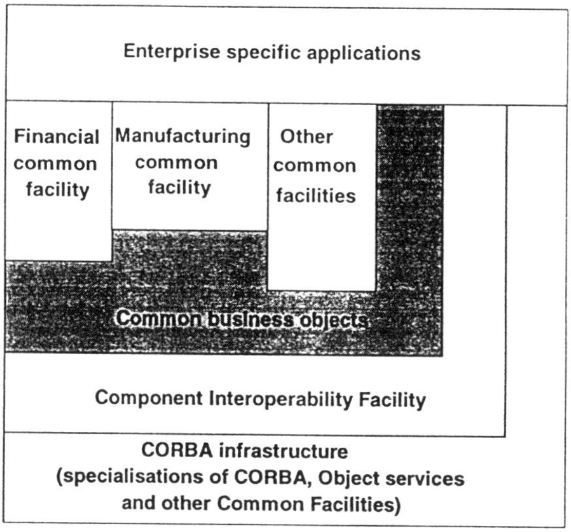

Figure 9: Business Application Architecture. CFRFP-4, OMG 95-12-13

The CORBA infrastructure provides an environment for communication between distributed objects. However, 100% of a business application needs to be hand coded in this environment. It should be possible with a component architecture to buy 80% of the application components and only have to write 20% of the code. A Component Interoperability Facility would provide generic superclasses for business objects. Common business objects crossing domains would be standardized, and domain frameworks would be developed to use both the Common Business Objects and the Component Interoperability Facility (later the Business Object Facility (BOF).

4.2 It's Never as Easy as it Looks

At the end of 1995, OMG Domain Task Forces where created to emphasis the importance of user organizations and vertical domain software to the future of OMG. BOMSIG metamorphized into the OMG Business Object Domain Task Force (BODTF) with the authority to issue its own RFPs and Common Facilities RFP-4 evolved into BODTF RFP-1.

The leading response to the Business Object Facility portion of BODTF RFP-1 matured, after several collaborative efforts, into the Business Object Component Architecture (BOCA). BOCA was approved by the OMG Architecture Board and failed to get the required vote of the OMG membership required for adoption as an OMG technology.

The problems with adopting a standard in 1998 revolved around several phases of integration with and definition of other OMG standards had to evolve:

It was necessary to harmonize BOCA with parallel work in multiple areas:

- UML - The Unified Modeling Language (UML) for object-oriented analysis and design became an OMG Adopted Technology in 1997 through the united efforts of Rational Software, Microsoft, Hewlett-Packard, Oracle, Sterling Software, MCI Systemhouse, Unisys, ICON Computing, IntelliCorp, i-Logix , IBM, ObjecTime, Platinum Technology, Ptech, Taskon, Reich Technologies, and Softeam corporations.[34]

- MOF - The Meta-Object Facility[35] defines a simple meta-metamodel with sufficient semantics to describe metamodels in various domains starting with the domain of object analysis and design. Integration of metamodels across domains is required for integrating tools and applications across the life cycle using common semantics. This OMG Adopted Technology represents the integration of efforts currently underway by the Cooperative Research Centre for Distributed Systems Technology (DSTC), IBM, International Computers Limited, Objectivity, Oracle, System Software Associates, and Unisys corporations in the areas of object repositories, object modeling tools, and meta data management in distributed object environments.

- CORBA Components - The current OMG RFP for CORBA Components begins, "While abstract interfaces are at the heart of object-oriented technology, they are only one dimension of the complex space within which distributed object applications are designed and built. In recent years, the concept of component technology has emerged as a more complete mechanism for expressing object-oriented software entities and assembling them into applications. Two prominent examples of component models are JavaBeans, and ActiveX Controls." [36]

4.3 The CORBA Component Conundrum

While BOCA achieved a reasonable level of integration with UML and the MOF in 1998, the lack of clear definition of a CORBA component model caused some OMG members to question whether a standard should be approved when it depended on an underlying component model that was still in the process of initial specification.

The Gang of Four (IBM, Netscape, Oracle, and Sunsoft) initiated the CORBA component effort in 1997 stating that "a component framework must provide a standard way to ask questions at design time as well as run time about the external interfaces, presented as methods, properties and events. The CORBA component model must support interface composition, so that components and the applications that use them are decoupled, and can evolve independently while maintaining compatibility. It must be possible to pass component state and methods by value so that native language interfaces can be mapped naturally into CORBA distributed operations. The CORBA component infrastructure must interoperate with existing non-proprietary component standards, such as JavaBeans. The component framework must support the Internet deployment of multi-tier applications, with URL naming of CORBA objects, and easy access to CORBA objects and services from Java."[37]

Currently, the way components are composed and "snap together" is left up to the implementation (Java beans being one such implementation). Without a standard component model there are no true "plug and play" business components. When CORBA-Components come on-line, BOCA IDL mappings can be extended to utilize CORBA components, achieving true "plug and play". Without the BOCA, CORBA components provide a way to "snap together" implementations, but no business application architecture to snap them into.

In early 1999, the leading proposal for a CORBA Component Model is similar to Enterprise Java Beans with some significant differences. It is likely that the industry will be face with three component models to deal with (ActiveX, JavaBeans, and a CORBA Component).

4.4 BOCA Current Implementation Status

The BOCA consists of several key concepts:[38]

- CDL: BOCA proposes a Common Specification Language (CDL), a way to write down, in a textual form, business object specifications that use the meta-model. With a way to textually express the meta-model, BOCA provides a way for writing publishable business object standards.

- IDL Mapping: The BOCA IDL mapping capability provides the mapping from the meta-model to OMG IDL interfaces. IDL interfaces necessarily contain technology details that need to be shielded from the business developer but are necessary for interoperability. Given a particular business object model, interfaces must be expressed in a consistent way that supports the underlying framework and interoperability. The IDL mapping specifies the form and content of business object interfaces based on the meta-model.

- Interoperability Framework – These are the CORBA interfaces that business objects have to support and use to achieve technical interoperability. The framework provides the technical underpinnings for BOCA objects using the meta-model. Standardization of the Interoperability Framework depends on the future adoption of a CORBA Component Specification standard.

Distributed business objects would not be possible without the underlying distributed object infrastructure. The CORBA Meta-model, ORB and IDL are the basis on which the BOCA and framework is built. Supporting the framework are the library of CORBA services used by business objects in well defined ways.

Software is available from Data Access Technologies[39] that will generate business object components into the IBM San Francisco Project Java Framework. An annotated UML designed autogenerates CDL and MOF metadata. These products can be used to generate Java classes in IBM's proprietary framework. Enterprise Java Bean frameworks will be available soon and BOCA will generate Enterprise Java Bean code. When the CORBA Component Facility is available BOCA will generate CORBA components.

4.5 Work in Progress

The 1999, the OMG BOCA effort refocused into a Business Object Initiative (BOI) addressing the characteristics of object-oriented analysis and design for enterprise computing systems. The OMG BOI Roadmap document noted that enterprise systems are closely tied to the business processes of an institution. As a result, the design of these systems will closely reflect the business domain of the enterprise. Several important characteristics need to be addressed in the design process:

- "The object types defined represent artifacts of the entities, processes, rules and events that occur in the enterprise business environment.
- "The number of object types is very large, sometimes numbering in the hundreds or thousands.
- "The associations among the myriad object types are numerous and the semantics of these associations are particularly crucial to ensuring the ability of different components to interoperate. The greater incidence in enterprise-scale distributed object systems of interactions among objects implemented by different development teams further magnifies the need for precision in this regard."[40]

Since the OMG had approved the Unified Modeling Language (UML) as a standard in 1998, BOI proponents argued that the important question was what, if anything, needed to be added to UML to properly specify a business object component system. What needed to be added to specify systems that needed to respond to high level business rules and events? What was important for building loosely coupled components that would be created by multiple development teams? How would UML be used to specify plug and play component models? These questions led to creation of four Request for Proposals (RFPs):

RFP 1: A UML Profile for Enterprise Distributed Object Computing (EDOC). This UML profile[41] must support specification at the design level of information required by all of the emerging OMG industry component models. It must distinguish between business process objects, business entity objects, and business rule objects. And it must support modeling business events.

RFP 2: A UML Profile for CORBA. This RFP calls for a UML profile supporting analysis and design semantics that are unique to CORBA.

RFP 3: A Human-Readable Textual Notation for the UML Profile for EDOC. This RFP calls for a Human Usable Textual Notation (HUTN) that would allow object models expressed in terms of the UML Profile for Enterprise Distributed Object Computing to be expressed textually.

RFP 4: A Mapping to CORBA of the UML Profile for EDOC. This RFP mandates that the mapping specify how an object model expressed in terms of the UML Profile for EDOC would be expressed in CORBA terms, including how the CORBA objects would use the CORBA Services.

These RFPs allow for competing proposals for UML specification of business object component systems and human readable text manifestation of those specifications, essential requirements for automating the creation of components from design. Presumable, portions of the original BOCA specification will be resubmitted for standardization in an environment where there is broader understanding within the OMG of BOCA issues and the opportunity to be fully consistent with the UML standard and the emerging OMG component standard.

5 Future Directions – XML and the WebBroker

In January 1998, Manola presented "Towards a Web Object Model" to the OMG Internet Special Interest Group.[42] This paper was developed under a DARPA contract to determine how the Web would become a distributed object computing environment. As the editor of the ANSI X3H7 Object Features Matrix, an extensive comparative analysis of object models developed over the last decade, Manola was ideally suited to the task.[43]

Conclusions were that the standardization of the Extensible Markup Language (XML), associated XML infrastructure standards, and the the World Wide Web Consortium's (W3C) Document Object Model (DOM), would provide a native Web environment for distributed XML objects. In April, 1998, a proposal was submitted to the W3C for a WebBroker as a lightweight alternative to COM and CORBA distribution models. The abstract stated:

A "necessary technological foundation exists to create a unified distributed computing model for the Web encompassing both document publishing and distributed software object communication. For lack of a better term, this model is referred to here as "WebComputing." Applications designed for the WebComputing environment exhibit a mix of features from both the Web publishing and the traditional distributed objects paradigms, blended into a unified model. The goal of this model is to extend the current Web application model such that the benefits of distributed object computing systems such as the OMG's CORBA and Microsoft's COM+ can be realized in a Web native fashion. The objective is to have a system which is less complicated than the above mentioned distributed computing systems and which is more powerful than HTML forms and CGI."

A Resource Description Framework (RDF) Model and Syntax Specification became a W3C Proposed Recommendation in January 1999. Together with Uniform Resource Identifiers (URI) which provide object identity and Namespaces, RDF provides the capability to implement an object model of an interoperable, distributed Web objects. It enables interoperability between applications that exchange machine-understandable information on the Web.

"RDF can be used in a variety of application areas; for example: in resource discovery to provide better search engine capabilities, in cataloging for describing the content and content relationships available at a particular Web site, page, or digital library, by intelligent software agents to facilitate knowledge sharing and exchange, in content rating, in describing collections of pages that represent a single logical "document", for describing intellectual property rights of Web pages, and for expressing the privacy preferences of a user as well as the privacy policies of a Web site. RDF with digital signatures will be key to building the "Web of Trust" for electronic commerce, collaboration, and other applications."[44]

The Web is driving many companies towards XML as a messaging paridigm within and between systems. Since it is a tagged data format with variable length records, allowing semantics to be defined separately from the data, one can envision systems which dynamically recognize and unravel XML packets of information and transform them into useful internal messages within a business component.

Consider an example from a health content provider on the Web. A request for an article from the New England Journal of Medicine causes the content server to server up an XML copy of the article. This XML package is then sent to the pricing server which looks at the XML and determines the pricing for the article. It appends pricing information to the XML package and passes the expanded information set to the advertising server. This server, in turn, appends the appropriate ads and sends the XML to the personalization server which appends the appropriate personalization information. Finally, the entire packet of XML information arrives at a Web server which transforms the XML into the appropriate HTML to ship to the client browser.

There are major benefits to this approach that radically reduce programming and maintenance for such applications:

- XML software is rapidly appearing on the Web to generate, process, and interpret XML, significantly reducing programming requirements.
- Complex XML interactions can execute very fast while human readable format significantly reduces debugging costs.
- Data ordering and data field lengths can be interpreted dynamically, drastically reducing transaction errors in operations.
- An organization or standards body can centrally define semantics and post them on the Web. XML tools can dynamically access and interprete this information.
- XML allows separation of presentation from semantics and data formatting. Multiple presentations of the same data can be generated through XSL style sheets.
- A single XML object can be a globally distributed complex concept via URL pointers, or an autonomous agent roaming the Web, interpretable and runnable on any Web server, or both simultaneously.

The natural direction for business object component systems in the Web environment will be to use XML distributed objects as the basis of the Workspace Tier of a business object component shown in Figure 5. As a tagged data model suitable for serializing objects, an XML Workspace Tier of a business object component is an ideal package, or kit of information, to pass around the enterprise as a workflow object. Various components in an enterprise system could “process” this XML kit, provide added value as appended XML information, and ship it on to the next service specified in a workflow graph.

6 Conclusion

When the development of a standard Business Object Component Architecture is complete, we will have a standard analysis and design language, a standard business specification language, a standard plug and play component environment, a standard meta-object facility for designs, applications, and repositories, and standard interfaces for distributed object. Tools will be provided to generate business systems from design into heterogeneous distributed runtime environments. Code changes may be reengineered into design supporting round trip engineering. A lightweight WebBroker may render distributed object computing as easily deliverable and as ubiquitous as HTML pages. This will position the software industry for the twenty-first century and launch a global effort to break down the barriers to implementing Moore's Law for Software.

7 References

[1] Portions of this paper were previously published as Sutherland, Jeff. Why I Love the OMG: The Emergence of a Business Object Component Architecture. *ACM StandardView 6:1:4-13, March 1998*

[2] Data Access Technologies, Inc., Electronic Data Systems (EDS), National Industrial Information Infrastructure Protocols (NIIIP), SEMATECH, Inc., Genesis Development Corporation, Prism Technologies, IONA Technologies. *Business Object Component Architecture (BOCA), Revision 1.1.* OMG Document: bom/98-01-07.

[3] X3H7 is now part of NCITS T3: Open Distributed Processing Technical Committee. See the NCITS X7 Technical Committee Home Page at http://enterprise.systemhouse.mci.com/X3H7/default.html.

[4] Open Distributed Processing Home Page, http://enterprise.systemhouse.mci.com/WG7/default.html

[5] The term "domain" refers to a realm of business interest such as transportation, manufacturing, or finance. It is also used in this document to refer to more specific areas of business interest such as marketing, sales, shipping, etc.

[6] OOPLSA Workshop on Business Object Component Design and Implementation, http://www.jeffsutherland.org/oopsla99/index.html

[7] Geerts, Guido. *The Timeless Way of Building Accounting Information Systems: The 'Activity' Pattern*. OOPSLA Workshop on Business Object Design and Implementation, 1997.

[8] Jacobson, Ivar, Maria Ericsson, Agneta Jacobson. *The Object Advantage : Business Process Reengineering With Object Technology*. Addison-Wesley, 1995.

[9] Digre, Tom. Business Application Components. In Sutherland J., D. Patel, C. Casanave, G. Hollowell and J. Miller (Eds). Business Object Design and Implementation: OOPSLA'95 Workshop Proceedings. Springer, 1997

[10] pcwebopedia.com. *Moore's Law*. http://pcwebopedia.com/Moores_Law.htm

[11] Moravec, Hans. *Robot, Being: mere machine to transcendent mind*. 1998

[12] Kent, William. X3H7 Objectives and Operations. X3H7-93-023, 18 January 1993.

[13] Manola, Frank (Ed.) *Object Model Features Matrix*. X3H7-93-007v12b, 25 May 1997.

[14] Sutherland, Jeff. *ANSI X3H7 Standardization Targets*. X3H7-94-35, 24 Sep 94.

[15] W3C. Distributed Object Communication on the Web. W3C Note 11-May-1998. http://www.w3.org/TR/1998/NOTE-webbroker

[16] Sutherland, Jeff. Business objects in corporate information systems. ACM Comput. Surv. 27, 2 (Jun. 1995), pp. 274 - 276.
[17] Casanave, Cory. OMG Business Application Architecture White Paper. OMG bomsig/95-4-1
[18] OMG Business Object Domain Task Force. Common Facilities RFP-4: Common Business Objects
and Component Interoperability Facility. OMG TC Document 95-12-13.
[19] Cox, Brad. *Object-Oriented Programming: An Evolutionary Approach.* Addison-Wesley, 1986.
[20] Taylor, David. *Object-Oriented Information Systems: Planning and Implementation.* John Wiley & Sons, 1992, pp. 320-322.
[21] META Group, Inc. Making the Case for Use Case. *Advanced Information Management*, File 324, 13 February 1995.
[22] Love, Tom. Object Lessons : Lessons in Object-Oriented Development Projects. SIGS Publications, 1993.
[23] Sutherland, Jeff and McKenna Jeff. Ensembles. Easel Corporation, 1993. http://www.jeffsutherland.com/papers/ensembles93.html
[24] Sutherland JV, Pope M, Rugg K. The Hybrid Object-Relational Architecture (HORA): An Integration of Object-Oriented and Relational Technology. *Proceedings of the 1993 ACM/SIGAPP Symposium on Applied Computing*, Indianapolis, 14-16 Feb 1993. Deaton E et al (Eds) ACM Press, pp 326-333.
[25] Herzum, Peter and Sims, Oliver. The Business Component Factory. John Wiley & Sons, 1999 (in press).
[26] Szyperski, Clemens. Component Software: Beyond Object-Oriented Programming. ACM Press, 1998.
[27] VMARK Software. Allied Signal Company wins the Computerworld Object Application Award at Object World. Press Release, 21 August 1995.
[28] Brodie, Michael. *The Emporer's Clothes are Object Oriented and Distributed.* GTE Laboratories, 1997.
[29] Microsoft. The Renaissance of Distributed Computing. White Paper, November 1996 (www.microsoft.com/pdc/html/p&s.htm).
[30] Sutherland, Jeff. An Executive Overview to Object Technology (tutorial). Object World, Boston, Sydney, San Francisco, Frankfurt and Executive Symposium on Object Technology, Toronto, 1995.
[31] Jones, Capers, Programming Languages Table, Release 8.2. Software Productivity Research, March 1996.
[32] Zincke, Gerald. How to Achieve 7.52 Function-Points per Person-Day with Object Technology. Addendum to Conference Proceedings, OOPSLA 12thAnnual Conference, 5-9 October, 1997. ACM Press SIGPLAN.
[33] OMG BOMSIG. OMG Business Application Architecture, Revision 2. OMG 95-04-01.
[34] Rational Software, Microsoft, Hewlett-Packard, Oracle, Sterling Software, MCI Systemhouse, Unisys, ICON Computing, IntelliCorp, i-Logix , IBM, ObjecTime, Platinum Technology, and Ptech. UML Proposal to the Object Management Group in response to the OA&D Task Force's RFP-1, Version 1.1. OMG Document: 97-08-11.

[35] Cooperative Research Centre for Distributed Systems Technology (DSTC), IBM, International Computers Limited, Objectivity, Oracle, System Software Associates, and Unisys. Meta Object Facility (MOF) Specification Joint Revised Submission. OMG Document: 97-10-2.
[36] OMG. CORBA Component Model Request For Proposal. OMG Document: orbos/96-06-12.
[37] IBM Corporation, Netscape Communications Corporation, Oracle Corporation, Sunsoft, Inc. CORBA Component Imperatives. OMG Document: orbos/97-05-25.
[38] Frankel, David. UML, BOCA, and MOF: Presentation to the Lifesciences DTF at the Orlando Meeting. OMG Document lifesci/98-06-02.
[39] BOCA CDL Development Kit for OMG IDL, Pre release revision 0.51. Data Access Technologies, Inc., 1998.
[40] Frankel, David S.; Seidewitz, Ed; Rutt, Tom (Eds). Roadmap for the Business Object Initiative: Supporting Enterprise Distributed Object Computing. OMG Document bom/98-12-04, Version 3.0, 21 December 1998.
[41] UML Profile is defined in the Roadmap for the Business Object Initiative. It is essentially a subset, not necessarily a proper subset, of UML.
[42] Manola, Frank. Towards a Web Object Model. Position Paper for the OMG-DARPA-MCC Workshop on Compositional Software Architectures. Object Services and Consulting, Inc., 1998.
[43] Manola, Frank (Ed.) X3H7 Object Features Matrix. NCITS X3H7 Technical Committee Document X3H7-93-007v12b, 25 May 1997.
[44] W3C. Resource Description Framework (RDF) Model and Syntax Specification.

Agent-Oriented Workflow: An Experience Report

Pamela M. Rostal
Compuware Corporation
Minneapolis Professional Services Division
3600 West 80th Street
Bloomington, Minnesota 55431
E-mail: prostal@acm.org

ABSTRACT: *This article is an experience report showing how autonomous software agents are being used to implement the business process and entity components that compose a workflow-intensive call center application. It starts by recounting the business background, requirements, and early approaches. The next section details the knowledge representations used to depict the process model, the domain model and the rule base. This is followed by a discussion of agent types and how they collaborate to meet business needs. The fourth section consists of an example demonstrating how a group of agents might keep a hypothetical work queue in equilibrium. The final section shows how interface agents might facilitate rule specification.*

1. Introduction

Business applications are built to support corporate objectives by automating appropriate activities so that employees can concentrate on tasks requiring human abilities. As such, business processes represent a collaboration between people and software with parallel goals. By modeling the elements of a business application as agents, business sponsors can define the system portion of a process in anthropomorphic terms, and developers can deliver software that integrates optimally with the rest of the enterprise.

Four years ago, a Minnesota company set out to meet its needs for adaptability, flexibility and productivity improvement by re-engineering its consumer relations department with the goal of eliminating paperwork and automating all routine tasks. After a year of business analysis, thirteen major processes were targeted for computerization, a software development team was assembled, and a phased release plan was developed. The initial product release supported a single process within a framework that would eventually evolve to handle all thirteen types of work.

After 18 months in service, the application had proved its worth by delivering savings of over $1 million and improving productivity by 36% in the company's Dallas call center. Considering the highly interactive nature of many call center activities, the goal of achieving a six-fold improvement within ten years remains a significant challenge. This paper presents a high-level experience report of ongoing efforts to integrate ideas from multiple disciplines into an automated solution that evolves continually to meet business needs.

1.1 Background

Consumer relation's personnel at this Twin Cities company handle over 10,000 requests for information, clarification and data correction every week. Often, employees must obtain additional information from the caller to determine exactly what service is required; however, in cases where the consumer's request is clear and the system information unambiguous, little human decision-making is needed. These were the first situations slated for automation.

Business process flowcharts indicating dozens of decision points had initially pointed to an expert system solution. Although an expert system might have handled rule specification better, several practical disadvantages prevented its adoption for the call center project:

- It presented a significant learning curve for developers who already knew business application languages (time costs),
- It had to be integrated with the body of code that actually automated the employees' work (both complexity and time costs)
- The product and annual support contracts had to be purchased (financial costs)

The return from adopting a commercial expert system rather than encapsulating business logic into internally developed code was not significant enough to warrant the investment.

Because of these difficulties, attention shifted to a workflow management approach. According to the Joint Workflow Management Facility Revised Submission [OMG 98], "A Workflow Management System provides procedural automation of a business process by management of the sequence of work activities and the invocation of appropriate human and/or IT resources associated with the various activity steps." The advantages of commercial workflow products were perceived as:

- The ability to invoke small independent modules of process application code
- Graphical process definition languages to facilitate specification of workflow conditions by non-programmers
- Encapsulation of both code and conditions in a single product

The selected system supported the assignment of roles to employees and the specification of work movement among them, but seemed less appropriate when a single person performed all activities associated with the request, as was often the case in the call center.

A more serious impedance mismatch occurred, however, because the distributed object-oriented business model did not integrate well with the monolithic workflow management system, which required duplication of data unless it was the controller of all data and objects. Wolfgang Schultze's presentation to the Business Object Domain Task Force (BODTF) on January 16, 1997, details the differences between workflow technology as specified by the Workflow Management Coalition, and business process components as envisioned by the Object Management Group (OMG) [OMG 97]. The OMG's statement that "there are no object-oriented frameworks to enable different Workflow Management products and workflow aware applications to work together, which is resulting in incompatible 'islands' of process automation" acknowledges these differences. [OMG 98]

Despite the industry situation, however, four employees attended weeklong training sessions from the vendor, and multiple consultants visited the project site over the next year and a half. After several attempts to produce adequate workflow-business component collaborations, developers redirected their efforts toward delegating workflow logic to small process components capable of requesting services from specialized business entity components. These components constitute a society of both reactive and deliberative agents that collaborate with each other and a user-created knowledge base to respond to a consumer's request in as little time as possible. Thus, workflow functionality is distributed across many business components, rather than being centralized in the workflow management system.

1.2 Call Center Workflow Requirements

Despite the redistribution of responsibilities, however, the requirements remained the same. The workflow management system was supposed to have been the repository for all non-structural business rules. Its requirements, as specified by the business sponsor, represent a customized version of the workflow requirements presented by Marc-Thomas Schmidt in last year's Business Object Workshop [SCHMIDT 98]. These requirements can be summarized as follows:

- Associate work with resources that have appropriate capabilities (#5 in Schmidt's article), automating any work that meets the stated criteria
- Rearrange priorities assigned to work types if one kind becomes too prevalent, so that resource usage remains optimized (#1)
- Keep individual workloads current by reminding users of work they placed on hold, even to the extent of sending reminders to correspondents when a response is delaying resolution (#3 and 4)
- Allow its rules to be changed by non-technical personnel who have clearance (#1 and 2)

The agent approach has been successful in meeting the first requirement, and will be tested on the third during the next release. A mechanism for meeting the second requirement is currently being developed, but the business has not specified exactly how it should work. A hypothetical example is presented in the "Deliberative or Opportunistic Agents" section. The fourth requirement is a subject for future research, which is detailed in the "Future Agent Functionality" section of this paper.

2. Knowledge Representation

[HAY 97] defines a business rule as "a statement that defines or constrains some aspect of the business. It is intended to assert business structure or to control or influence the behavior of the business." This implies that multiple business component views are required to convey a complete picture. The structural rules are reified in the attributes of the business entities themselves, while business behavior is codified in the process components and constrained by knowledge base rules. Johansson et al. [JOHANSSON 97] diagrammed the relationships among the domain model, the rule base, and the process model as shown in Figure 1.

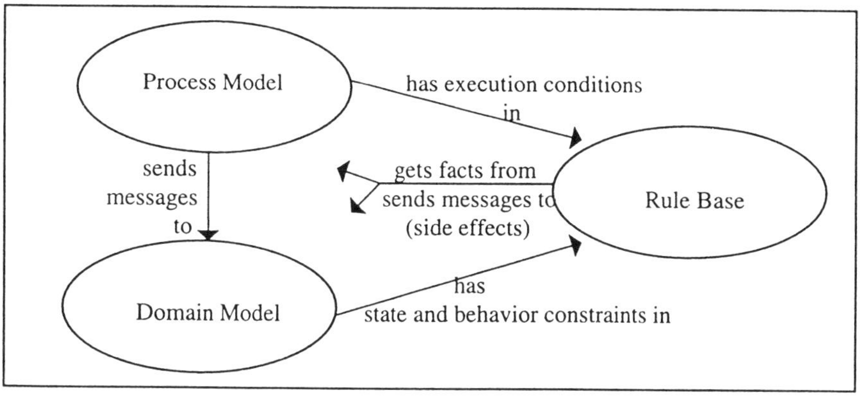

Figure 1 Johansson's Knowledge Representation Relationships

2.1 Process Model

The process model captures the way work is done in the organization, as defined by the business process re-engineering output. Its participants are both people and autonomous business processes implemented as agents. Within the system, the process agents pass messages to business entity agents. The message recipients respond by executing the requested methods if possible, or alternatively, by returning reasons for failure. Methods may be implemented by base business entities if the behavior is part of the entity's essence, but often, subclasses or interfaces provide the required aspect-oriented behavior.

In the Minnesota project, flowcharts were used to specify processes during the re-engineering effort. Accompanying text enhanced the understandability of the flowcharts by adding additional context for the required decisions. These documents became the basis for requirement specification of the software processes. Each automated activity was delegated to a business process component whose responsibility was to script the calls to the specialized business entities.

The specialized business entities are analogous to Sims and Eeles' workspace layer distributed objects between the enterprise layer and the user interface screen [SIMS 98]. In Building Business Objects, the workspace layer acts as a facilitator to prepare the business entity for display and provide any services required for user interaction with the business entity.

Generalizing the concept of a facilitator between a process and an entity allows process-specific behavior to be factored out from the base entity object. Associating a business entity with its context-specific behavior only when relevant allows retrieval of a process-specific subset of rules, thus improving rule-processing performance. It also allows the possibility of polymorphic activities, or process steps, in different contexts. When an activity is complete, an audit entry records the result, and the activity returns control to the calling business component. Figure 2 uses UML to illustrate the relationship cardinality and the distribution of responsibilities across business objects and layers.

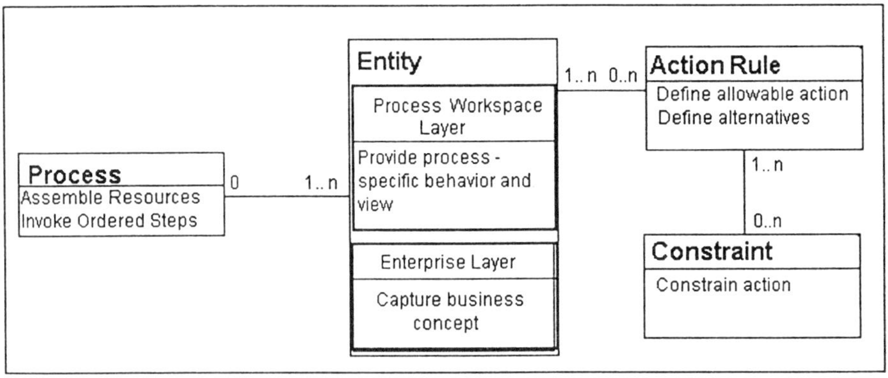

Figure 2 Business Object Responsibilities in a Process

If the work needs to interact with a user again, it can be put back into the user's queue. Upon completion of another user-interface process, the user can invoke additional processes to return control to the software agents in the system.

2.2 Domain Model

The domain model was fashioned using object role modeling principles supported by the Infomodeler CASE tool, most recently acquired by Visio. Business partners specified the attributes of each entity and its inherent behavior. Every business entity was designed for manipulation at the client machine, followed by transportation to the server for storage. As such, each entity implemented the user interface and resource layers described by Sims and Eeles [SIMS 98]. In addition, each entity was essentially a mobile agent with user interface behavior in one environment and persistence behavior in another.

Process logic was minimal, so it was not adequately addressed in the first release. Aspects of business process logic were incorporated into the input screens, the database library and the delegator server whose original reponsibility had been only to direct the entities as they passed through to other application servers.

As new functionality was added, the data-centric entities were easy to implement, but displaying and processing them became increasingly difficult. Hence, the decision to re-architect the application.

Following the pattern suggested by Herzum and Sims in [HERZUM 98], the new process components contain one or more screens, one or more processes, and references to the appropriate interface for each business entity in the process. The resource layer has been made much more generic, and one approach currently being evaluated is to move most, if not all, of the business entity persistence logic into Oracle packages containing stored procedures and triggers.

2.3 Rule Base

The lifecycle rule base described in [ROSTAL 98] was enhanced to incorporate more complex conditions and is moving toward inclusion of the business process context information mentioned earlier. In the enhanced version, the process provides the business entity with its context, allowing the entity to retrieve its action options, evaluate its state, and execute the appropriate behavior. While the lifecycle subsystem requires a great deal of further development, it has worked satisfactorily during its first year of operation governing the behavior of three domain entities. Developers were able to correct a processing defect without recompiling code, which was the primary intent of separating the knowledge base from the object's definition.

This separation of process rules from static object implementation is what gives the business entity agents a semblance of intelligence. Although they are not learning agents, their activities are dynamically linked in response to changing environmental conditions, so that succeeding generations of agents become more favorably adapted to their environment.

3. Why Agents?

Adaptation to a changing environment is just one of the benefits of implementing business components as agents. Distributing workflow responsibilities across layers of agents allows developers to craft each type of agent to optimize its functionality, but this ability is predicated on a common understanding of agency. The definition of an agent given by Jennings and Wooldridge [JENNINGS 98], is general enough to allow a wide range of functionality, yet specific enough to keep development efforts focused on a single purpose for each agent. Since the authors opined that most researchers would find it acceptable, the following definition governs the use of agents in the project:

> "...an agent is a computer system situated in some environment, and that is capable of autonomous action in this environment in order to meet its design objectives."

The agent's autonomy implies that it has control over its response to an incoming message - the sender can only request a service, not mandate its outcome. This flexibility is illustrated in Figure 3, which shows the work agent consulting its rule base before determining how it should respond to an incoming message based on its current state. In that way, it resembles the human trainee confirming a hunch before finalizing a decision.

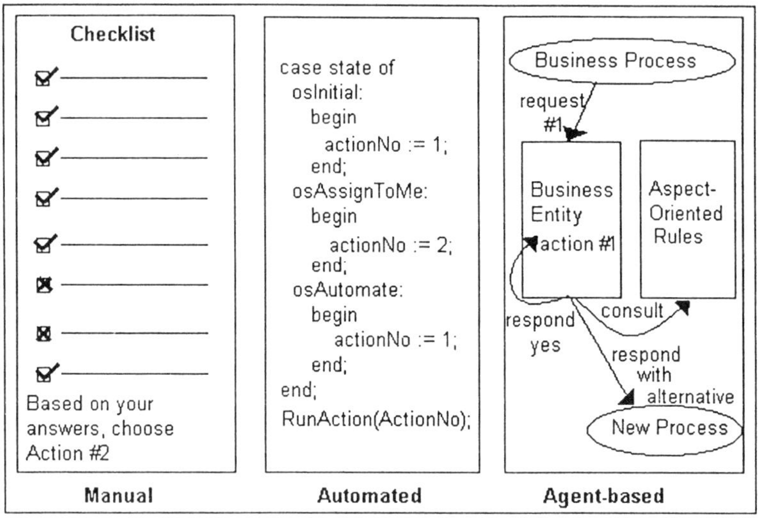

Figure 3 Process Implementation Comparison

If the rule changes, the trainee responds differently as soon as the change is communicated, just as the agent does. The agent also resembles the automated system, however, because it never forgets, misinterprets or grows bored with the rules it is given. By combining the characteristics of both human and automated processors, the agent-based system delivers the best of both worlds.

3.1 Which Agents?

Elizabeth Kendall et al.[KENDALL 98] classify the types of agents used in this system as either reactive or deliberative. Whereas "a reactive agent reacts to changes in its environment or to messages from other agents," a deliberative or intentional agent is strong because "it is able to reason on its intentions and beliefs, to create plans of actions, and to execute those plans." [MOULIN 96] The reactive agent is weak because it has no internal model of itself or the world around it. It reacts to events and causes pre-programmed changes to its environment. The work agent is a deliberative agent, corresponding to a business entity operating in the context of a business process, that reasons about itself and its environment to determine how best to respond to the consumer's request. Kendall suggests that a society of deliberative agents, each with knowledge of specific business processes, would exemplify an ideal application for agent technology.

3.2 Deliberative Agents

Consider the real-world example of handling a consumer's request for information as diagrammed in Figure 4. The user has instantiated a process to create and define a piece of work, and would now like to have it assigned to himself. Before assigning itself to the user, the work agent must consider whether it requires a designated specialist. This could be the case if it deals with a special-handling consumer, or deals with a specialized type of information. It must also consider whether the user has the appropriate security to proceed farther. All of this takes place during the "Considering Assign" state.

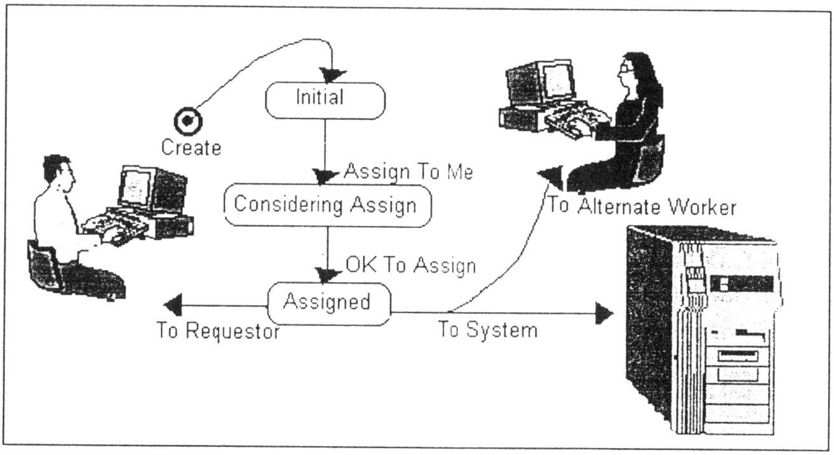

Figure 4 Worker asks Work to Assign Itself to Him

The deliberative work agent analyzes each of the following aspects of its environment model to determine whether it can assign itself to the requesting worker:

- The list of involved consumers to determine if they are special-handling consumers. If so, assign the worker who should handle them. (This may require a negotiating agent to resolve conflicts as to which worker should be assigned if multiple consumers on the same request require special handling by different workers.)
- Information about the consumer's request to determine whether responding to the consumer will require specific expertise. If so, assign the worker with that expertise.
- Identifying information about the requesting worker to determine whether he has clearance to do this type of work. If so, assign the worker; if not, assign the system to examine whether automation is appropriate.

If further conditions apply, users add them as rules to the knowledge base so that additional properties will be evaluated against their required values. Regardless of its decision, the work persists itself.

If the work decides that the user is not the best candidate, it responds to the input process that it could not meet the worker's request, and the input process displays the message to the user. Otherwise, the input process creates and runs a new process to display the work to the user. Upon either action, the input process terminates.
Reactive Agents

Both the input process and the process it creates upon termination could be considered reactive agents. They can be instantiated by the user's clicking on a menu item or a button, as an effect of a deliberative agent's actions, or as part of another process's executing its actions. Reactive agents can only react to external stimuli; they cannot make decisions about whether or not the stimulus is appropriate given their current state. Processes always behave the same way because they cannot reason on their beliefs as they have no internal symbolic model of the world. They provide context for work agents so that work agent deliberations can exclude any action that is not allowed in the current process. This allows work agents to reach a decision much more quickly than if every possible action were contemplated.

The collaboration among multiple diverse, independent agents, each acting according to its own set of internal rules, gives rise to a complex society of agents capable of generating emergent behavior. To deal with emergent behavior, reactive agents monitor various aspects of the system and instantiate deliberative agents to modify the rules for succeeding generations of work agents.

Figure 5 shows an employee who is ready to work on his next assignment. The rules on the right could be presented during training, and the user could choose where the next assignment comes from, or an agent could read the rules from the knowledge base and execute actions on behalf of the user. All work is drawn from the queues in order from highest priority to lowest priority. The circled words represent variables that user administrators can modify whenever their policies change. The numbers are circled because the order of queue searching is also a variable that administrators can modify.

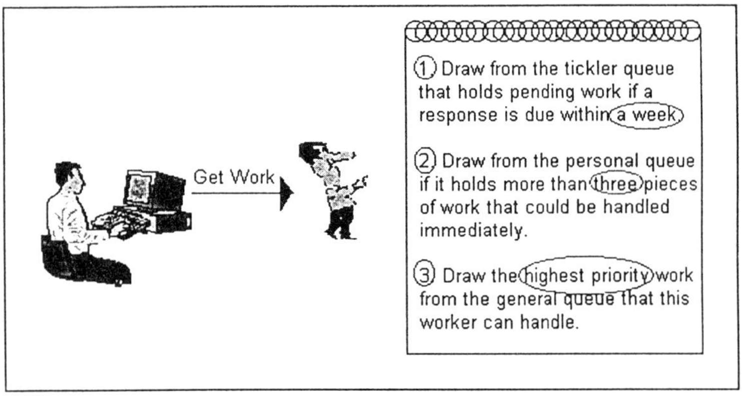

Figure 5 Using a Deliberative "Get Work" Agent

3.3 Deliberative or Opportunistic Agents

As the user's agent draws work from the general queue, a simple reactive agent monitors queue composition against a user-specified ideal. When the system moves far enough away from this ideal, (as when the employee just took a piece of work that left the queue too rich in urgent work), the reactive agent notifies a deliberative or opportunistic agent to remedy the situation. The difference between these two classes of agent is that deliberative agents use data in the knowledge base to modify the system according to prescribed strategies. An opportunistic agent does not know a predefined action to take under given circumstances, but knows the constraints that define when the system is out of equilibrium [KENDALL 98]. An opportunistic agent can take any action that keeps the system within its constraints.

This system uses deliberative agents that manipulate priorities so the copious work that can be done by many employees can move ahead of normally higher priority work done by just a few. This action allows the queue to move toward the ideal composition profiled by the user administrators.

The formula for calculating priority is:

Age Factor * Age	Age is # of days since work arrived
+ Legal Factor * (0 or 1)	Legal is 0 if no impact, 1 if impact
+ Financial Factor * (0 or 1)	Financial is 0 if no impact, 1 if impact
+ Rank Factor * Rank	Rank ranges from 1 to 5 (Figure 5)
+ 100	Constant
- DueDate Factor * Days until duedate	Due date - Today's date
Priority	Calculated priority

4. Queue Management Example

This example shows how the calculation above might be used to regulate the work queue. Figure 6 shows a hypothetical model of the the target system. The administrators have decided that almost anyone can work on Type A work, but only the most experienced can perform Type E work. Any Type E worker can also do Type A-D work.

Rank	Ideal Composition	Workers	Normal Volume	Due In	Speed
5	20% Type E Work	5% can do	7%	3 days	Slow
4	20% Type D Work	15% can do	10%	3 days	Medium
3	10% Type C Work	25% can do	3%	5 days	Very Fast
2	30% Type B Work	50% can do	30%	3 days	Medium
1	20% Type A Work	90% can do	50%	4 days	Fast

Figure 6 Hypothetical Work Model

Suppose new federal legislation generates a spike in the amount of Type C work, so that instead of being 3%, it now becomes 15% of the total. Even though the work can be processed very quickly, the queue is out of equilibrium as dictated by the administrators' ideal world. The reactive agent monitoring the queue detects the spike and alerts the deliberative agent to take corrective action. The deliberative agent follows the rules in the knowledge base and adjusts the rank of Type C work to 4, moving type D work down to 3. The monitor waits a prescribed amount of time before contacting the deliberative agent again so that the queue has time to be affected by the new rule. After an hour, if Type C work does not represent 10% of the total work in the queue, the monitor agent can request that the rule adjuster moderate the queue again. It can move Type C up to a rank of 5, moving type E down to 4. This means that most of the workers who are capable of doing Type C work will now draw Type C unless there is still some very old Type D or E work that is well past its due date. If, after another hour, the queue equilibrates, Type C can drop to a rank of 4, and Type E can regain its top status. Finally, after another hour, Type C can return to its normal rank of 3.

Although the example was simple, it shows the power that the priority-changing agents can wield over what work will be returned when someone needs a new assignment from the general queue. If, even after elevating Type C work to a rank of 5, the queue had not come to equilibrium within an hour (or the prescribed time interval), a notification to the manager in charge of assigning responsibilities to workers would highlight the situation. The manager could then call in additional workers, or overtime could be offered to clear the Type C work before the next day.

This is where people interact with the agents, remedying situations for which the agent does not have a ready solution. At some point, an opportunistic agent might assist the rule-modifier and promote any worker who has had training on Type C work but had not officially been promoted yet. The opportunistic agent might have observed that the business administrator had applied this solution, and use a neural network to determine which other workers might have the ability to handle Type C work. It could then recommend that those workers be given training so that they might be available for the next Type C glut.

This simple approach might be modified by changing the available remedies for excess work, but it will serve as a first step toward a self-regulating workflow system that frees its business administrators from endless cycling through examining reports, making changes to the rules, and observing the effects.

5. Future Agent Functionality

Defining and constraining the behavior illustrated in the example is not an easy task. Although the development process has been fairly successfully adapted to Sims and Herzum's full-lifecycle component model [HERZUM 98], constraint definition remains an open issue in the call center application. Currently, rules are entered directly into the database without the aid of a user interface. Therefore, users must call developers, define the rules, confirm that the developer has interpreted the rule specification correctly, and finally verify that the change was effected properly.

Accommodating this use of natural language for rule specification is one of the development staff's goals. Therefore, research is being done to determine whether an interface agent might be the most appropriate mechanism for defining workflow constraints. This approach also insulates users from process definition language changes and inconsistencies across tool vendors.

Collaborating with the user to jointly develop and test the constraint, the interface agent could learn about various constraint structures, and could teach the user to construct rules in ways that make them more amenable to automated interpretation. Thus, the process would remain virtually unchanged except that, instead of a developer, the user would converse with an interface agent.

The motivation for this approach came from Apple Computer which developed "Data Detectors" that detect structures in any user-selected text and then provide the user with a menu appropriate to the selected structure [NARDI 98]. Applying a comparable strategy to a "Rule Detector" might allow process changes communicated by e-mail to be selected and automatically entered into change control or the database. It could also be used to select rules embedded in existing policy manuals for inclusion in the rule base. Although much research remains to be done in this area, the use of interface agents appears to be a feasible solution to the problem of rule specification.

6. Conclusion

This paper has shown that agents are not just esoteric concepts for the consideration of artificial intelligence buffs. As the examples show, they represent a reasonable approach to delivering functionality that is appropriate, flexible and adaptable. Their autonomy and mobility make them an ideal implementation model for a distributed component architecture. Making their internal model of the world dynamic in response to rules in the database makes them flexible. The fact that each agent can be implemented as a reactive, deliberative and opportunistic type offers developers the chance to refine its default behavior to optimize its fitness for use in a particular application. The fact that these agents are small and single-purpose means that adaptive workflow behavior can be ensured using a standard business object approach. Implementing them as loosely coupled business entities and processes serves to deliver the functionality *du jour*, while ensuring that they will continue to respond when tomorrow's enterprise changes.

References

[HAY 97] David Hay, Keri Anderson Healy, "GUIDE Business Rule Project Final Report," October, 1997.

[HERZUM 98] Peter Herzum and Oliver Sims, "The Business Component Approach", position paper for the Business Objects IV Workshop at the 1998 ACM SIGPLAN conference on Object-oriented programming, systems, languages, and applications, http://jeffsutherland.org/oopsla98/sims.html.

[JENNINGS 98] Nicholas R. Jennings and Michael J. Wooldridge, *Agent Technology*, Springer-Verlag, New York, 1998. Page 4.

[JOHANSSON 97] Sven Erik Johansson. Benedikte Harstad Kallak, Thomas Beech Pettersen, Jan Erik Ressem, "Expert Workflow," Practitioner's Report in Addendum to the 1997 ACM SIGPLAN conference on Object-oriented programming, systems, languages, and applications (Addendum) , 1997, Pages 45 - 49.

[KENDALL 98] Elizabeth A. Kendall, P. V. Murali Krishna, Chirag V. Pathak, C. B. Suresh, "Patterns of intelligent and mobile agents," *Proceedings of the second international conference on Autonomous agents*, 1998, Pages 92 - 99.

[MOULIN 96] B. Moulin and B. Chaib-draa, "An Overview of Distributed Artificial Intelligence," in *Foundations of Distributed Artificial Intelligence*, eds. G. M. P. O'Hare and N. R. Jennings, New York, 1996. Pages 3-5.

[NARDI 98] Bonnie A. Nardi, James R. Miller, David J. Wright, "Collaborative, Programmable Intelligent Agents," *Communications of the ACM*, Vol 41, No. 3, March, 1998

[OMG 97] Wolfgang Schultze, "Relationship of Business Objects and the Workflow Facility," document BOM 97-01-16, Presentation to the Business Object Domain Task force OMG Technical Meeting, Tampa, FL, January 16, 1997.

[OMG 98] *Object Management Group (OMG) Business Object Domain Task Force (BODTF) RFP #2 Submission for a Workflow Management Facility*, 7/4/98, p. 1-9

[ROSTAL 98] Pam Rostal, "From Business Objects toward Adaptive Agents," position paper for the Business Objects IV Workshop at the 1998 ACM SIGPLAN conference on Object-oriented programming, systems, languages, and applications, http://jeffsutherland.org/oopsla98/rostal.html

[SCHMIDT 98] Marc-Thomas Schmidt, "Building Workflow Business Objects," position paper for the Business Objects IV Workshop at the 1998 ACM SIGPLAN conference on Object-oriented programming, systems, languages, and applications, http://jeffsutherland.org/oopsla98/mts.html.

[SIMS 98] Peter Eeles and Oliver Sims, *Building Business Objects*, Wiley Computer Publishing, 1998.

Business Processes are not Represented Adequately in Business Applications and Frameworks!

Hans Albrecht Schmid

FB Informatik, University of Applied Sciences, Konstanz, Germany

e-mail: schmidha@fh-konstanz.de

Fernando Simonazzi

LIFIA, UNLP, La Plata, Argentina

Abstract. In principle, there is wide agreement on the requirement that business processes and their characteristics, as described from the business domain, should be represented by objects in information systems. This paper describes important characteristics of business processes. It demonstrates, by three examples, that state of the art business applications and frameworks do not represent business processes and their characteristics by objects. An outlook is given how this can be done.

Keywords: Business process, business procedure, business activity, business applications, business object frameworks

1 Introduction

During the last years, the object-oriented community has put much emphasis on the structuring of business applications, in particular in the context of user-event driven graphical user interfaces and of client/server computing (see e.g. [OMG97] [SPCHM97] [OH97] [CNM97] [F97] [IBMSF98]). There is a wide agreement: that a business object is a representation of a thing from the business domain; that business objects are classified into business entity objects like an account, and business process objects like withdrawing an amount from an account; that the business object abstraction, which models the real world, is represented by an object in the information system [B95] [C95]. On the other hand, the business community has described and specified, in the context of business process engineering, what business processes are and which characteristics they have (see section 2 for a description).

There seems to be a gap between the two camps. The object-oriented community agrees that business processes and their characteristics should be represented by objects in the information system. The business community describes business processes and their characteristics. Bringing together the statements from both camps, the conclusion is: business processes and their characteristics, as described from the business domain, should be represented by objects in a business application or framework! This requirement is, in principle, not new; it is a specialization of the more general requirement for the "natural representation of an application domain by software structures", which is one of the driving factors for object-oriented techniques.

However, state of the art business applications and frameworks do not meet this requirement. They do not represent business processes and their characteristics (explicitly and directly) by objects. Typically, they represent a business process somehow as a part of the graphical user interface and within its classes, often only implicitly in the control flow. We call an explicit, direct and clear representation that reflects the way as business processes and their characteristics are described by the business community, an adequate representation. We will show in this paper that state of the art business applications and frameworks do not represent business processes adequately.

To prove this, we describe important characteristics of business processes in section 2. In section 3, we analyse several prominent examples for state of the art business applications structures and framework: client/server application development [OH97], and systematically application development with strategies and patterns [CNM97] [F97]. In section 4, we summarize the state of the art. In section 5, we will give an outlook on how business processes may be represented adequately.

2 Business Processes and their Characteristics

Business objects are classified mainly into business entity objects and business process objects. A business entity object, like a product, an invoice, or an account, which is compared to the "nouns of the model world, represents the static state of the enterprise" [C95]. That means it is a passive object which may not change its state by itself. In contrast, a business process object, like buying a product or withdrawing an amount from an account, "represents the flow of work" and "acts on the business entities to cause the business to function" [C95]. That means a business process object represents an activity, that, typically, changes the state of the business entities as a result.

Let us consider business processes in more detail. A business process often involves multiple users and activities that take place over different time-slices [AF98]. To get more manageable parts, a business process is decomposed in business procedures.

A business procedure (called "process thread" by [AF98]) is triggered by an external event and produces some result which has a value for the business. Typically, business procedures are the units of activity, which a business application provides for execution. They are run by clerks.

For example, two business procedures are change customer address, which is a triggered by the event of receiving an address-has-changed letter from a customer; cancel health insurance policy, which is triggered by a customer giving notice.

A business procedure is composed, typically, of smaller units, which we call business activities. Whereas change customer address, consists of only one business activity, change the customer address; cancel health insurance policy, consists of five business activities. These are: check validity of notice; if notice is not valid notify customer; if notice is valid check if policy is a good risk; if notice is valid and risk is good, approach customer to take notice back; if required, cancel policy. As this example demonstrates, a business procedure typically determines the, often non-strict or conditional, sequence in which the business activities, from which it is composed, are to be executed. There are also cases, in which it is up to the choice of an end-user in which sequence a set of business activities is executed.

A business activity (called "elementary business process" by [AF98]) is a logical unit of work that "is performed by one person in one place at one time", which adds measurable value to the business. A business activity needs not to be triggered by an external event; it is typically triggered by the termination of a preceding activity. Since it is a logical unit of work, it is either performed completely, or it has no effects at all; in both cases, it leaves the business data in a consistent state.

A business activity is often composed by subactivities (and a subactivity might be composed itself by subactivities if required). For example, the business activity "check validity of notice" consists of five subactivities, which are executed in a fixed sequence: search the customer, select the correct customer from search result, select the policy, display the policy, and compare policy and notice. The differences between a business activity and a subactivity are that:

- a subactivity is not a logical unit of work
- a subactivity presents, typically, one screen
- within a subactivity, the sequence of processing is mainly driven by user input events.

Note that a business process contains both modal dialog elements (constituted by the sequencing of activities, respectively, subactivities) and non-modal dialog elements (event-driven subactivities). This is a major source of complexity, which has not been discussed in the literature.

Another important characteristic of a business activity and a subactivity is, as the examples also show, that it uses fixed (classes of) business entities, like a customer or a policy, and requests services from them. A business activity or subactivity may create the business entities that it uses, or it may access existing entities that its get passed from another activity or subactivity.

We conclude that the important characteristics of a business process, which need to be represented by business applications and frameworks, are

- the hierarchical decomposition of a business procedure in activities and subactivities,
- the (often non-strict or conditional) sequencing of activities and subactivities,
- the creation of business entities or the access to existing business entities.

3 Business Processes in Application Architectures

3.1 Club-Med Example

In: Client/Server Programming with Java and Corba [OH97], Orfali presents the example of a travel agency mini-application. The application allows the booking (incl. canceling) of vacations with a club med vacation village. The application is, according to our definitions, a business procedure that consists of two business activities, the booking of vacations, and the canceling of vacations. Each of them is a logical unit of work. The booking activity consists of three subactivities: present all club villages and select a club, select a vacation week in the selected club, book the selected week for the desired number of persons. The canceling activity consists of two subactivities: display the bookings, and cancel a booking. Each activity presents its subactivities in a fixed sequence (though each of the subactivities provides also a possibility to return directly to the first subactivity).

Each subactivity presents a screen (see Figure 1) of its own for data display and data entry. During a subactivity, data are entered in text fields or by selection from a list box. When a subactivity is terminated by pressing a confirm or cancel button, the data entered are stored, and the screen belonging to the following subactivity is shown.

Obviously, the business procedure has the characteristics that are described (from a business engineering viewpoint) in section 2:

1. a hierarchical structure of the business procedure: a business procedure is composed by business activities each of which is composed by business subactivities

2. a sequencing of the business subactivities: subactivities can only be processed in a prescribed sequence and not in a deliberate sequence following the end-users choice.

Let us see how these characteristics are represented in the software structure of the information system. The club-med application is a three tier client-server application written in Java. The presentation tier runs as an applet on the client and is connected by Corba to the server. The business process is part of the presentation, though some efforts were done to separate it from the presentation. The business entity tier runs (with business entities tailored to the specific application) on the server. The database forms the third tier.

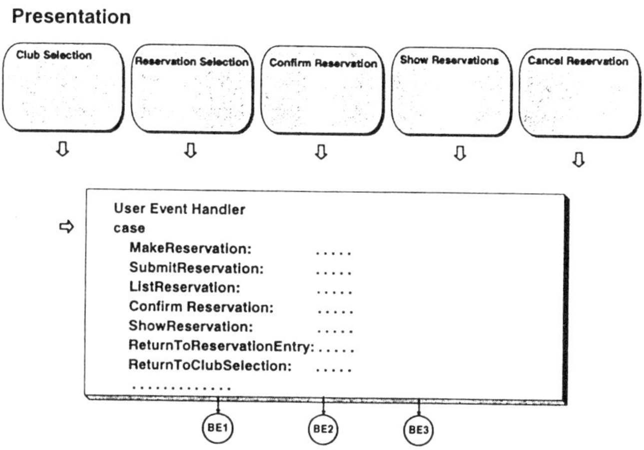

Figure 1 Structure of the club-med client application

Figure 1 presents the structure of the client tier applet. All business entities are created globally and accessible in the applet. There is one window (this is called panel for an applet) associated to the application. In it, the screens of all subactivities are presented. This is done by attaching a card layout manager that contains all subactivity screens, to the panel. Each subactivity screen is like a card in a deck of cards, only the topmost one being visible.

Attached to the window is one event handler, which handles all the events originating from all the different subactivities. One cannot see without a detail analysis of the screens and of the control flow, to which subactivity an event belongs, and if, on an event, the subactivity is terminated or an action in the subactivity is done.

For each screen, an auxiliary class is provided. It has methods to build up the screen-layout, to get data from business entities and to display them on the screen, and to fetch input data from the screen and put them in temporary variables or business entities. From this description, we see that an auxiliary class corresponds somehow to a business subactivity.

Upon a user-input event, e.g. when a button is pressed, the event handler calls methods from the auxiliary class belonging to the displayed screen. Upon an event that terminates a subactivity, the event handler: switches the screen by calling a cardlayout manager method that moves the screen to be shown next the topmost position of the "deck of cards"; calls methods from two auxiliary classes, from one to store the input data, and from the other one to display data on the new screen. Thus, the switch from a subactivity to the next one is done implicitly.

The described application structure does not represent explicitly

- business procedure, business activities and subactivities
- their hierarchical structure
- the sequencing of subactivities
- which screen belongs to which subactivity
- which business entity is created and/or accessible by a subactivity.

Though the application code is quite well structured, one has to analyze the dynamical flow of control in the application to get an understanding of these structures.

The conclusion is that the business process objects are not represented by the software structure adequately.

3.2 Application Logic Tier

In Analysis Patterns [F97], Fowler recommends to introduce an application logic tier, in addition to the presentation tier, which "is only concerned with the user interface, and has no knowledge of underlying domain tier", and the domain tier, which is "a direct model of business objects applicable to the whole domain independent of individual applications and data sources".

The application logic tier is described as follows: "A selection and simplification of the domain model for an application. Contains no user interface code but provides a set of facades of the domain tier for the user interface. Converts .. types...". He proposes to "prepare a facade for each presentation. The facade has a feature for each element on the corresponding user interface. Each presentation thus has a simple interface to the domain model that minimizes any processing for the presentation other than the user interface."

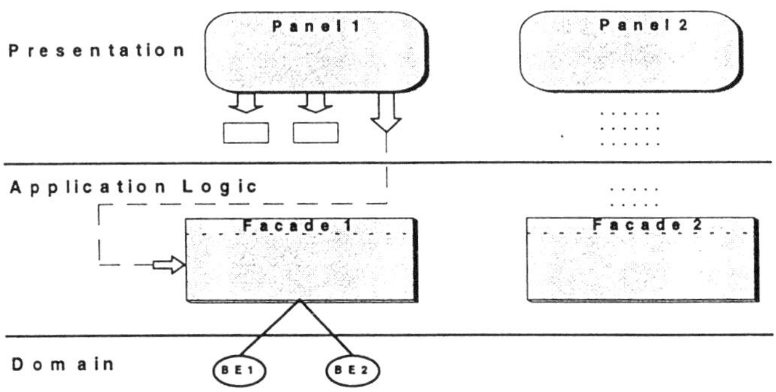

Figure 2 Presentation, Application Logic, and Domain Tier

Figure 2 illustrates the presentation, application logic, and domain tier. For each panel, it shows a facade object. A facade method is called by an event (represented by a double arrow) caused by a GUI widget in a panel, or by an event handler of the panel, as illustrated in Figure 2.

In a business procedure like change customer address, a business entity from the domain tier, the customer, is presented by the presentation tier for display and editing of some fields. In this case, a facade has two main responsibilities: when the customer view on the screen is built up, the facade will call methods of the customer business entity to get the attribute data and to convert them, if required, and transfer them to the customer view; when the presentation generates a user event indicating the termination of the editing activity, it will transfer, similarly, the edited data from the view to the customer entity. In other cases, a facade method may contain a sequence of calls to methods of different business entities. For example, it might calculate a result with data from different business entities that is to be displayed by a result view on the screen.

A sequence of requests to methods of a business entity is a (small) part of a business process (often called business logic). Thus, separating such a sequence into the method of a business logic object, which belongs to a separate tier, is certainly a step towards representing a business process adequately. However, it does not go far enough, since all methods of a facade represent only a small piece of a business process, typically a business subactivity or a part of it.

Our conclusion is that a facade class of the application logic tier, which represents a business subactivity or a part of it, does not represent

- the hierarchical composition of a business procedure in activities and nor subactivities
- the sequencing of business activities and subactivities (Fowler [F97] does not describe how to do this. But it is, similarly to Orfalis approach, contained implicitly in event handling methods).

Though introducing a separate facade tier is certainly a step towards representing business processes adequately, the other steps are still missing. Application logic facades are a valuable mechanism for the mapping from presentation objects to business entities, but they do meet only a part of the requirements.

3.3 Point of Sale Application

In Object Models [CNM97], Coad presents with his co-authors an object-oriented analysis and design of different example applications, from business applications through real-time applications. Though the emphasis is on the analysis side, the design is carried out until a complete class structure is available. Strategies and patterns guide the analysis and design process. In the strategy 25, the object model is partitioned into four components, problem domain, human interaction, data management and system interaction. The problem domain contains business entities, and the human interaction is the user interface domain. Thus, a business process component or domain is missing. An analysis of the example applications confirms that they do not contain business process objects.

For "Connie's convenience store", a complete application to conduct the business of a store is developed. The application contains several human interactions (to use Coad's terminology), which are business procedures. Let us analyze the most important business procedure in the system, "cashier sells items". There is no class that represents this business procedure, but a class Sale and a class Sale Window. Sale represents the result of a sale (i.e. the list of sold line items with quantity and price, etc., the total, sales tax, etc.).

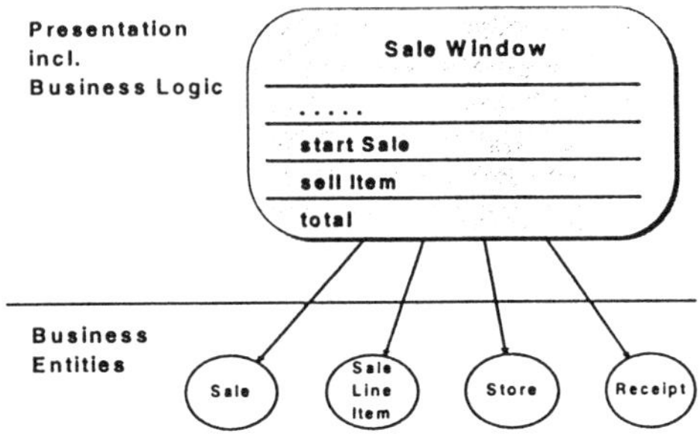

Figure 3 Sale Window and the business entities which it knows

The class Sale Window (see Figure 3) is a user interface window class that is used to display the receipt. However, Sale Window drives the "make sale scenario"; it contains shorter scenarios, like start sale, sell item, total, pay by check, end sale in the form of methods. Sale Window knows (explicitly) all business entities like sale, sale line item, etc. on which it operates. When Sale Window calls a method like sell item, this method adds, after several other calls to methods of other objects, a line item line to the receipt, and Sale Window displays it.

This shows that a user interface object, Sale Window, represents implicitly the business activity "cashier sells items". The methods that the window contains, like sell item, might be considered as subactivities or as reactions on user events in the activity.

Our conclusion is that business processes are not represented. However, it should be relatively easy to separate the business activity with the "scenarios" from the window class. Then, business activities and their creation of business objects and the access to existing ones would be represented adequately, except for

- the hierarchical composition of a business procedure in activities and nor subactivities
- the sequencing of business activities and subactivities.

4 State of the Art Summary

The examples given demonstrate the state of the art of well-structured business applications and frameworks. Our conclusion is that, according to the state of the art, only the part of a business subactivity that embodies the reaction on a user input event like the pressing of an OK-button, is represented as a unit, typically as a method that is called by an event handler. In some cases, all units that form a subactivity are included as methods in a class, like a facade class [F97] or a sale window class [CNM97]. Such a class corresponds "somehow" to a business subactivity, but it does not represent one directly.

However, the examples given show, from a business community point of view, business areas with well-defined business procedures that are composed of activities and subactivities, which create and use well-defined business entities. The software state of the art does neither represent the business procedures, activities and subactivities by objects, nor does it represent their composition, nor (explicitly) the possible sequence in which business (sub-)activities are executed. The only way how the sequencing of business (sub-)activities is represented is by the dynamical control flow. Nor does the software state of the art represent (statically visible and explicitly) which business activities or subactivities create business entities or have access to already existing ones.

Thus, we have shown that state of the art business applications and frameworks do not represent business processes adequately. Only in a business area with business procedures the flow of which is only driven by user-events, but has no prescribed order and sequencing of activities, this might be adequate.

5 Representation of Business Processes

Business applications and frameworks should represent business procedures, activities and subactivities and their composition explicitly. This can be done by introducing classes that represent business procedures, business activities and business subactivities. From these, we build a business activity tree (see Figure 4), following the composite pattern [GHJV95]. It has a business procedure as the root and business subactivities as leaves. A business subactivity contains the actions that are performed as reactions on user input events during the subactivity. A business activity or subactivity creates or accesses business entities, and invokes their operations.

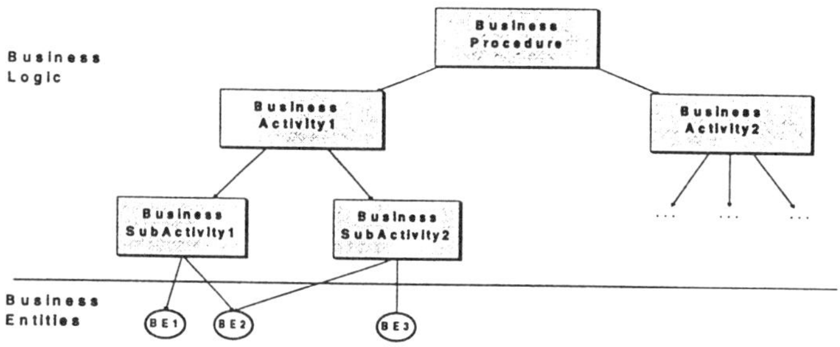

Figure 4 Business activity tree

Each business procedure, activity and subactivity as well as business entities have a view that presents the business object to the end-user.

The business activity tree is executed dynamically. A business procedure, activity and subactivity is started by calling its start-method. This method makes the respective view visible. Then, it either starts an activity or subactivity that it contains, or it makes the business entities visible and waits for user input events. When a user causes an event that terminates a subactivity or activity, like by pressing a commit-button, the subactivity or activity first performs the required processing before it returns control to the parent business activity or procedure which called it. For example, it might transfer back input data from the view of a business entity into the business entity and save it. When this is done, the subactivity or activity notifies by an event its parent that it is committed. The parent activity or business procedure then takes the required actions; it makes the child invisible and, for example, it might start the subactivity or activity to be executed next.

A business activity tree can be realized efficiently. We have implemented a simple and lean business activity tree framework in Java and validated it in cooperation with a German insurance company. The business activity framework contains abstract classes for business procedures, activities and subactivities. It has a business procedure as the root and business subactivities as leaves.

6 Conclusions

We have demonstrated that state of the art business applications and frameworks do not represent business processes adequately. Mainly, three characteristics of business processes are missing:

- the hierarchical composition of a business procedure in activities and nor subactivities
- the sequencing of business activities and subactivities
- the association of business entities to business activities or subactivities.

These are very important characteristics, which you have to know and understand when you describe a business process. If these characteristics are not represented adequately in a business application or framework, a developer needs to transform this - easily understandable - "real world" structure into a different and much more complex software structure. This is slow and error-prone. But the real problems come up with the maintenance of such software structures. Suppose, you have to insert an additional subactivity between two existing ones. Conceptually, this is quite simple; but implementing this simple task in state of the art software structures is overly complex. Another problem is that reuse of business (sub)activities is conceptually very simple, since you take a subactivity, insert it within a different activity and reuse it in this way. But implementing reuse of business (sub)activities in state of the art software structures is nearly impossible.

Thus, there is much to be gained by making the software representation correspond better to business processes and their characteristics. We have given an outlook how this can be done.

7 Acknowledgments

Our thanks are due to Angela Barth-Kuepper who supported the preparation of this paper.

8 References

[AF98] P.Allen, S.Frost: Component-Based Development for Enterprise Systems, Cambridge University Press, Cambridge, Great Britain, 1998

[B95] C.Burt (ed.): OMG BOMSIG survey with published definition of a business object. OMG document 95-02-04. See www.omg.org

[C95] C.Casanave: Business-Object Architectures and Standards; in [SPCHM97]

[CNM97] P.Coad, D.North, M.Mayfield: Object Models; Prentice-Hall, Englewood Cliffs, NJ, 1997

[F97] M.Fowler: Analysis Patterns; Addison-Wesley, Reading Mass., 1997

[GHJV95] E.Gamma, R.Helm, R.Johnson, J.Vlissides: Design Patterns: Elements of Reusable Object-Oriented Software; Addison-Wesley, 1994

[IBMSF98] IBM Technical Support Organization: San Francisco Concepts and Facilities, IBM Redbook, SG24-2157-00, 1998

[OH97] R.Orfali, D.Harkey: Client/Server Programming with Java and Corba; John Wiley & Sons, Chicester, UK, 1997

[OMG97] Object Management Group OMG: Business Object DTF, Common Business Objects; 1997

[SPCHM97] J.Sutherland, D.Patel, C.Casanave, G.Hollowell, J.Miller (eds.): Business Object Design and Implementation; Springer, Berlin, 1997

Are Workers Knowledge Rich Business Objects?

Nigel Phillips
Centre for Information and Organisational Studies
School of Computing Information Systems and Mathematics
South Bank University
London
e-mail phillinp@sbu.ac.uk

Abstract: Learning from the science of complexity is seen as centrally important by the Business Objects Design and Implementation Workshop and the Knowledge Management Coalition (KMC). There is much common ground between the concerns of these two groups. Central to both is the concept of Complex Adaptive Systems. A meta-model of organisations based on the Organisations as Complex Evolving Systems (OACES) framework is developed. Combined with extensions to Business Object Architecture proposed by Sims and others this is seen to lead to an Enterprise Meta-Model that provides a common core architecture for KM, BO and Workflow Management.

1 Introduction

The Object Management Group (OMG) seeks (among other things) to develop standards for a technological infrastructure that creates a level playing field that allows software vendors to compete across all platforms purely on functionality and performance. It seeks to achieve this by providing interoperability mechanisms that enable components constructed by different vendors at various levels of granularity to work together. It is hoped that this will lead to a large market in plug-n-play shrink-wrapped components that can be customised and assembled by users to provide unique solutions to their business requirements. The Knowledge Management Coalition (KMC) seeks (among other things) to develop standards for knowledge management (KM) that will enable buyers to compare competing KM tools and with which KM tools vendors can differentiate their products. Part of this effort involves developing standards for the technological infrastructure and an appropriate architecture to support KM.

Where the two approaches meet is in the area of enterprise modelling and in particular the modelling and effective management of processes, workflows, business objects and workers. There are some interesting parallels between current debates within the OMG and KMC. Both find UML in its current form inadequate for enterprise modelling and are seeking extensions to improve matters. The current business object model is static and doesn't scale very well. Both see a need to support mobile objects and agents. Both see a need to support incremental evolutionary development of business processes and software. At stake is a huge "business-to-business electronic commerce" market that "combines the Internet infrastructure with standards for business-oriented components"(OMG, 1998).

- ***Observation 1**: The relationship between the KMC and the OMG is similar to that between a domain expert and an information systems developer. Both seek to reduce the 'semantic gap' between vendor and buyer but there is a clear danger that they will re-enforce it if their standards are incompatible.*
- ***Observation 2:** An organisation's model of its enterprise distributed computing facilities and the process that develops and maintains it represents a large investment in knowledge management.*
- ***Observation 3:** Enterprise distributed computing development is validated against an organisation's knowledge of itself and its environment.*
- ***Observation 4**: Process and transaction are core concepts in both approaches.*

Assertion 1: *The business object architecture and the knowledge management architecture need a common core of shared concepts that define the organisational meta-model of both.*

The Knowledge Management process adopted by an organisation provides the context and content against which the requirements, analysis and design phases of the systems development life cycle for business objects must be validated. Similarly the process of designing business objects and associated workflows represents a major source of learning and knowledge explication. Clearly the better the fit between KM architecture KMA, Business Object Architecture BOA and Workflow Management Architecture WMA the more effective knowledge extraction and validation will be.

The Knowledge Management Consortium KMC (see below) reference-model views the workers of an organisation as a type of Business Object (BO) one that adds value to a business through the application of knowledge rather than one that adds information through the application of data. Accommodating this view into the current OMG BOA is difficult because the current architecture is data driven.

Extending the OMG BOA to four tiers as proposed by Herzum and Sims 1998, would improve the fit between the OMG BOA and KMC KMA but its essentially data driven view needs to be addressed. There are currently two rather contradictory views of workflow and workflow management. A central issue is whether process control is centralised or distributed. If the former, how is local knowledge accommodated, and if the later how is a single coherent view achieved? Should there be a single architecture that accommodates both views or is it necessary to make a choice?

The KMC seeks to build on the theory of complexity, in particular the work of Holland (Holland, 1995) in developing its model of organisation. The Business Object Workshop has for many years been seeking to develop the ideas of Complex Adaptive Systems CAS as a foundation of the BOA also building on Holland (1995) among others (Sutherland, 1998). Many of the fundamental ideas emerging from the computational study of CAS have a strong intuitive resonance with our conception of social organisation. There are however dangers in performing a too literal mapping between these computational results and social systems as note by Holland (1998) among many other. Introna (1998) defines this problem as needing to determine the level of ontological incommensurability between the computational and the social. Viewing Organisations as Complex Evolving Systems (OACES) has been suggested by Eve Mittleton-Kelly as a means of achieving this.

Assertion 2: *Complexity theory and in particular its application to social systems in the form of Organisations As Complex Evolving Systems (OACES) is ideally suited to provide common core to the KM, BO and WM architectures.*

Assessing each of these architectures against the four key principles of the OACES model suggests that a single coherent architecture that can accommodate centralised, distributed and mobile workflows and associated business objects is possible. Further more, it leads to an Enterprise Meta-Model that clearly defines the responsibilities of the KMA, BOA and WMA. Three central concepts in this architecture are rule spaces, domains of control and knowledge rich business objects.

The rest of this paper is structured as follows: Section 2 introduces four core concepts of OACES. Section 3 provides a brief introduction to the KMC intentions and framework and relates it to the four principles. Sections 4 and 5 discuss the implications for business object and workflow management section 6 presents the Organisational Meta-Model and its implications for the three architectures.

2 Organisations as Complex Evolving Systems - OACES

OACES has been suggested by Eve Mitleton-Kelly as a means to move from a few generic characteristics or principles common to all complex adaptive systems to a framework of ideas for applying these principles in social systems (Mitleton-Kelly, 1998). The term complex evolving system (CES) is used to distinguish human systems from other complex adaptive systems (CAS) taking account of the privileged position of human systems conferred by language use that enables adaptation through learning, and tool use that enables evolution through change of structure.

There is considerable common ground between the ideas express in OACES and those aspects of complexity theory adopted by the KMC - see for instance Firestone, (1999) Swanstrom, (1998). For the purpose of this current argument four main concepts are paramount: Self-similar and self-affinine structures, complicit co-evolution, closed feedback loops in open systems and the space of possibilities. Only a brief description will be given here and elaborated in-terms of each architecture below. A more detailed discussion of some of these elements can be found in Phillips and Patel, 1997.

2.1 Self-Similar and Self-Affinine Structures

Fractals are now familiar self-similar structures. Mandlebrot (1999) points out that the term self-similar should only be applied where the patterns are identical except for scale, where all axes of a pattern are not transformed to the same degree from one scale to another the term self-affinine is more appropriate. In human social systems fractal structures tend to be self-affinine. That is there are strong affinities between them but they are not identical except for scale. Aggregation and composition hierarchies are self-affinine structures. Workflow objects can also be viewed as self-affinine fractal structures (Shultze, 1996) and conform to the recursive "COMPOSITE" pattern (Gamma 1995).

2.2 Complicit Co-Evolution

The adaptation of an organisation has been traditionally thought of against a fixed environment - like water flowing into the shape of its container. This view is extremely limiting when considering CAS. Adaptation in CAS is more like a 'lava lamp' each change in an element effecting change in all its neighbours creating new opportunities and new constraints. Stewart and Cohen (Stewart, 1997) introduce the term complicity to describe this bi-directional dependency. If there is a complicit relationship between two systems then a change in either will lead to change in the other: and change in each is constrained by the other.

In information systems development the term "coupling" has a very similar meaning. A CAS creates boundary structures to protect itself from too many interactions with its environment, limiting the number of complicit relations at each scale of granularity. The relative ability of complicit CAS defines a fitness landscape that is continuously deforming as each change leads to the waxing and waning of fortunes of individual CAS. Note that complicit evolution is not necessarily competitive, systems can co-evolve to their mutual benefit.

2.3 Closed Feedback Loops in Open Systems

Information, energy and material flow through a CAS, but it maintains its identity through a closed cycle of behaviours - a work cycle. A work cycle transforms the information, energy and material as it flows through the system. Within the boundary of a system a work cycle is a workflow within the system. That is, there are workflows at all levels of granularity of a system but they tend to be orthogonal (the lower level workflow is a point from the perspective of the high level workflow) at the system boundary for each level of granularity. See figure 1.

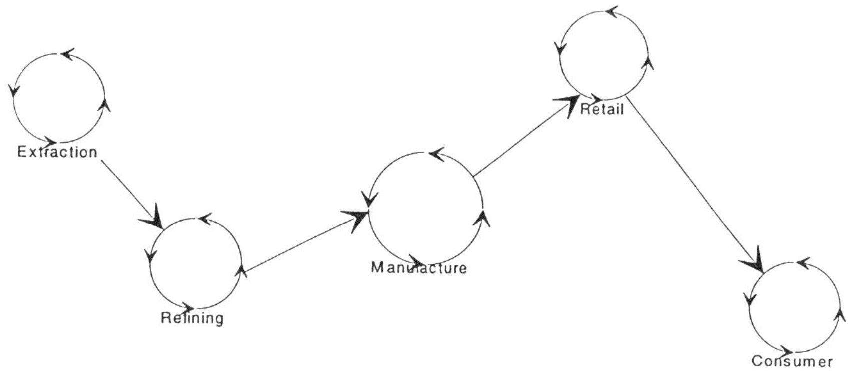

Business flow: Organisations as closed loops in an open economic system

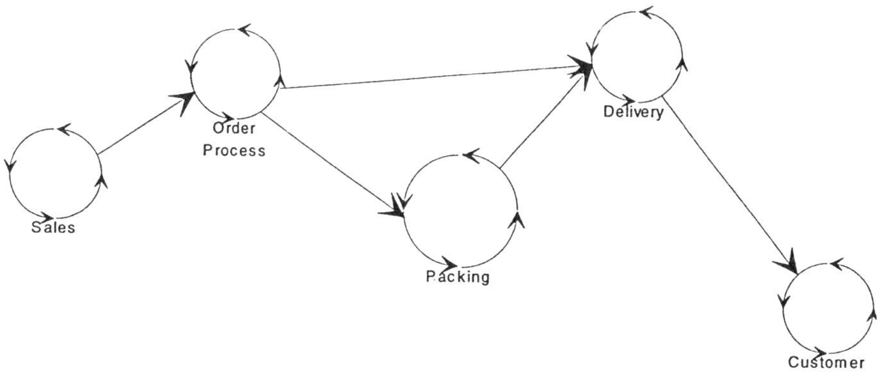

Enterprise workflow: Business units as closed loops in an open enterprise system

2.4 The Space of Possibilities

At any one time there are a great many ways in which an organisation can change. A CAS is constrained in how it can move in relation to its fitness landscape by the possible states it can achieve with its repertoire of behaviour. To reach other parts of the landscape it needs to change its structure and behaviour. Each possible structure and behaviour a CAS might have makes up its space of possibilities. That part of the space of possibilities accessible from its current state by taking a single step is the adjacent possible sub-space. A CAS explores its adjacent possible sub-space by trying out different rules sets or changing its structure. Change in CAS appears discontinuous. A CAS makes small changes in rules and structure constantly. A Successful CAS grows; extending its structure as it goes. As it grows, it becomes unstable and needs to develop new higher level structures and rule sets to stabilise itself. Unsuccessful CAS shrink, as they shrink it becomes harder to maintain their current structure, and again new forms must be found.

Together these four principles form the basis of an organisational meta-model. An organisation is formed from self-affinine structures, within which recursively nested closed loops of rule-based behaviours process information, energy and material to maintain and extend themselves. Complicit organisations co-evolve with each other by exploring their space of possibilities by making changes to their rule sets and structures. Continuous small changes can lead to sudden discontinuous shifts when size makes a particular structure unstable.

The relationship between a business and its information systems is clearly complicit. If their co-evolution is to be seamless and business driven then the IS/IT architecture must support the natural structures in the organisation meta-model.

3 Knowledge Management Architecture

The concept of knowledge management first mooted ten years or so ago (although arguable as old as man. See Swanstrom, 1998) has recently been enjoying celebrity status in the business community. As is typically the case in these circumstances there is considerable disagreement about what exactly KM is - a situation widely exploited by vendors re-badging everything from digital watches to Windows NT as a knowledge management tool. The Knowledge Management Consortium KMC is a buyer/user driven not for profit organisation that is seeking to develop a comprehensive set of standards against which such claims can be judged. The KMC takes CAS as a core concept in its organisational model building, based on the work of John Holland (Holland, 1995, 1998) who has developed mathematical models of knowledge sharing. At its highest level concerns are split between the Natural Knowledge Management System (NKMS) and the Artificial Knowledge Management System (AKMS) and between a number of domain hierarchies - KM of Organisations,

KM of Science and KM of Society. KM of Organisations is the newest and fastest growing branch of KM with sub-branches KM of Business, KM of non-profit Organisations, KM of Government and KM of Educational Institutes (Swanstrom, 1998).

NKMS is primarily concerned with creating the right conditions to foster natural human knowledge management, while the AKMS is concerned with the development of computer-based tools to support the NKMS effort. The relationship between the two is of fundamental importance. NKMS focuses on people rather than on hardware or software. In particular, it views people within an organisational boundary as knowledge rich fully-fledged business objects.

The central concern of AKMS is the development of IS/IT infrastructure that supports an enterprise in applying KM as a science. It views the people in an organisation as creators, acquirers and transmitters of knowledge, and seeks to develop structures that support them in these processes. As well as business level knowledge there is also meta-knowledge: knowledge about knowledge of the business and meta-meta-knowledge etc. An AKMS must be able to provide a single coherent image of the knowledge and knowledge management activities of the whole enterprise through an Enterprise Model (EM) and access to this model needs to be available from any where in the organisation. Therefore a distributed computing environment is assumed and the target functionality is that of a Distributed Knowledge management System. It is proposed that these facilities should be supported by an Active Knowledge Manager facility that extends the functionality of current Object Request Brokers to maintain the EM (Firestone, 1999).

4 The Business Object Architecture

The OMG's Object Model Architecture, Common Object Request Broker Architecture and Business Object Architecture BOA are clearly foundations on which the KMC would like to build in developing a AKM DKMS environment. For this to be possible the BOA must deliver the necessary abstractions and independence from underlying technology to enable a DKMS to be built. The current BOA is not considered sufficiently mature for this to be possible.

The current standard model of a business object component consists of three sub-components: the resource manager, the process manager and the presentation manager. The resource manager encapsulates the rules for using the technology. It is responsible for maintaining the state of the object making it persistent, and ensuring it is coherent. The process manager encapsulates the business rules. It is responsible for managing interactions with other objects. The presentation manager encapsulates task rules. It is responsible for managing interactions with users including the creation, modification and destruction of business objects.

A fourth sub-component has been proposed - the workspace component would manage task-related interactions and encapsulate the rules of operation. It is proposed that this addition would reduce the coupling between tasks and processes and enable the business component to be treated as a single coherent object at all stages of the life cycle Herzum and Sims 1998. The four sub-components can then be viewed as four tiers each with its own rule set and management requirements.

These four tiers can be seen as providing different layers of abstraction over the underlying data. This data driven approach can be seen as a natural consequence of the OMG's bottom-up interoperability focus. From a KM perspective, business objects need to be responsibility driven to reflect their roles within the organisation. The BOA spans these two areas of concern within the information system. The enterprise tier is where the responsibility driven business requirements interface with the data driven technology requirements.

A clearer conceptual model can be obtained if the tier concept is replaced with that of a layer, where each layer defines a different rule space (similar arguments have been suggested by Schmid, 1998). The layers can then be considered as protocols that translate between knowledge processing and data processing. The user tier becomes the knowledge resource layer. The workspace layer implements the local business rules for using the knowledge resource. The enterprise layer implements the global business rules for using the workspaces and ties these to the technology through an object layer to the data resource layer (See figure 2 Section 6).

Each layer defines a rule space that constrains the flow of information, energy and material through the organisation. Workflows represent the rules by which value is added and are defined within each rule-space, which form domains of control. The passage of workflow through these rule-spaces ties together the knowledge and data processes of the organisation.

Such an architecture would offer support for mobile objects and agents while continuing to support static agents. Allowing knowledge agent and data agent to be relative concepts also allows for much finer grained adjustment and more incremental development. There are three closed loops in this architecture. The data resource is passed by the enterprise workflow to the workspace workflow. Knowledge is applied to the data by the knowledge resource, and it is then handed back by the workspace workflow to the enterprise workflow. Each workflow, enterprise and workspace is a closed loop.

5 Workflow Management Architecture

Workflow provides a set of dynamic views of the organisation. A workflow is a long running transaction and is described by a graph where the nodes represent particular tasks carried out on a stream of Units of Work (UOW). The routing of a particular UOW is determined by the outcome of the task at each node it visits. How monitoring and control are implemented differentiates the approaches to workflow modelling. Essentially this means the difference is in where knowledge of the graph is encapsulated. The Workflow Management Consortium WfMC model is built around the idea of a workflow engine providing centralised planning and control. This can be deployed either as a single monolithic system or as a number of co-operating static agents. This approach has been severely criticised because of its failure to support good practice in distributed development (see for instance, Santanu, 1997, Schulze, 1996). Distributed models can take a variety of other forms. The static agent approach assumes sets of task nodes have their own local controllers each with knowledge of its portion of the graph. The mobile agent approach assumes that rules for navigating the graph are encapsulated in the Unit of Work and it determines its path and instructs workstations what to do according to its state. There are a variety of ways in which these two approaches can be hybridised. Where for instance a mobile object is given knowledge of what to do next by the static agents it visits.

Workflow management is concerned with deploying resources to perform tasks and developing rule sets for the effective execution of those tasks to achieve the aims of the organisation. The central issue is not how workflow systems are implemented, but how the rules that they embody are partitioned, and how these are tied in to the BOA.

From the AKMS perspective, what is important is that local business rules can be decided locally independent of (though constrained by) the global rules and that this as far as possible should be de-coupled from the technological rules. This maximises the opportunities for exploring the adjacent possible sub-space. The workflows at one level of granularity become the objects called on by the workflow at a higher level of granularity. Adopting the idea of streams Units of Work through rule spaces, the physical embodiment of the rules in the system becomes transparent to the business object designer. Rule spaces can then be conveniently divided into sub-spaces that form domains of control for local rule development. Where the focus is clearly scoped by the layer where the sub-space resides separating worker, business unit, enterprise and object and resource development.

6 An Enterprise Architecture

Taking the CES organisation meta model, and combining it with the ideas of rule spaces and domains of control that bind knowledge rich business objects with data rich resource objects, provides a coherent enterprise architecture. This architecture provides a common core that should inform the development of KMA, BOA and WMA that will enable them to complicitly evolve to their mutual benefit.

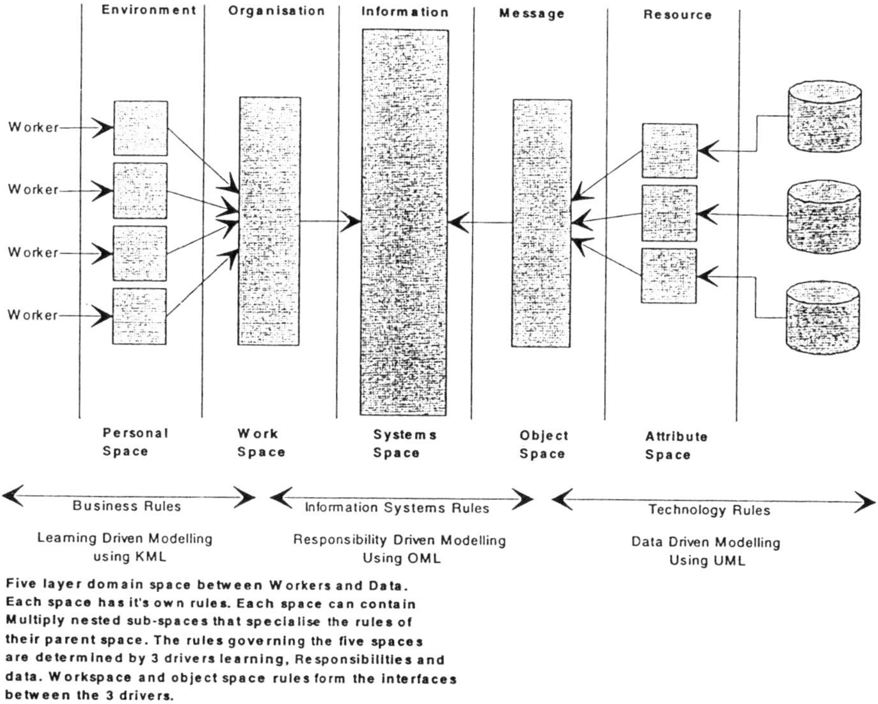

Figure 2 The Five Layer Domain Space of the Business Object Architecture.

Each space has its own rule set. Spaces can be further divided into sub-spaces with their own rule sets but within anyone Space sub-space rules must be specialisations of Space rules. Attribute space defines the rules for accessing resources. Resources are clustered into objects according to the rules of object space. Objects are clustered into information systems according to the rules of systems space. Organisations cluster information systems interfaces according to the rules of the workspace. Workers cluster interfaces of the workspace according to the rules of their personal space.

Workspaces are constructed to perform the functions necessary to meet the organisations goals workers are assigned specific tasks and responsibilities are assigned to them which are reflected in their personal spaces. Workflows represent streams of UOW through the various spaces. The rules of each space and sub-space are evolved to optimise the value added to the UOW by the knowledge rich business objects. Whether these streams are static or mobile or a combination of both should be transparent when viewing the behaviour of a workflow in or between spaces.

This approach has clear implications for analysis and design of Business Objects as indicated in figure 2. Evolution of the rules in the personal and workspace layer's should be driven by the KM process. These need to be supported in the systems space by responsibility driven design such as offered by the Open Modelling Language from the Open Consortium (Firesmith, 1998). While data resources need to be managed for data efficiency and require a data driven design such as UML.

7 Conclusions

The KMC and the Business Objects Design and Implementation Workshop share a number of common concerns regarding what the fundamental nature of BOA should be. Common to both is the realisation of the central importance of Complex Adaptive Systems theory. This paper has presented an organisation meta-model based on four principles of the OACES framework and argued that this architecture should form a common core for the KMA, BOA and WMA.

It has become apparent in researching this paper that the common ground between the KMC and this workshop is considerable and that there is much that might be gained from developing formal links between them.

If KMC is the client and OMG is the server then BODIW is the broker that can enable them to interface transparently.

8 References

Firesmith, 1998	Firesmith, D. Krutsch, S. Stowe, M, Hendley, G. Documenting a Complete Java Application Using Open. Addison-Wesley, 1998.
Firestone, 1999	Firestone, J. Enterprise Knowledge Management Modeling and Distributed Knowledge Management Systems. Executive Information Systems Inc. White Paper No. Twelve. http://dkms.com/EKMDKMS.html.
Holland, 1995	Holland, J. Hidden Order: How Adaptation Builds Complexity. Addison-Wesley, 1995.
Holland, 1998	Holland, J. Emergence - From Chaos To Order. Oxford University Press, 1998.
Hurzum, 1998	Hersum, P. Sims, O. The Business Component Approach. Proceedings of the Business Objects Workshop IV 1998.

Introna, 1998	Introna, I. Complexity Theory and Social Systems: Is there a match? Proceedings of Organisations As Complex Adaptive Systems. ISBN 0902683403.
Mandelbrot, 1999	Mandelbrot, B. A Multifractal Walk Down Wall Street. Scientific American, Febuary 1999.
Mitleton-Kelly, 1998	Mitleton-Kelly, E. Organisations As Complex Evolving Systems. Proceedings of Organisations As Complex Adaptive Systems. ISBN 0902683403.
OMG, 1998	OMG Document bom/98-10-01, Roadmap for the Business Object Initiative: Supporting Enterprise Distributed Computing.
Santanu, 1997	Aantanu, P. Park, E. Chaar, J. Essential Requirements for a Workflow Standard. Proceedings Business Object Workshop III, 1997.
Schmid, 1998	Schmid, H. Riebisch, M. Heverhagen, T. Liessmann, H. A Business Objects Framework Architecture. Proceedings of Business Object Workshop IV 1998.
Schulze, 1996	Schlze, W. Bohm, M, and Meyer-Wenger, K. Services of Workflow Objects and Workflow Meta-Objects in OMG-compliant environments, Business Objects workshop II, 1996.
Stewart, 1997	Stewart, I. Cohen, J. Figments of Reality. Cambridge University Press, 1997
Sutherland, 1998	Sutherland, J. Business Object Component Architectures: A Target Application Area for Complex Adaptive Systems Research. Proceedings of Business Objects Workshop IV, 1998.
Swanstrom, 1998	Swanstrom, E. What is Knowledge Management? Knowledge Management Consortium (Draft to be published John Wiley and Sons).

A Dynamic Business Object Architecture for Bridging the Communication Gap between Business Management and IT Professionals

Kitty Hung [1], Matthias Kraner [2], Srba Cvetkovic [3]
Department of Computer Science
The University of Sheffield
Regent Court, 211 Portobello Street,
Sheffield, S1 4DP
United Kingdom
Email : [1] k.hung@dcs.shef.ac.uk , [2] Matthias_Kraner@credo.shef.ac.uk ,
[3] Srba_Cvetkovic@credo.shef.ac.uk

Abstract: Business organisations are constantly facing competition. There is a growing awareness amongst many organisations that a strategic approach has to be adopted to retain competitiveness. Nowadays, information technology (IT) underpins the implementation of most business strategies. However, IT solutions frequently fail to deliver business benefits. One of the main causes of failure is the communication gap that exists between the business management and IT professionals. Whilst this program continues to be the subject of extensive inter-disciplinary research, a reliable, generally applicable, low cost, low risk and any easy to implement solution, is yet to be found.

This paper seeks to exploit the potential contribution how some new and emerging technologies may offer to bridging, or at least reducing, this gap. A novel conceptual model, called Dynamic Business Object Architecture (DBOA), has been developed starting from the well know and already established concept of Strategic Management Planning (SMP). The SMP implementation is based on the combination of Object-Orientation (OO), Business Objects (BOs), Business Object Architecture (BOA) and Dynamic Systems Development Method (DSDM). The DBOA approach was then evaluated through an extensive case study carried out in the credit insurance sector.

The principal findings of the case study clearly demonstrated the capability of DBOA to reduce the communication gap significantly by ensuring the IT professionals retain their business focus throughout the development lifecycle. In addition, the DBOA minimised the risk of omitting any of the essential stages throughout the implementation process. Moreover, DBOA provided a review mechanism for 'continuous improvement' of business performance, thus further enhancing the reliability of this approach. The case study provided an early indication that DBOA may also be generally applicable as its implementation required only a few relatively minor sector specific modifications. This particular finding supports the claim that DBOA can be expected to provide a low cost and an easy to implement solution to the communication gap problem.

1. INTRODUCTION

In the ever changing and competitive world of business, organisations are facing increasing challenges both internally such as staff skill shortages, and externally such as marketing competitiveness. Organisations compete to survive, or to position themselves as leaders in their particular sectors. To achieve this, various steps and measures are being taken by organisations which involve changes, at different degrees, in the structures and/or people in organisations. There is a growing awareness amongst many organisations that a strategic approach has to be adopted to retain competitiveness. Many organisations have admitted that to achieve results, it is their primary task to take strategic approaches to determine their business directions and to take proper steps to effect changes. It is an experience of many organisations that business strategies can help them handle changes and achieve their business goals more successfully.

Although the principles of business strategies may look straightforward, achieving them is extremely difficult. Once they are applied to the actual day-to-day business operations, their complexity prevents many organisations from implementing them successfully and highly skilled staff to monitor the transition are required. However, according to Ovum's Management Report [source: http://www.ovum.com], there is currently a shortage of management cum operations professionals who possess the skills to monitor the smooth transformation from business strategies to business operations and to ensure the business operations can support the business strategies.

1.1 Business Problems vs. Software Solutions

Recognising the fast pace of advancement of information technology (IT), an increasing number of organisations have started adopting IT to assist them in implementing their business strategies. IT is also seen as a means of alleviating the skill shortage problems experienced in terms of human expertise. Many companies have therefore increased their investment in IT. IT thus underpins the implementation of most business strategies. However, current IT practices are still emphasising software performance and user interface techniques rather than business solutions. For this reason, the expectations from the business remain severely neglected. Consequently, IT solutions frequently fail to deliver business benefit. Brown [Brown et al 1996] suggests that since IT professionals are still very much focused on software products, they may not be able to understand the real business problems, and thus may fail to deliver business solutions. Whilst this communication problem continuous to be the subject of extensive interdisciplinary research, a reliable, generally applicable, low cost, low risk and any easy to implement solution, is yet to be found. This paper focuses on the communication gap between business management and IT professionals.

1.2 Bridging the Communication Gap

Based on experience of business consultants, the underlying problem of the communication gap could be improved by a control mechanism that has the ability to:

(1) *encourage business management and IT professionals to have mutual understanding and mutual consultation with each other;*

(2) *effectively link the business strategies directly to the day-to-day business operations;*

(3) *reflect the way that the day-to-day business operations match the business strategies;*
(4) *ensure that the day-to-day business operations are properly defined in the software applications;*
(5) *review the effectiveness of the software against the business performance;*
(6) *review the business performance against business objectives.*

1.3 Motivation of the Investigation

New and emerging techniques are used to implement this control mechanism to see whether they could tackle the communication problem. Business Objects (BOs), Business Object Architecture (BOA) [OMG 1995] and Dynamic Systems Development Method (DSDM) [DSDM 1995] have been examined to identify their capability to improve the interaction between business management and IT professionals.

Equally, the structure and clarity of business strategies are regarded as vitally important when interpreted and explained by business management to IT professionals. This 'raison d'être' has prompted an investigation into the study of organisational Strategic Management Planning (SMP).

1.4 Related Work

In recent years a number of new research areas have emerged concerning the improvement in business performance that can be achieved by brining closer together business users and software developers. Those attempts have focused on making software more 'user' oriented. Business users are invited to participate actively in software development activities. The objective is to ensure that software delivered meets the business requirements. The literature abounds in more or less the interaction between the business users and software developers, but they have quite different motivations from the approach proposed in this paper. The following sub-sections will cite some of this work and evaluate its effectiveness if used for supporting the control mechanism as described in Section 1.2.

1.4.1 Usage Centric Approach

The Usage Centric Approach [Constantine 1996] emphasises the user's needs but only addresses the improvement of Human Computer Interface (HCI) by better eliciting user interaction requirements; and does not address how software can better support business strategies.

1.4.2 Business Process Reengineering

Business Process Reengineering (BPR) is defined as the fundamental rethinking and radical redesign of business processes to achieve improvements of business performance in regards to costs, service and speed [Hammer et al 1995]. However, most of the time, business processes do not accurately reflect business strategies. Due to the absence of linkage between these two levels, it may be difficult to ensure that reengineered business processes would meet business goals. Jacobson [Jacobson et al 1994] sees BPR as a way to take a comprehensive view of the entire existing operations and redesign it in a way that uses a new technology to serve this purpose. However if the existing operations do not match the business objectives, business goals may not be achieved no matter what new technology is used. BPR lacks a clear link with business strategies and hence may fail to highlight the key strategic factors which may contribute to the achievement of business objectives.

1.4.3 Requirements Engineering

Requirements Engineering (RE) is the elicitation, definition, modelling, analysis, specification and validation of what is needed from a computer system. It is a process which draws on techniques from software engineering, knowledge acquisition, cognitive science and social science to improve software engineering practice [Thome 1993].

Rolland [1996] proposes a framework to identify the business and its requirements. This architectural framework contains models of business structure, organisational information, system life cycle and different dimensions of business processes. RE framework is designed to encourage software developers to appreciate business needs. However such an approach only concentrates on the operational level rather than the business strategic level. If business strategies are not clearly reflected by business operations, business objectives may not be achieved.

1.4.4 Incremental Delivery

Hsia [Hsia et al 1996] proposes an Incremental Delivery (ID) technique to effectively divide a software system into partial, but individually operational components which can be delivered to customers on an incremental basis. The ID decomposition philosophy is a technique of partitioning a software system from the utility point of view (i.e., the external view). The external view allows a system to be grouped into usable subsystems (called increments). The incremental delivery philosophy would significantly modify software development (requirement analysis, system partitioning and system integration), giving it a user-centred perspective, thus encouraging user involvement. Although the communication gap between IT developers and business users may improve through the incremental process, it is still on 'application-specific' rather than 'enterprise-wide' approach. IT professionals may still have difficulties in identifying the overall business objectives which the software should be designed to help in achieving.

1.4.5 Dynamic Systems Development Method

The Dynamic Systems Development Method (DSDM) is a management philosophy for the Rapid Application Development (RAD) [Martin 1991]. It claims to be suitable for urgent business needs in a rapid changing world. Systems developed through DSDM can deliver business advantage rapidly and adaptively [DSDM 1995, 1997]. DSDM emphasises that user involvement is imperative, and that satisfying business requirements is more important than the quality of system operational characteristics. In DSDM, all changes are reversible and estimates should be tight from the outset with frequent deliverables through the iterative prototyping life cycle. However the above two techniques only provide a project management approach. Neither of them takes into account enterprise-wide business goals. Likewise, DSDM lacks actual software development techniques.

1.5 Drawback of Related Work

Despite the fact that the User Centric Approach, Requirements Engineering, Business Process Reengineering, Incremental Delivery and Dynamic Systems Development Method all emphasise business users' involvement, no model is used to implement business strategies. Reaching the business strategic level is crucial given that business management have an opportunity to describe their business situation and business goals to IT professionals. Software applications would more likely be able to support the business hence would become more realistic as business solutions.

2. DYNAMIC BUSINESS OBJECT ARCHITECTURE

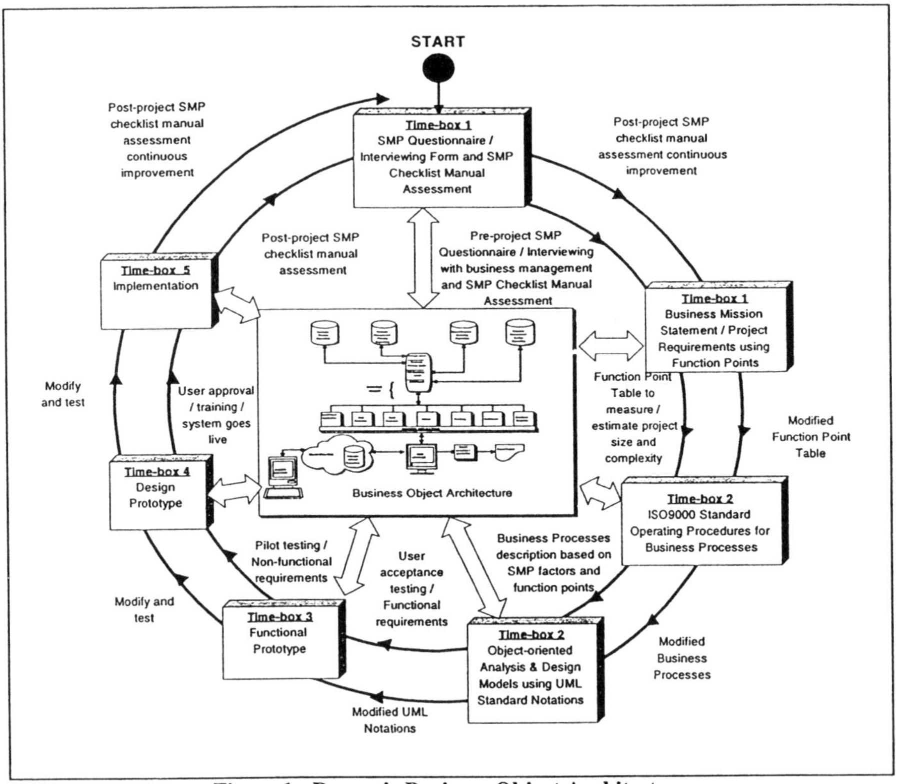

Figure 1 : Dynamic Business Object Architecture

A Dynamic Business Object Architecture (DBOA) is proposed in this paper. DBOA, integrating BOs, BOA and DSDM, is a novel conceptual model which is presented as a tool for supporting organisational SMP. The techniques provided seek to bridge the communication gap between business management and IT professionals. The key linking abstraction in the DBOA approach is a new, coarser-grained and semantically richer notion of BOs together with associated management processes, an iterative prototyping life cycle and substantial business management involvement. DBOA attempts to provide organisations with a complete project development life cycle and a review mechanism to evaluate software development against business performance. A change of business performance would indicate to organisations a need to modify their business in terms of strategies, processes and software applications to achieve their ultimate business goals. DBOA also seeks to offer a thorough, systematic and coherent way of minimising risk at each stage of the development process, which on some occasions might be omitted due to the negligence or incompetence of people who perform the processes.

Figure 1 shows the DBOA model. BOA is situated at the centre surrounded by the DSDM life cycle. The white arrows between BOA and DSDM indicate that the BOA model can always be re-architectured at any stage of the life cycle. Among each life cycle, there is an incremental prototyping approach through a number of distinct phases moving clockwise from the top.

The starting point is represented by a black dot. Each life cycle contains five Time-boxes arranged in the following order:-

Time-box 1 :
- An SMP 'Open-ended' Questionnaire is used to conduct the SMP 'Open-ended' Question interviews with the business management to capture the organisational business situation and to identify business objectives.
- An SMP 'Closed' Questionnaire is used to conduct the SMP Checklist Manual Assessment exercise with the business management, to measure business performance and to identify business strategies – if they exist; or to establish the business strategies otherwise.
- A Business Mission Statement is established to identify the business requirements based on the results of the SMP Checklist Manual Assessment exercise. A Function Points Table is used in the Project Requirements document to estimate project development time and resources required.

Time-box 2 :
- A set of ISO9000 Standard Operating Procedure forms are used to define the business processes in response to the Business Mission Statement and Project Requirement Statement.
- The OO Modelling technique using UML Standard Notation is used to model the Business Processes.

Time-box 3 :
- A Functional Prototype is produced for testing by the business users. Users' comments and feedback are used to modify the functional prototype and to develop a Design Prototype.

Time-box 4 :
- A Design Prototype is developed for further testing and modification. At this stage, non-functional requirements such as the integration of the newly-developed application and the existing legacy or non-legacy

database system should be carried out. Pilot Testing also takes place at this stage.

Time-box 5 : -The system is implemented after the modification of the Design Prototype and the Pilot Testing are completed. User approval is sought and user training is conducted before the system goes live.

In every DBOA post-project phase, an SMP Checklist Manual Assessment exercise is conducted to review the business performance and to modify the business processes, system modelling and application development accordingly. To fulfil the spirit of 'continuous improvement', the SMP Checklist Manual Assessment exercise should take place periodically. It is recommended a six to twelve month interim period as in most companies, Trading and Profit/Loss Account Statement and Financial Reports are usually produced either six months (half yearly) or twelve months (yearly). Financial figures reflect company's profitability and they are useful as indicators in the improvement of business performance. As depicted in Figure 1, the 'continuous improvement' spiral continues to move on cycle-after-cycle. It is anticipated that the contribution of DBOA would be to provide a tool for IT professionals, notably inexperienced consultants and developers, to use the DBOA to practise their profession more proficiently in a relatively short period of time. This may help combat the skill shortage of human experts.

3. IMPLEMENTATION OF DBOA THROUGH A CASE STUDY PROJECT

This section will present an extensive case study using DBOA. The purpose of applying DBOA in a real business environment is to validate this approach in a practical situation.

3.1 Project Initiation

The case study was carried out in a credit insurance company. The company was established in 1976 and has been in profit since opening. However the company's profits had fallen in recent years. The priority goal was to retain the company's market position and to stop the decline in projects. DBOA was recommended to the company and it was explained to the management how it could link their business and IT strategies together.

3.2 Project Plan

The overall project plan was divided into six discrete phases namely: (1) Feasibility Study; (2) Business Study; (3) Functional Prototype; (4) Design Prototype; (5) Implementation; and (6) Post-Project Review. The deliverables (i.e., the reviewable products / documentation etc.) produced by each project phase will be used as the basis of project review and control. They also give those involved in the project a remainder of what the deliverables will cover, when, and by whom, they will be developed.

3.3 Prototyping Strategy

In this project, a prototyping strategy was to produce a version of working system to give an idea to the business users of how the prospective application would look like. The functional and design prototype deliverables were produced in a piecemeal fashion, allowing the users to test and change their requirements. It is expected prototypes will evolve from earlier prototypes, and into the final production version.

3.4 Time-boxing

DBOA was developed with heavy emphasis on the importance of Time-boxing to help project to be delivered on time hence within budget.

3.4.1 Time-box 1 : Feasibility

The duration of Time-box 1 in this project was four weeks. During the Feasibility study phase, activities carried out were as follows:-

- *Joint Requirement Planning (JRP) / Joint Application Development (JAD)*
- *Closed Strategic Management Planning (SMP) Checklist Manual Assessment*
- *Business Mission Statement*
- *Purpose and Scope*
- *Project Requirement*
- *Project Estimation using Function Points*

At the end of this project phase, it was found that the company was weak in the Product Differentiation Strategy. The priority was to concentrate on how to improve this strategy. The management agreed in the identification of the right kinds of technological approaches which could help improve business performance through product differentiation. It was decided to adopt the internet technology to automate and streamline business processes, with a view to speeding up the response time to customers. The project was called "Online Credit Limit Application via the Internet/Intranet ('OCLAVI'). The new services offered were envisaged as round-the-clock, global and multilingual. This would differentiate the company from its competitors who only provide nine-to-five services, local time, Monday-to-Friday. Furthermore most of the competitors use only English or the official language in their own country to communicate with customers.

3.4.2 Time-box 2 : Business Study

The duration of Time-box 2 was 4 weeks. During the business study phase, detailed business functions and business rules were captured. An 'OCLAVI' Business Object was developed. It contained the usual four levels of Business Strategies, Business Processes, OO Modelling and Database Management Systems. The ISO9000 Standard Procedure was created. Within the procedure, business processes were defined. All the processes and necessary tasks were based on the Business Mission Statement and Project Requirements, drafted as a result of the SMP Checklist Manual Assessment exercise. OO models using UML notation were used to model the business processes.

3.4.3 *Time-box 3 : Functional Prototype*

The duration of Time-box3 was seven weeks. The objective of the Functional Prototype was to produce a version of the working system from analysis and design notation to implementation.

During this phase, the OO models drawn up using UML notation were mapped into a web enabling tool. The emphasis at this stage was on the development of data fields and the associated screen handling. This was not more than a 'rough' prototype, but it was able to demonstrate the essential features of the interface and some of the functionality of the new system. Interfaces were created with the feature sufficient to enable a CLA transaction to progress to the users, through a standard Internet browser.

An IT internal review meeting was held for testing prior to the prototyping session with the business users. A range of modifications and improvements were made, with suitable care to ensure that the UML models were kept consistent with the web tool implementation. The final activity to take place in this Time-box was a JAD session to review the prototype with the business users.

3.4.4 *Time-box 4 : Design Prototype*

The duration of Time-box 4 was seven weeks. The main objective of this phase of the Design Prototype was to provide the bulk of the essential functionality of the application. The Functional Prototype had been largely concerned with the design of the user interface and with business functionality, and paid little attention to such non-functional requirements as integrating the newly-developed application and the existing database system.

Another important focus of the activities carried out in this phase was to update the ISO9000 procedure manual in response to the changes resulting from the prototyping session. The developers also had to update the OO models to ensure that the design models correctly reflected business processes, hence ensuring the delivery of a business application that could effectively support the business. Since the 'OCLAVI' Business Object had been developed as a conceptual model to pave the way for software system analysis, design and implementation, the changes suggested by the business users were applied to the modification of the BO. Such a cycle proceeds iteratively so that the model can be checked and altered, as and when is required. Essential to this phase was the designing and building of the system. Hence by the end of this phase the system, in principle, should contain absolutely all functionalities in a form suitable for testing in the final JAD session. There should be no components of functionality left 'un-implemented' if the schedule is to be met.

The schedule in Time-box 4 was quite similar to that in Time-box 3. First the IT developers modified the system in accordance with the users' changes of requirements elicited from the previous JAD session. The new prototype was tested again after the modification. Then, an internal IT department review meeting was held to discuss progress and modifications. Much care was taken to keep adequate records and check on what could potentially have become a quire frantic rate of change. Version control was the real issue. There were three versions of application in this project, namely: (1) Prototyping version; (2) Pilot testing version; and (3) Production version.

Towards the end of Time-box 4, a JAD session was held to test the Design Prototype with the users. The users were invited to try to submit a mock Online CLA through the test bed linked between the Web browser, Company's Web server and the Insurance Underwriter's database. All the databases had been copied from the live systems to the test systems so that if the CLAs were approved, the users would get online decision on their screens. Otherwise, the application would be forwarded to the deferred decision folder pending further processing. The users could also download the decision reports on deferred CLAs previously submitted.

This time, the JAD session revealed the requirements for a few minor changes, such as tidying up the position of the data fields, setting the margins of the documentation and changing the report format. After the meeting, the IT department staff reviewed the prototype again and created a Pilot testing version. This time, not only the users within the project development team, but also company's customers were invited to test the application. After the Pilot testing, the Pilot version was modified further before being converted to a release version for implementation in Time-box 5.

3.4..5 Time-box 5 : Implementation

The duration of Time-box 5 was five weeks. The activities in this Time-box were mainly designed to test the reliability of the system in collaboration with the users, and to perform any final debugging that was required. No extra requirements from the users were accepted within this Time-box. If the user had wanted to make any further changes, the project team would have had to reschedule the project development life cycle. Other activities at this stage included obtaining the users' approval for the release of the application, issuing user guidelines, organising user training programmes, setting up a Web production server, connecting to the Internet Gateway, configuring firewall security for the Intranet access, linking Company's Web server to the Intranet server, creating a rollout plan, notifying customers of the Web Site registration procedure, and setting up customer user names and passwords. Finally, the test site was moved from the text bed to the production server. A data take-on procedure was performed and the system went live.

3.5 Post-Project Review

The 'OCLAVI' project had been delivered on time, within budget and was operational. In order to measure the level of improvement in business performance as a result of this project, a preliminary Post-project review exercise was executive five weeks after the system had gone live. Seven management team members assembled together to conduct the Post-project SMP Checklist Manual Assessment exercise. Evidence in the form of financial statements, sales volume figures, and staff records, were examined.

A comparison between the Pre-project and Post-project SMP Checklist Manual Assessments exercise was executed in order to evaluate the DBOA project against business performance and to see whether or not the DBOA approach had improved the business performance. This exercise had shown there was a 13% improvement in the overall business performance. The variation between the two assessments are listed in Table 1.

SMP Checklists	Assessment Date : March 1998 % of objectives met	Assessment Date : November 1998 % of objectives met	Margin
Low Cost Strategy	50%	60%	+10%
Product Differentiation Strategy	25%	50%	+25%
Product Efficiency Strategy	46%	60%	+14%
Insurance Market Competitiveness Strategy	50%	63.3%	+13.3%
Customer Services Strategy	67.5%	72.5%	+5%
Human Resources Strategy	68%	76%	+8%
Information Systems Effectiveness Strategy	50.8%	66.6%	+15.8%
			Average Margin : +13%

Table 1 : Comparison between the Pre-project and Post-project SMP Checklist Manual Assessments

After the Post-project SMP Checklist Manual Assessment exercise, notes were made concerning the level of improvement (or decline) in business performance. The number of new factors meeting business objectives and failing to meet business objectives were both recorded. Problem areas were outlined and flagged for future investigations.

As part of the 'continuous improvement' practice, the Project Requirement Statement and Function Points Table were updated in accordance with the conclusions from the exercise. After meeting with the business management and obtained the necessary recommendation from them, the IT staff then updated the ISO9000 procedure. The components inside the BOA repository modules were modified in accordance with the new instructions as set out in the procedure. The software application was also modified based on the modified design work.

3.6 Evaluation of the Case Study

The project team considered that DBOA had been an effective tool to assist them in running the project better. The IT department staff found that DBOA had offered a way of addressing business problems first before bogged down in the details of technical issues. When the IT department staff developed the software application, they understood the reasons why it had to be done in a particular way to tackle business problems. Management and business users considered the 'OCLAVI' project using the DBOA approach a satisfactory one. They experienced fewer problems compared to previous projects not using DBOA. The 'OCLAVI' project was delivered on time, within budget and operated satisfactorily.

The project team felt that the 'Open-ended' questionnaire design had enabled IT department staff to capture the business scene more holistically. It had also encouraged those involved to express their feelings more sincerely and hence had enabled IT department staff to understand the business situation better. The SMP interview had provided an opportunity for business management and IT department staff to communicate better with each other.

The SMP Checklist, in a 'Closed' questionnaire format, had transformed the loose, unstructured and hard-to-measure information obtained from the interviews into tight, structured and easy to measure strategic factors. The SMP Checklist Manual Assessment exercises during the Pre- and Post-project phases had provided an opportunity for IT department staff to measure business performance at different stages. Hence, software applications could be modified accordingly for 'continuous improvement'. The measurement of business performance could also help the organisation to evaluate its investment in software development against business gains.

The ISO9000 operating procedure had integrated business strategies with business processes. Such an integration had enabled a correlation to be formed between business strategies and day-to-day business operations. The use of OO modelling techniques to model the business processes had provided a means of transforming business abstraction into software development. Software application would thus be more statistically based and business focused. In the case study, UML notation was used to model the 'OCLAVI' project and project team considered that UML was capable of modelling the business processes in this respect.

The DSDM project management technique had brought business management and IT department staff closer together. The iterative and evolutionary prototyping approach had enabled the frequent testing of the system to minimise the risk of failing to deliver the system on time and within budget.

Overall, the tripartite integration of: (1) business strategies; (2) software development; and (3) project management had made IT department staff aware that when business strategies and software applications are linked together to form a single pool of knowledge and developed in an iterative project development life cycle, software applications produced are likely to be more effective in supporting the organisational SMP. Project team also considered DBOA easy to implement and the learning curve was not steep. On the whole, the outcome of the project has revealed that DBOA has demonstrated merits in reducing the communication gap between business management and IT department staff, by enabling the development of software application embracing the knowledge acquired from the business. Both business management and IT department staff appreciated that DBOA is an ideal tool for fostering communication between them and provides the techniques to enable IT department staff to acquire business knowledge, objectives and requirements. The management also welcomed the opportunities to review the project against business performance. This could help them justify their investment in IT against their business benefit.

4. CONCLUSIONS

This paper has proposed a Dynamic Business Object Architecture (DBOA) which integrates business and IT domains aiming to bridge the communication gap between them. DBOA is a conceptual framework with all the steps and techniques necessary to monitor the implementation processes, which will minimise the risk associated with human error or negligence encountered when implementing business strategies. Further, DBOA is intended to ensure a smooth transition from the business strategic level to software development level. It also seeks to provide a mechanism to review software development against improvement in business performance subsequent to its implementation.

DBOA shows certain advantages with respect to the origination of BOs and demonstrates that BOs have the potential to become powerful modelling techniques to support organisational SMP by implementing business strategies into software applications. DBOA allows both business management and IT professionals to work together towards business objectives.

DBOA was applied to a case study project in a business organisation to demonstrate the practical application of the approach. The results of the case study provided an early indication the primary benefit of DBOA was to be able to reduce the communication gap significantly by ensuring the IT professionals retain the business focus throughout the development lifecycle. In additional, it minimised the risk of omitting any of the essential stages of the implementation process from capturing business situation to delivering software application.

Additionally, the review mechanism substantiates the spirit of 'continuous improvement' in business performance which makes DBOA adaptive and responsive to environmental changes. The above features of DBOA distinguish it from other BO models in terms of the level of object abstraction and scope of adaptation. The paradigm of DBOA paves the way for new directions of Business Object development. Evan though after the case study, rather than the many that would be needed to support a strong claim for the usefulness of DBOA, the fact that it was regarded as useful in developing a needed strategic software system is evidence in its favour. DBOA provides a new conceptual modelling method which we advocates as a useful guideline for developing an automated strategic tool.

5. REFERENCES

[Boehm 1986] Boehm, B. "A Spiral Model of Software Development and Enhancement" in *the ACM SIGSOFT Software Engineering Notes,* August 1986.

[Booch 1994] Booch G. *Object-Oriented Analysis and Design.* Benjamin-Cummings Publishing Company Inc. 1994 (2nd Edition). ISBN 0-805-35340-2.

[Booch et al 1998] Booch G, Jacobson I and Rumbaugh J. *The Unified Modeling Language User Guide.* Addison-Wesley, Mass, USA 1998. ISBN 0-201-57168-4.

[Brown et al 1996] Brown C and Asch D. *Managing Strategy.* Macmillan Press, NY.

[Constantine 1996] Constantine, L. "Objects As If People Mattered" in the *OOPSLA'96 Conference, San Jose, CA, October 1996.* Source: http://www.acm.org/sigplan/oopsla/oopsla96/oopsla96.html.

[DSDM 1995] DSDM Consortium. *Dynamic Systems Development Method Version 2.0.* Tresseract Publishing, Surrey, UK, 1995.

[DSDM 1997] DSDM Consortium. *Dynamic Systems Development Method Version 3.0.* Tresseract Publishing, Surrey, UK, 1997.

[Faulkner et al 1995] Faulkner D and Rowman C. *The Essence of Competitive Strategy.* Prentice Hall International (UK) Ltd., Exter, UK. ISBN 0-13-291477-8

[Hsia 1996] Hsia, P., Hsu, C., Kung, D., Hepner, M. and Wang, J. "An Object-Oriented Approach to Incremental Delivery of Software Systems" in the *OOIS'96 Conference, London, 1996*, Springer, London, 1996, pp 431-446. ISBN 3-540-76132-2.

[IFPUG 1996] *International Function Point Users Group.* Ohio, USA. Source: http://cuiwww.unige.ch/OSG/FAQ/SE/se-faq-s-2.html#S-2.

[Jacobson et al 1994] Jacobson I et al, *The Object Advantages: Business Process Reengineering With Object Technology*, 1994 (Addison-Wesley, New York), ISBN 0-201-42289-1

[Martin 1991] Martin, J. *Rapid Application Development.* Macmillan, NY, 1991. ISBN 0-02-376775-8

[OMG 1995] *OMG, Object Management Group - Object Management Architecture Guide*, 1995 (John Wiley & Sons, Inc., New York). ISBN 0-471-14193-3.

[Rolland 1996] Rolland, C. "Challenges in Object Oriented Modelling: From Conceptual Modelling to Requirements Engineering" in *the OOIS'96 Conference, London, December 1996*, Springer, London 1996, pp3-17. ISBN 3-540-76132-2.

[Thome 1993] Thome, B. *Systems Engineering – Principles and Practice of Computer-Based Systems Engineering.* John Wiley & Sons, NY., 1993. ISBN 047 1935522.

Distributed Management of Component Framework Specifications

Junichi Suzuki and Yoshikazu Yamamoto
Department of Computer Science,
Graduate School of Science and Technology,
Keio University
Yokohama City, 223-8522, Japan
+81-45-563-3925
{suzuki, yama}@yy.cs.keio.ac.jp

Abstract. *The emergence of the Internet has radically changed how to develop and circulate software. It drives rapid software development using plug-compatible components, and also requires distributed software development allowing developers to collaborate in widely disparate places. This paper describes our SoftDock system that leverages distributed component development. It supports the iterative and consistent evolution of component model specifications by combining several emerging standard technologies. We believe our work shows a blue print of a next logical step in the business component research.*

Keywords. *Business components, Business objects, Distributed software development, Model interchange, Model engineering, UML, XML, DOM, CORBA.*

1 Introduction

The emergence of the Internet has radically changed how to develop and circulate software. The development cycle at "Internet speed" requires less time-to-market and more frequent updates, while maintaining high levels of functionality and quality. The notions of component and business object are the key for this issue. A business component is defined in (Herzum et al., 1998) as follows:

> *A business component is the IS representation, from requirements analysis through deployment and run-time, of an "autonomous" business concept or process. It consists of all the software artifacts necessary to express, implement and deploy the given autonomous business concept as an equally autonomous, reusable element of a larger information system.*

It addresses rapid software development and adaptability to survive in changing environment including technological and business changes.

Also, the current software development projects are becoming more network-centric, because effective and economical communication mediums are available, and because the knowledge and skills required for a large project often cannot be found in one location. The team communication among developers critically impacts the quality of their deliverables in the situation where they spread across geometrically distributed places (Dutoit et al., 1998). The friction of distributed, and therefore delayed, communication typically forces the information overhead in teams, thereby works to slow development. It is highly required to develop components independently of physical places and assemble them.

For the above driving forces and requirements, unfortunately, there are few collaborative platforms to manage rapid evolution of business component models. Such an integrated framework requires several challenges for supporting distributed business component development:

- Modeling components and relationships (dependencies, associations, etc.) between them, which involves the modeling language that defines interchangeable semantics of components.
- Describing and interchanging component model information, which involves the model exchange format.
- Providing a uniform means to access and circulate components, which involves a set of published interfaces and communication protocol.
- Ensuring the integrity of component models, which involves the model tracking and storage facility.

This paper describes our SoftDock system which is a platform for distributed software development (Suzuki, 1999a-1999c). SoftDock supports the model-based component development and management. It allows developers to share and manage component model specifications collaboratively, through requirements analysis to deployment, and then produce software from the model.

Our system addresses the above four issues by combining some standard technologies. It provides a solution to the first issue by using the Unified Modeling Language (UML) (OMG, 1999a), to the second one by providing an application-independent interchange format for UML models, called UXF (UML eXchange Format) (Suzuki, 1998a and 1999d), and to the third and fourth issues by distributing UXF descriptions through DOM (Document Object Model) interface (W3C, 1998a) implemented on top of CORBA (Common Object Request Broker Architecture) (OMG, 1998b).

The SoftDock system provides following benefits:

- *It addresses model-based component development.*
  SoftDock allows developers to specify component models independently of implementation technologies such as programming language, network facility and operating system.
- *It leverages model reuse by tool interoperability.*

SoftDock allows component models to be interchangeable and reusable between different development tools with different strengths, throughout the lifecycle of software development. With this capability, development teams do not have to lock-in any specific tools.

– *It addresses cost-effectiveness.*
The seamless tool interoperability and model reusability reduces the information overhead between tools, project members or development phases. Also, SoftDock has the potential to reduce cost, i.e. time and money, by incorporating promising open standards. Using promising standards helps risk management.
– *It has the potential to speed up model development.*
The above characteristics increase the model continuity and improve developers' productivity. SoftDock has great potential to streamline distributed business component development.

The remainder of this paper is organized as follows. Section 2 overviews enabling technologies for SoftDock: UML, XML, UXF, RDF, DOM and CORBA. Section 3 describes the SoftDock architecture and its implementation. We conclude with a note on future work, in Section 4 and 5.

2 Foundation Technologies for SoftDock

This section briefly overviews backgrounds, motivations and benefits of enabling technologies used in SoftDock.

2.1 Unified Modeling Language (UML)

The Unified Modeling Language (UML) is the union of the previous leading object modeling methodologies; Booch, OMT and OOSE. It is a standard object-oriented modeling language that defines most of the semantics and their notations required for representing software constructs. UML provides nearly nine types of independent diagrams for modeling a given problem domain in terms of various perspectives. UML has been widely accepted by academic and commercial developers, and used for representing various software models including real-time system models, hypermedia models, business models, engineering design models, multi-agent models, etc.

2.2 Component Model Interchange: UXF and XMI

Model interchange is a quite important capability in software development, because there are few application-neutral exchange format between development tools. The most important factor in interchanging model information is that the semantics within the model should be described explicitly and transferred precisely. To address this issue, we developed UXF (UML eXchange Format), which is an interchange format for UML models (Suzuki, 1998a and 1999d). Object Management Group also completed the XMI (XML Metamodel Interchange) format (OMG, 1999). Both UXF and XMI are based on eXtensible Markup Language (XML) (W3C, 1998b), and serves as a communication vehicle for component model information between development tools or developers (Suzuki, 1998a and 1999d).

UXF is carefully designed to be simple and well-structured enough to encode, publish, access and interchange UML models. We are now using UXF in the SoftDock system, because it preceded XMI at the time of beginning of our project, and because it is much simpler than XMI. However, we are considering to support XMI as well in SoftDock (see Section 4). Note that due to space limitations, the basics and benefits of using XML as an interchange format are not covered here. Please see (Suzuki, 1999c and 1999d) for more in-depth discussion.

2.3 Distributed Component Model Interchange: DOM and CORBA

SoftDock manages component model information written in UXF through the Document Object Model (DOM) interface implemented on CORBA (Common Object Request Broker Architecture). DOM defines general-purpose interfaces to manipulate a parsed tree structure of a XML document. It provides a set of APIs for the following capabilities:

- *Structure navigation*, which is the navigation of document structures such as accessing and searching elements or attributes.
- *Structure manipulation*, which is the manipulation of document structures such as adding, changing and removing elements or attributes.
- *Content manipulation*, which is the manipulation of document contents such as putting or getting values to elements and attributes.

The DOM interface is defined with the OMG Interface Definition Language (IDL), a primary component in the CORBA specification (see below), because it is designed to be programming language neutral. DOM does not intend to be implemented with CORBA, but implementing DOM interfaces on CORBA is reasonable strategy for our goal to distribute component models on the network environment (Suzuki, 1999a).

Common Object Request Broker Architecture (CORBA) is a standard for object middleware used in the heterogeneous environment. It provides a standard way to interoperate distributed objects. CORBA defines the interfaces and components that organize Object Request Brokers (ORBs). An application accessing the service of a remote object uses an ORB to send a message and receive the results. A series of interfaces in CORBA allows the distribution of

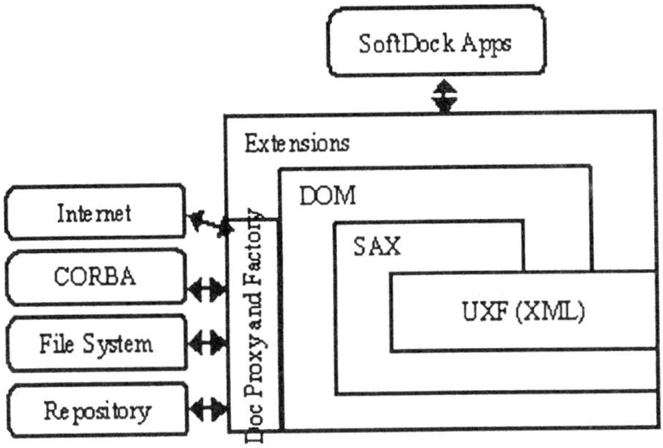

Figure 1: SoftDock Architecture

remote objects on multiple platforms in a transparent way to applications. One of the key components in CORBA is OMG Interface Definition Language (IDL), a language to define the interface of a remote object. It is programming language neutral by providing a mapping to various languages. Another important component is Internet Inter-ORB Protocol (IIOP), which is a standard on-the-wire protocol based on TCP. IIOP leverages the interoperability between different ORBs as well as between objects on a single ORB. The benefits from combining DOM and CORBA are described in (Suzuki, 1999c).

2.4 Component Metadata: RDF

Metadata is data about data, or specifically descriptive information about software models, e.g. objects, components, packages, etc., in the context of our system. It is used to index, retrieve, manage, interchange or automate model information. The concept of metadata is becoming important in the web community. The Resource Description Framework (RDF) specification (W3C, 1999) has been completed by the World Wide Web Consortium (W3C). RDF allows us to define metadata of arbitrary web resources including an entire web document, a part of a document, a collection of documents and even an object that is not directly accessible via the web. RDF is an XML-based format.

In the SoftDock system, we use RDF to define metadata of various software models. However, it can integrate any other metadata description languages that are based on XML. For example, we have used the IMS Meta-Data specification (IMS, 1999), which is a metadata description language for educational resources, in order to build a distance learning/training system for teaching software modeling based on SoftDock (Suzuki, 1999c). Section 3.2 shows component metadata is used for describing its non-functional aspects.

3 The SoftDock System

This section describes the foundation architecture, system organization, design strategy, deployment and applications of the SoftDock system.

3.1 Architecture and System Organization

Figure 1 shows the SoftDock architecture, which describes the relationships between different APIs to access component model specifications encoded in UXF. UXF descriptions are manipulated through either DOM or SAX (Simple API for XML) interface (SAX, 1998). SAX is a de-facto standard parser interface, the interface between a XML parser and its applications, which has been developed in the XML community. SAX is an event-based parser interface, while DOM is tree-based (Chang, 1998). DOM compliant parsers often use SAX-based parsers internally. Any parsers supporting either DOM or SAX can be plugged into our architecture without affecting other components in the system. The extension part in the architecture provides a series of utility objects that are useful for building various SoftDock applications (see Figure 1). One of the most important objects in this part is a document proxy. Its responsibilities are:

- Fetching remote model specifications consistently.
- Connecting a parser interface with external environments such as the Internet, CORBA, file systems and repositories.

The design details of document proxy is described in Section 3.3.

Figure 2 shows our current system organization. All the UXF descriptions are stored in the resource server. The SoftDock system provides the connectivity with a web server and CORBA environment. The HTTP connection provides the oneway communication between clients and servers, which aims to allow client applications including web browsers to refer model information within a resource server through a web server. Whenever a UXF description is updated in resource server, SoftDock pushes the updated description to a web server.

The IIOP connection provides the two-way communication between clients and servers, which aims to allow developers at separated places to refer, create and modify arbitrary model specifications. Client applications include CASE tools, documentation tools, design metrics tools, source code generators, reverse engineering tools.

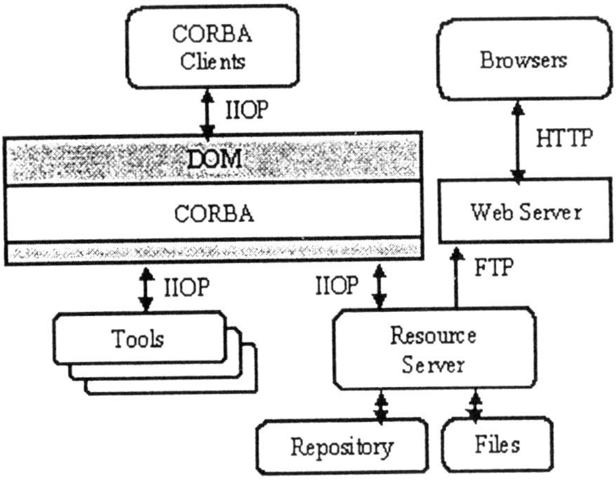

Figure 2: The current SoftDock system organization

3.2 Description of Business Components

There is an emerging consensus about business components, apparent in (Herzum et al., 1998 and Herzum, 1998), though there has never been any standard consensus (Sutherland, 1998). It proposes four major dimensions for business components:

- The concept of the business component itself.
- The business component system –the groups of business components that cooperate to deliver the system functionality.
- The internal architecture of the business component.
- The business component system development process.

The SoftDock system supports the categorization and internal structure of business components.

(Herzum et al., 1998) defines the layered categorization of business components:

- *Business process components*, representing business processes and workflows
- *Business entity components*, representing components upon which business processes operate.
- *Utility components*, fine-grained components used by the above components.

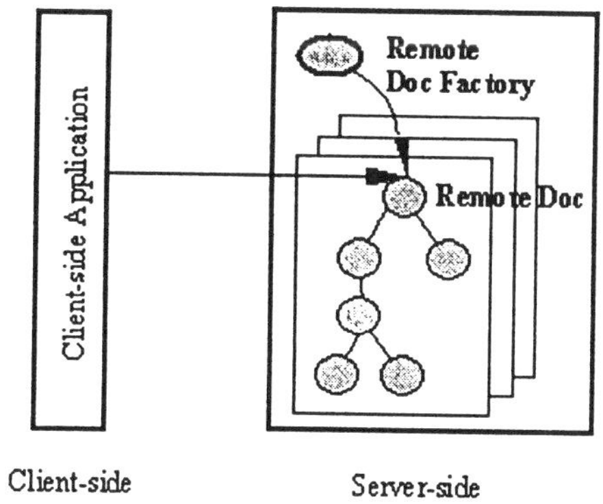

Figure 3: Access to a remote UXF description

A business component at a given level can depend on business components at any of the levels below. SoftDock supports business entity component and utility components by modeling and describing them with UML. Business process components are partially supported by specifying business processes and workflows using UML sequence and activity diagrams. The complete support of business process components is future work, because UML does not have enough model elements to specify business processes and workflows. We are investigating an extension to the UML metamodel for modeling them (see Section 4).

(Herzum et al., 1998) also defines the layered internal structure of each business component: *a presentation layer, a workspace layer* supporting a business transaction, *an enterprise layer* defining business logic, rules and interaction between components, and *a resource layer* supporting transaction, persistence, security and other services. Our system currently supports the description of an enterprise layer.

For the above supports, we extended UXF and introduced the notion of component metadata. UXF is extended to describe the enterprise level of three kinds of components. A sample description is shown in the Appendix. Currently, we suppose all the business components are modeled with UML and UXF, though we are aware the current UML is not sufficient to specify them. What model elements should be prepared for defining business components is beyond the scope of this paper. When further standard consensus or UML extension is emerged, we will plug-in it to the SoftDock system.

Component metadata contains important information to circulate and assemble components. It is described with RDF, and linked to a corresponding

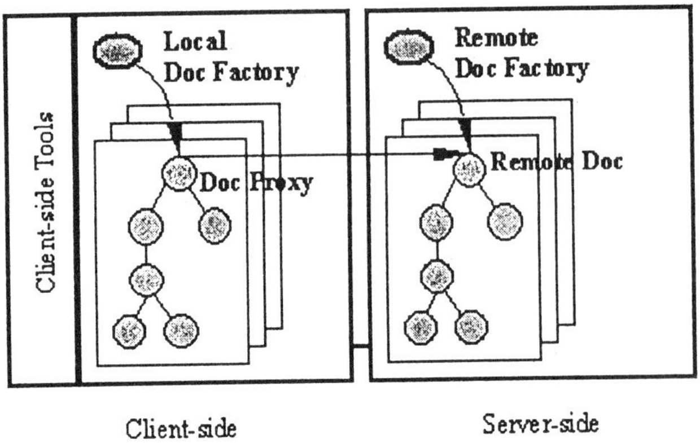

Figure 4: Local cache of a remote UXF description

component description (see Appendix). Section 3.3 describes how they are transferred and handled in SoftDock.

3.3 Design and Implementation

This section describes design strategies we chose for the IIOP communication subsystem depicted in Figure 2.

3.3.1 Model Management Interfaces

As described earlier, SoftDock allows client applications to access remote UXF-formatted model information through the DOM interface built on CORBA. Every UXF description is parsed into a tree structure according to its tag hierarchy with a DOM-compliant XML parser, and maintained as a set of CORBA objects (Figure 3). The CORBA objects are registered into the Basic Object Adapter (BOA), which is a server-side facility used for managing their lifecycle and dispatching incoming requests to them. Every root node (or object) of tree structures is published to client applications using the CORBA naming service, a white page service for CORBA objects. Client applications locate the root node of a target UXF description and then navigate its structure and contents.

This design strategy is straightforward, but it does not scale well in the situation where the size of a single UXF document is large or it has many tags. It raises object management problem and increased overhead problem. The object management problem means that an underlying ORB (or BOA, specifically) have to register huge amount of objects potentially. This is because a

```
#pragma prefix "jp.ac.keio.SoftDock"
#include <dom.idl>
#include <CosEventComm.idl>
module SoftDockExtention
{
  typedef long UID;
  interface UXFDescription
    :dom::Document,
    :CosEventComm::TypedPushConsumer,
    :CosEventComm::TypedPushSupplier
  {
    attribute UID nodeId;
    readonly attribute float revision;
    void externalize();
    sequence<string> content();
    boolean isLocked();
    oneway void lockNode(in CorbaDocProxy proxy);
    oneway void releaseNode();
    void update(in string docName,
                in UID    changePoint,
                in short  changeTypeId);
  };
  interface CorbaDocProxy
    :UXFDescripion,
  {
    attribute dom::Document remoteDoc;
    oneway metadata(in sequence<string> mdata);
  };
  interface CorbaDocFactory
  {
    dom::Document createDocument(in string docName);
    dom::Document cloneDocument(in UXFDescriiption doc);
    oneway void releaseNode(in UXFDescriiption node);
    void destroyDocument(in UXFDescriiption doc);
  };
};
```

Figure 5: Extended IDL definition for SoftDock

UXF tag is mapped to a DOM node, which is in turn mapped to a CORBA object. The overhead problem means that a remote method invocation is always required when referring to and/or changing any node in a remote UXF description.

To avoid the overhead problem, SoftDock allows a client application to cache remote UXF documents locally (Figure 4). It provides the IDL interface extending the DOM APIs for fetching and maintaining remote UXF descriptions at client-side. Figure 5 shows three extended interfaces: `UXFDescription`, `CorbaDocAgent` and `CorbaDocProxy`.

`UXFDescription` represents a server-side root node of an entire UXF description. It is derived from `dom::Document` defined in the DOM specification, which provides the methods for accessing to the document's data and creating its internal elements. `UXFDescription` is also derived from `CosEventComm::PushSupplier` and `CosEventComm::PushConsumer`, which are the interfaces for push-style event notification in the CORBA event service. These interfaces are used to notify the change events between a remote UXF description and its local cache. The

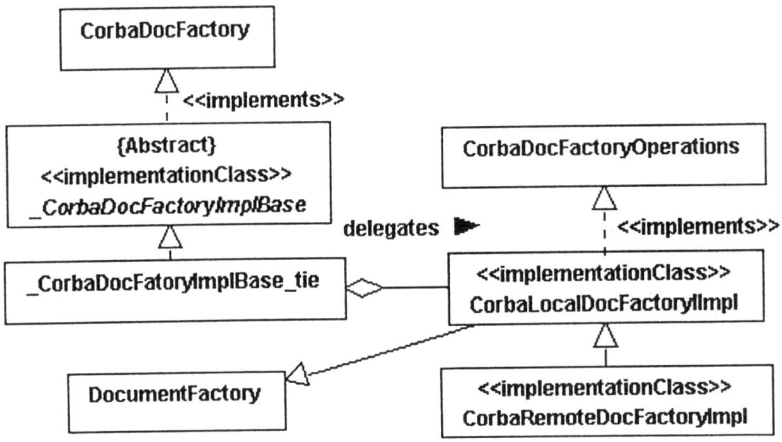

Figure 6: Class structure of the `CorbaDocFactory` interface and its implementations

document change notification is described Section 3.3.2. `UXFDescription` has an attribute `revision` to track its revision number and exposes five methods. `externalize()` translates a document's tree structure into a file, and `content()` returns its representation as a sequence of string data. `lockNode()` and `releaseNode()` are used to require and release a lock of the document passed as an argument. `update()` is used to notify any change of a UXF description (see Section 3.3.2).

The `CorbaDocProxy` interface is a client-side proxy for a remote UXF description, shown in Figure 4. This interface is derived from `UXFDescription`. It has references to root nodes of both a remote document and its local cache. The method `metadata()` transfers component metadata (see also Section 3.2).

The `CorbaDocFactory` interface represents the local and remote factory for a UXF description. The DOM specification does not define the way of creating an XML document instance, and therefore this interface provides factory methods for creating, cloning and destroying a document.

Figure 6 shows the server-side class structure of `CorbaDocFactory` and its implementations, which are generated by an IDL-Java compiler. `CorbaDocFactory` in Figure 6 is a Java interface class, which is a Java-side equivalent of the IDL `CorbaDocFactory` interface. `_CorbaDocFactoryImplBase` and `_CorbaDocFactoryImplBase_tie` are skeleton classes for `CorbaDocFactory`, which unmarshal parameters contained in method invocations.

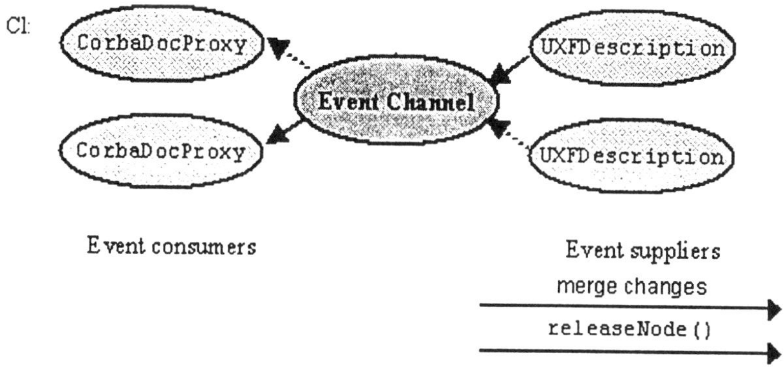

Figure 8: Synchronous (left) and Asynchronous interactions between client and server (right)

We are using the *tie approach* in which a skeleton asks for its delegate class to perform method invocations, instead to perform them by itself. `_CorbaDocFactoryImplBase_tie` delegates method executions to `CorbaLocalDocFactoryImpl` and `CorbaRemoteDocFactoryImpl`. These classes implement the `CorbaDocFactory` interface. They are the client-side and server-side factory classes for a UXF description respectively (see Figure 4).

3.3.2 Change Notification

When a server-side UXF description is updated, the change is notified to the corresponding `CorbaDocProxy` at client-side. This notification is performed by calling the `CorbaDocProxy`'s `update()` method. SoftDock transfers typed events through event channel based on the push model.

Event data is passed by means of the parameters defined in `update()`. The parameter `changeTypeId` shows what kind of change is occurred in an original description at server-side. The kinds of changes include copy, movement, insertion, deletion and modification of a node. An event channel is an intermediate object that allows multiple event suppliers to communicate with multiple event consumers in the decoupled manner. An event channel is both a consumer and supplier of events. It is a standard CORBA object, and the communication with an event channel is accomplished using normal CORBA requests. In SoftDock, `UXFDescription` transfers a push-style change notification to an event channel, and then the event channel pushes the change to `CorbaDocProxy` (Figure 7).

3.3.3 Synchronous and Asynchronous Accesses

The caching mechanism described above allows SoftDock to support both synchronous and asynchronous manipulation of a UXF description.

The synchronous editing is performed as shown in the left of Figure 8. A client-side `CorbaDocProxy` locks a remote document using its method `lockNode()` to prevent modifications by other applications. Once the document is locked, its metadata is transferred to its `CorbaDocProxy`. Then, it accesses and manipulates the remote document based on the obtained metadata. After editing the remote documents, `CorbaDocProxy` releases the lock with its method `releaseNode()`. The synchronous editing is a simple model and ensures the document's consistency by preventing overwrites. However, it does not scale well in the situation where many learners are accessing a remote document frequently because every access requires a lock even if the document is not changed.

In contrast to the exclusive lock, our system provides an alternative lock, *shared lock*, which allows a group of applications to share a single lock on a document. This lock enables the asynchronous remote editing. Users can continue to work even when they are offline, e.g. using mobile computers, and merge changes later. Merging a change to the original description, a client application uses the method `update()` of `UXFDescription`. The asynchronous editing can reduce the number of remote method invocations. The right of Figure 8 shows the interactions between client and server in the asynchronous mode. This mode works best in environments in which participants know each other's activities, or just refer the remote document.

3.4 Deployment

SoftDock has been deployed with:

- DOM compliant XML parser: We have used XML4J (IBM), and are replacing it with our own parser.
- CORBA compliant ORB: We are using two different ORBs, ORBacus (OOC) and Fnorb (DSTC), which are Java-based and Python-based ORBs respectively. The IIOP protocol ensures the interoperability between these ORBs.
- Web server: Our in-house web server, OpenWebServer (Suzuki et al., 1998b, 1999e and 1999f), is used for the HTTP connection (see Section 2).
- Programming languages: CORBA server applications are written with Java, while its client applications are with Java and Python. Our web server is developed with Java.
- Operating systems: CORBA server applications are run on Linux and Windows NT, while its client applications are on Windows 95, Windows NT.

3.5 Applications

We have interchanged some simple component models in SoftDock, e.g. CurrencyBook component, which is designed based on the OMG Finance DTF's Currency specification (OMG, 1998c), Invoice component, Customer component and InvoiceManager component.

SoftDock has a command-line and graphical (Java applet-based and Tk-based) model reference/revision tools. Also, we have developed model documentation tools and connectivity glues for commercial CASE tools. These tools fetch a UXF description from a resource server and translate it into HTML, RTF, PDF, PostScript or proprietary formats used in Rational Rose and MagicDraw.

4 Future Work

We are extending our system from several viewpoints.

As described in Section 3.2, our work has not addressed how business components should be modeled. SoftDock incorporates a minimum extension to UML and UXF. We are investigating some proposals for metamodel extensions and techniques for specifying business processes and workflow with UML (Bock, 1998, Wiegart, 1998 and Hruby, 1998). We plan to build some prototype applications for testing their feasibility.

We are adding some capabilities to SoftDock, which allows more effective distributed model management. The first one is a transparent communication between a remote UXF description and its local cache to whether a target description is cached in client-side, while client applications currently have to know that in advance. The second capability is a yellow page service for each root node of UXF descriptions. It provides more semantics-aware search mechanisms than the current white page service. We are now designing it with the CORBA trading service. The third one is secure communication facility. We are considering to use IIOP over SSL. The fourth one is adding a different locking scopes to a UXF description, e.g. a lock for a collection of documents. We are also analyzing the system behavior in the asynchronous editing mode, and investigating the consistent distributed document management.

We also plan to align some other specifications such as the Document Repository Integration by the OMG Business Object DTF (OMG, 1998c), the XMI format (OMG, 1999b), and the Meta Object Facility (MOF) specification (OMG, 1997) for evaluating the possibility and implications of a highly interoperable and semantics-interchangeable infrastructure.

5 Conclusion

This paper describes our SoftDock system that leverages distributed business component development. It supports the iterative and consistent evolution of component model specifications by combining some emerging standard technologies such as UML, XML, DOM and CORBA. We describe our system architecture, design strategies, techniques and implications for managing component models effectively in the distributed environment. We believe our work shows a blue print of a next logical step in the business component research.

Appendix Sample Description of a Component and its Metadata

```
<UXF Version="2.0"
     xmlns:UXF="http://www.yy.cs.keio.ac.jp/~suzuki/project/uxf/">
  <!-- Component description -- >
  <UXF:BusinessComponent>
    <UXF:Name>Invoice</UXF:Name>
    <EnterpriseLevel>
      ...
    </EnterpriseLevel>
    ...
  </UXF:BusinessComponent>
  ...
</UXF>
<!-- Component metadata definition -->
<RDF
  xmlns="http://www.yy.cs.keio.ac.jp/~suzuki/RDF"
  xmlns:UXF="http://www.yy.cs.keio.ac.jp/~suzuki/project/uxf/">
  <Description about="http://www.yy.cs.keio.ac.jp/SoftDock/invoice.uxf">
    <UXF:ComponentCategory>
      Entity
    <UXF:ComponentCategory>
    <UXF:Dependency>
      <UXF:BusinessComponent>
        <Name>CurrencyBook</Name>
      </UXF:BusinessComponent>
      ...
    </UXF:Dependency>
    <UXF:Author>
      <UXF:Name>
      ...
    </UXF:Author>
    <UXF:Date>
      ...
    </UXF:Date>
    <UXF:Version>
      ...
    </UXF:Version>
    ...
  </Description>
</RDF>
```

References

[Bock, 1998] C. Bock. *Suggested Revisions to Activity Models for Business Process Modeling*. OMG document number ad/98-06-13, available at uml.systemhouse.mci.com/artifacts.htm, 1998.
[Chang, 1998] D. Chang and D. Harkey. *Client/Server Data Access with Java and XML*. Wiley, 1998.

[Dutoit et al., 1998] A. H. Dutoit and B. Bruegge. *Communication Metrics for Software Development.* In IEEE Trans. On Software Engineering vol. 24, no. 8, August 1998.

[DSTC] CRC for Distributed Systems Technology. *Fnorb ORB.* available at www.dstc.edu.au/Fnorb/

[Herzum et al., 1998] P. Herzum and O. Sims. *The Business Component Approach.* In the Proceedings of the OOPSLA'98 Workshop on Business Object Design and Implementation, 1998.

[Herzum, 1998] P. Herzum. *The Business Object Component.* OMG document, ormsc/98-09-01.

[Hruby, 1998] P. Hruby. Structuring Specification of Business Systems with UML (with an Emphasis on Workflow Management. In Proceedings of OOPSLA'98 Workshop on Business Object Design and Implementation, 1998. Systems)

[IBM] IBM. *XML parser for Java.* available at www.alphaworks.ibm.com/tech/xml4j.

[IMS, 1999] IMS Project. *IMS Meta-Data Specification, version 1.02.* February 1999, available at www.imsproject.org/

[OOC] Object-Oriented Concepts, Inc. *ORBacus for Java.* available at www.ooc.com/ob/.

[SAX, 1998] D. Megginson. *SAX 1.0: The Simple API for XML.* available at www.megginson.com/SAX/.

[Sutherland, 1998] J. Sutherland. OOPSLA'98 Workshop Report on Business Object Design and Implementation IV: From Business Objects to Complex Adaptive Systems. 1998, available at www.jeffsutherland.org/oopsla98/.

[Suzuki et al., 1998a] J. Suzuki and Y. Yamamoto. *Managing the Software Design Documents with XML.* In Proceedings of the 16th ACM Annual International Conference of Computer Documentation (SIGDOC '98), pages 127–136, Quebec City Canada, September 1998.

[Suzuki et al., 1998b] J. Suzuki and Y. Yamamoto. *Building an Adaptive Web Server with a Meta-architecture: AISF approach.* In Proceedings of SPA'98, Kusatsu, Japan, March 1998.

[Suzuki et al., 1999a] J. Suzuki and Y. Yamamoto. *Toward the Interoperable Software Models: Quartet of UML, XML, DOM and CORBA.* In the 4th IEEE International Software Engineering Standards Symposium (ISESS '99), pages 163–172, Curitiba, Brazil, May 1999.

[Suzuki et al., 1999b] Junichi Suzuki and Yoshikazu Yamamoto. *SoftDock: a Distributed Collaborative Platform for Model-based Software Development.* In the 10th International Workshop on Database and Expert Systems Applications (DEXA '99), Florence, Italy, September 1999, to appear.

[Suzuki et al., 1999c] J. Suzuki and Y. Yamamoto. *Building A Next-Generation Infrastructure for Agent-based Distance Learning.* In the International Journal of Continuing Engineering Education and Life-Long Learning, November 1999, to appear.

[Suzuki et al., 1999d] J. Suzuki and Y. Yamamoto. *Making UML Models Interoperable with UXF.* In P. Muller and J. Bezivin, editors, Unified Modeling Language, LNCS 1618, 1999, to appear.

[Suzuki et al., 1999e] J. Suzuki and Y. Yamamoto. *OpenWebServer: an Adaptive Web Server Using Software Patterns.* In IEEE Communications Magazine, Vol.37, No.4, pp. 46 - 52, April 1999.

[Suzuki et al., 1999f] J. Suzuki and Y. Yamamoto. *Dynamic Adaptation in the Web Server Design Space using OpenWebServer.* In Proceedings of SPA '99, Atagawa, Japan, March 1999.

[OMG, 1997] Object Management Group. *Meta Object Facility Specification.* OMG document ad/97-08-14, ad/97-08-15 and ad/97-09-04, available at www.omg.org/techprocess/meetings/schedule/Technology_Adoptions.html, 1997.

[OMG, 1998] Object Management Group. *Common Object Request Broker Architecture 2.2.* available at www.omg.org/library/c2indx.html, February 1998.

[OMG, 1998b] Object Management Group. *Currency Specification.* available at www.omg.org/corba/cfinchp.html, 1998.

[OMG, 1998c] Object Management Group. *Document. Repository Integration RFP.* OMG document dtc/98-09-01, 1998.

[OMG, 1999a] Object Management Group. *Unified Modeling Language Specification.* version 1.3R5, available at uml.systemhouse.mci.com, 1999.

[OMG, 1999b] Object Management Group. *XML Metadata Interchange (XMI) Specification.* OMG document, ad/98-10-05 and ad/98-10-06, available at uml.shl.com/xml/xmi.htm, 1999.

[W3C, 1998a] World Wide Web Consortium, M. Champion et. al., editors. *Document Object Model Level 1 Specification.* August 1998, available at www.w3.org/TR/REC-DOM-Level-1/.

[W3C, 1998b] World Wide Web Consortium, Tim Bray et. al., editors. *Extensible Markup Language (XML) 1.0.* February 1998, available at www.w3.org/TR/1998/REC-xml-19980210.

[W3C, 1999] World Wide Web Consortium, O. Lassila and R. R. Swick, editors. *Resource Description Framework (RDF) Model and Syntax Specification.* February 1999, at www.w3.org/Press/1999/RDF-REC.

[Wiegart, 1998] O. Wiegart. *Business Process Modeling & Workflow Definition with UML.* OMG document number ad/98-04-04, available at uml.systemhouse.mci.com/artifacts.htm1998.

Business Entity and Process Components

Hans Albrecht Schmid
Dept of Computer Science
University of Applied Sciences Konstanz
Brauneggerstrasse 55, D-78462 Konstanz
Phone: x49-7531-206-631 or -500, Fax: x49-7531-206-559
email: schmidha@fh-konstanz.de

Keywords: business applications, component, business component, business object, business entity, business process

Abstract. The topic of this paper is how to structure a business application in components. A business component is constructed by horizontal and vertical integration of business objects. Vertically, it integrates four layers of a business objects and consists of three (layered) constituent components. Horizontally, on each layer, it integrates a set of closely related business objects. Conditions are given to determine the business objects to be included. Business components are partitioned in business entity components and business process components, since they have different properties. It is shown that the domain layer of a process component should be on top of the presentation layer in a layered architecture.

Keywords: business applications, component, business component, business object, business entity, business process

1 Introduction

Few years after the introduction of the three layer architecture for business object applications and frameworks with: a presentation layer, a model or domain layer, and a persistence layer (compare [Burt 95] [OMG97] [SPCHM97]), it has been acknowledged that not all far-reaching expectations with regard to the reusability of business objects have been met. There are mainly two reasons: objects are often too small, and objects are often too tightly coupled with other objects such that they cannot be reused without the other objects.

Components (see [Sz98]), which have a nice and easy to use materialization in Java Beans, promise to improve the situation by two properties:

1. Components pack together small objects that are tightly coupled in larger units.
2. Components introduce new interface concepts that are suitable for composition.

Components describe not only the incoming interfaces, but also the outgoing interfaces. This is a necessity: if you would not know the outgoing interface of a component, how could you try to match it with the incoming interfaces of other components for composition. In addition, the outgoing interfaces are restricted. A component should not directly invoke operations of objects (or components) that do not belong to it.

The topic of this paper is how to structure a business application in components. Which influence do the properties of components have on the structure? Which business objects should be integrated in a component, which interfaces should components provide?

We distinguish a horizontal integration and a vertical integration of business objects in a component. The horizontal integration describes the inclusion of related business objects with the same kind of responsibilities in a component. Conditions based on syntactical and semantical properties of business objects are given that state clearly when business objects should be included together in a component.

The vertical integration is the integration of the different layers of a business object in a business component. The three layer architecture is extended to a four layer architecture, since the persistence layer should be partitioned in a data access layer and a data storage layer. A business component integrates the four layers: it consists, however, only of three layers of horizontally integrated constituent components, since the coupling among the model-domain layer and the data access layer is too strong to separate them into different components.

Business components are partitioned in business entity components and business process components, since they have very different properties. It is shown that the domain layer of process component should be on top of the presentation layer, which is quite surprising.

The characteristics of the constituent components of a business entity component (an entity view component, an entity domain and data access component, and an entity storage component) are analyzed as well as those of the constituent components of a business process component (a process view component, a process domain component, a process data access component, and a process storage component).

The collaboration among the constituent components of business entity components and business process components is different from the collaborations in a non-componentized architecture for business applications: the process domain constituent component invokes operation of the other constituent components; but these generate mainly events.

2 Horizontal Integration of Business Objects

This section analyzes the horizontal integration, that is the inclusion of related business objects with the same kind of responsibilities in a component (compare [ES98]). We demonstrate this regarding the domain-layer.

2.1 Components

A component differs from an object according to three characteris-tic properties: a component is a unit of independent deployment, a unit of third party composition, and has no persistent state [Sz98]. Since the term component is also used in a looser sense that allows the existence of dependencies, for example by the UML, we use the term strict component when confusion might arise.

To allow for independent deployment, a component must be self-contained. A component must have a well-defined (incoming) interface (or interfaces) that specifies its operations and their effects. These operations may be invoked freely from outside by other objects or components. However, a component may not invoke freely the operations of other objects (or components). Third party composition is possible only under two conditions: The outgoing interface(s) must be well-defined, and it must be possible to bind the invocations to different targets without a recompilation. A direct invocation (which is quite normal with objects) is not allowed, since it causes a coupling that is too tight. An object BO is said to directly invoke a method of an object BO1 if it contains a reference of type BO1 (or of a the type of a concrete superclass of BO1) and invokes an operation of BO1 via this reference.

A strict component provides the event mechanism (which is a form of the Observer pattern [GHJV95]) as an outgoing interface: it generates events that are bound to Listener-objects or Listener-components. In this way, the event-generating component has an absolutely minimal knowledge about the event-processing objects or components, both about its type and their dynamical availability. As a consequence, the „coupling is abstract and minimal".

Java Beans have an incoming interface with operations that are not restricted. As outgoing interface, they have the event mechanism.

2.2 Component Inclusion Conditions

Consider the business object Employee. If the Employee class is not derived from another class and does not have associations, in particular no aggregations or compositions (all these terms are used with the meaning as defined by the UML) with other classes, then the Employee business object is self-contained and independently deployable; it can be packaged and shipped as a component.

However, very often the structure of a business object Employee is more complex (see Figure 1). There are following cases:

- The Employee class is derived from another class, like Person.
- The Employee has a (possibly multivalued) attribute, like an Address, included in another object. One says that the Employee is composed with the Address. That means it contains a (set of) reference variable(s) referring to the Address object(s) and forwards operations to it. Additionally, an Address object depends in its existence on the existence of the Employee object.
- An object from a technical a base class is used for implementation of the Employee. For example, the 1:n relationship from a Employee to its Address might be implemented by a Set class from a collection library. Note that this is also a composition.
- A method of Employee, like GetSalary, invokes a method of another object, like SalaryCalculation.

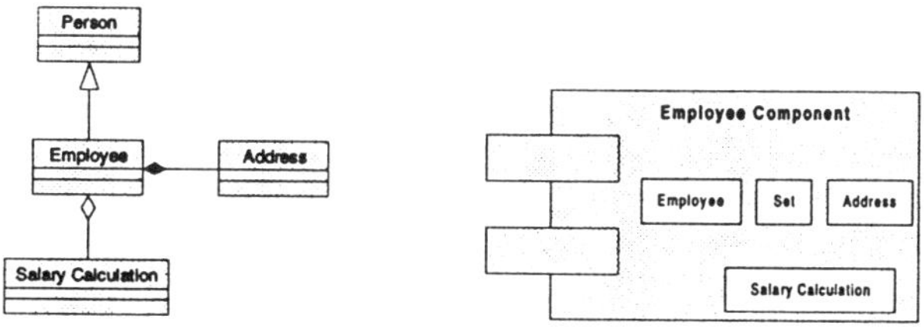

Figure 1 Employee kernel class and dependent classes and Employee component

In all these cases, the Employee is not self-contained: it invokes operations of other objects or uses methods inherited from other classes such that it cannot work independently. We need to include the objects from these classes, like Address, Set and SalaryCalculation, and the superclass Person into the Employee component (see Figure 1). We say that the Employee object forms the kernel of the Employee component; each component has exactly one kernel object. Address, Set and SalaryCalculation form dependent objects, Person forms a dependent class of the component (called focus object and embedded objects by [ES98]).

A consequence is that a component has not only one incoming interface, but may have multiple interfaces, like an Employee, and Address interface. It includes the interfaces of the kernel and dependent objects. Typically, only the kernel of a component has associations (in the sense of the UML, which are permanent or of a long durability) to the kernel of other components. Dependent objects of a component have associations to the kernel, but only temporary associations to outside objects or components.

In addition, the Employee component may generate events, like a Changed-Event, to notify listener objects or components about a change of its state.

Eeles and Sims [ES98] give intuitive guidelines and heuristics for a set of business objects forming a component. They state that

- a business component realizes a (a real-world) business concept, is autonomous and independent, and is large grained
- a kernel object
  - „represents something real and independent in the business domain“
  - „represents a potential unit of reuse and can have applicability outside the“ application „under consideration“
  - „is not usually aggregated, although it can aggregate other objects“
  - „often collaborates directly with other“ kernel „objects“ via associations

- a business component includes the kernel object and
  - „any objects associated with the“ kernel „object that are not themselves“ kernel „objects“
  - „any classes that represent attributes of the“ kernel „object“
  - „any classes from which the class of the“ kernel „object is inherited as long as those superclasses are not“ kernel „objects“.

We formulate three conditions that characterize when objects need to be included together in a component. The conditions are applied separately to the business entity layer (from which the given examples are) and business process layer. The conditions deliver in most cases similar results as the guidelines and heuristics. The first condition describes syntactical aspects of a tight coupling between two objects BO and BO1.

Component inclusion condition 1:
If a method of a business object BO directly invokes a method of an object BO1, then a component that includes BO should include BO1. Otherwise, there is a hard (both a code and an object reference) dependency between the component including BO and that including BO1. A hard dependency can possibly be loosened as described in section 2.3.

Component inclusion condition 2:
If a method of a business object BO invokes a method declared in a superclass S, then a component that includes BO should include S. Otherwise, there is a soft (only a code) dependency.

For each of the related objects or classes of the Employee example (see Figure 1), either condition 1 or 2 is met. Therefore, the respective objects or classes are included with the Employee in one component.

Note that these conditions allow the inclusion of a class, or of objects from the same class, in several components. Consider a class Employee and a class Customer that are both derived from a class Person. Then class Person should be included both in the Employee component and the Customer component (see Figure 2).

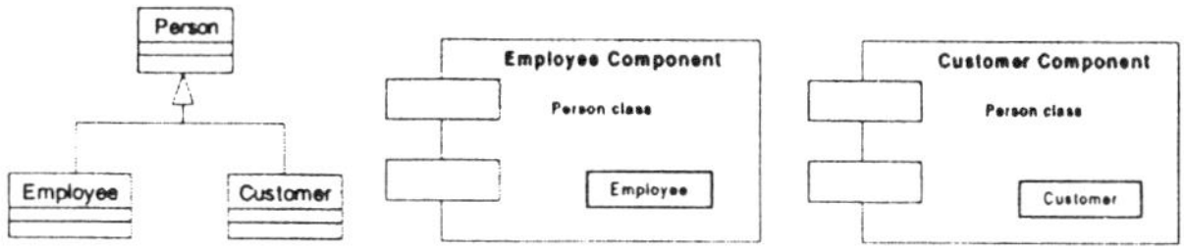

Figure 2 Class Employee and Customer, and Employee and Customer components

Another case is that a business object BO1 is included in one component as a kernel object, and in another component as a dependent object (which is excluded by the guidelines of Eeles and Sims [ES98]). Consider an aggregation: a Car consists of four Wheels, besides other objects (see Figure 3). When the operation getPrice of a Car is invoked, it invokes the operation getPrice of a Wheel. Thus, following the syntactical inclusion condition, a Car component should include the Wheel objects. However, a Wheel can also exist without a Car. Thus, one should provide also a Wheel-component, e.g. for use in a car supply shop.

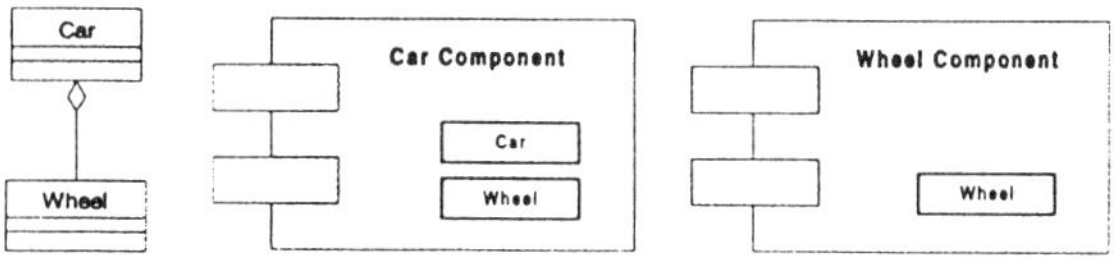

Figure 3 Car and Wheel classes, and Car and Wheel component

However, consider a composition: an Employee has an Address (see Figure 4). Following the syntactical inclusion condition, a Employee component should include the Address objects. But an Address cannot exist without a Employee. Therefore, we need not provide also an Address component.

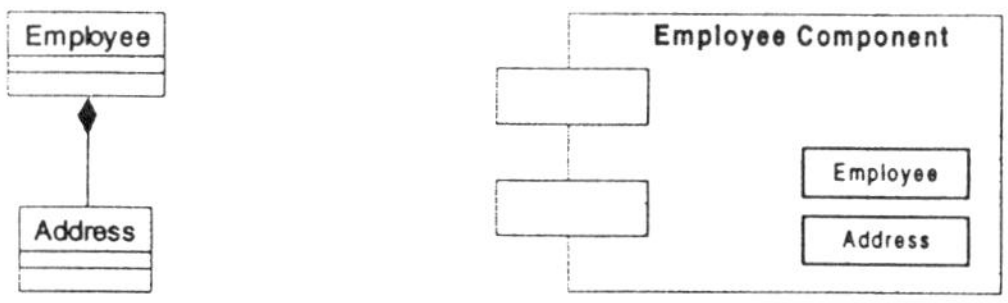

Figure 4 Employee and Address classes; and Employee component

This example shows the importance of a semantical aspect, the existence-dependency condition, which is known from semantical data models and used in UML to distinguish between an aggregation and a composition.

Component inclusion condition 3:

If the existence of an business object BO1 is dependent on the existence of an business object BO, then a component that includes BO1 must include BO. It makes no sense to allow exceptions to this rule.

2.3 Loosening the Coupling

The component inclusion conditions are closely related to the classification of association among classes in a UML class diagram. Typically,

- condition 1 is met by linked objects BO and BO1, i.e., objects from classes, which are related by some kind of directed association (including aggregation and composition) from class BO to class BO1. The reason is that a link between two classes is typically used to directly invoke an operation of BO1.

- condition 2 may be met by an object BO the class of which is derived from a class BO1.
- condition 3 is met by objects from classes that are related by composition.

In a typical application class structure, all classes are related by associations. Consider a class diagram that represents a Company as an aggregation of Departments, which consist of Employees. The company is in bi-directional associations to customers, and other classes.

The consequence is that practically all classes, or very large sets of classes, namely all classes on a directed path of (directed) associations, would have to be included in a component. For example, a company component would have to include objects from all classes, since there is a directed path of associations from Customer over Company to Department and Employees. For this reason, we would have to loosen the tight coupling among entities like company, department, employee, and customer in a componentized architecture.

You may possibly modify the form of the collaboration in order to loosen a tight coupling among components, which violates the component inclusion condition 1. There are three options:

1. You may decouple a business object BO from BO1 by introducing an outgoing interface IF1. Then, a method of BO invokes methods that are specified by the interface IF1. Now, BO cannot collaborate only with BO1, but with all components and classes that implement the interface IF1. Note that this kind of collaboration is not supported by the Java Bean model and by Bean builder tools. You may implement it, nevertheless, with a Bean by using a property with the type IF1. Thus, this is a grey area (also with regard to the discussion in [Sz98]) that requires clarification.

2. You may decouple a business object BO from BO1 by using the event mechanism as outgoing interface of BO. With the Observer (Listener) registration mechanism, an unknow number of components or objects may react on this event. However, it is often questionable, if this approach to the loosenig of a tight coupling is be semantically adequate, even if it were technically possible. Consider, for example, the association between a Company and its Department. To replace it by a coupling by events does not seem to be adequate.

3. Another approch to the loosening of a tight coupling among business objects is to replace associations (e.g. outgoing references in the analysis class diagramm) by attributes that are unique identifiers of other components (in the design class diagramm). For example, the aggregation between Company and Department may be replaced by a multivalued attribute department number in the company component. Then, there is no coupling on the class and object level of the business entities. An object that uses the decoupled components, like a business process, reconstructs the association by fetching the corresponding objects with help of the key attribute, and by keeping a directed association to each of them. This approach is often used.

A weak coupling, as described by the component inclusion condition 2, cannot be loosened by similar transformations. Same as an existence dependency between components, as described by the component inclusion condition 3, it can only be avoided by a restructuring of objects and classes within the components.

3 Layer Structure of Business Components

The three layer architecture identifies three different kinds of responsibilities for a business object: a presentation, a model or domain, and a persistence responsibility (see Figure 5) and allocates them each to a different layer. The domain-related behavior, of e.g. an Employee, is separated from its presentation in a view, and from the way how the attributes are made persistent. A layer defines both the conceptual partitioning and the use structure of a software system; only an object in a higher layer may invoke operations of an object in a lower layer, except for callbacks that follow the Observer or a similar pattern [GHJV95].

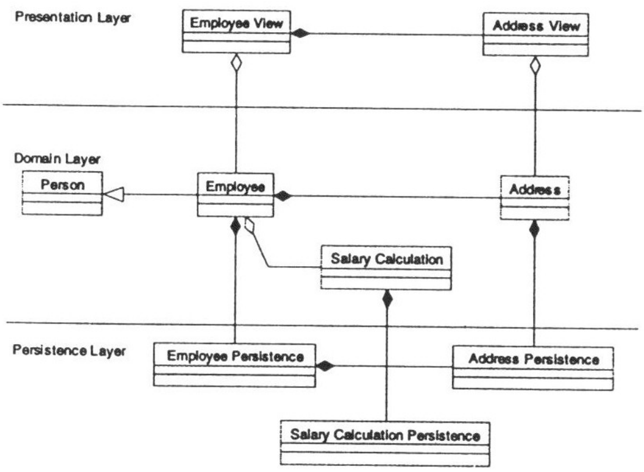

Figure 5 Three-layer architecture

Each layer integrates horizontally, similarly as described for the model or domain layer in section 2, a corresponding kernel object and dependent objects. However, not all dependent objects need to be represented on each layer explicitly.

Consider the Employee. It consists of

- a presentation layer with a view component integrating an Employee View and Address View's. The view of the Set class is implicitly contained in the display of multiple Address View's. If the SalaryCalculation is an auxiliary class, no SalaryCalculation View object is required.
- a domain layer with a domain component integrating an Employee domain object, a Set domain object, several Address domain objects, and a SalaryCalculation domain object.
- a persistence layer with an persistence component integrating an Employee Persistence object, a Set Persistence object, and Address Persistence objects. If SalaryCalculation is a stateless object, no SalaryCalculation Persistence object is required.

An application that uses a component like an Employee, uses typically all responsibilities of the Employee, from displaying its view to accessing the persistent data, and not only the domain-related one. Therefore, a business component is introduced as an organizational unit that vertically integrates the corresponding components on each layer.

In the following sections, we show that the persistence layer should be partitioned in two layers, and how to structure a layered business component.

3.1 Partitioning of Persistence Layer

The responsibility of the persistence layer is to store and retrieve entity domain components in a relational or another database. It has a large number of responsibilities that are partitioned in two groups: Attribute mapping is concerned mainly with object attributes, change management, attribute to column mapping, attribute to relation mapping, and type conversion; row mapping is concerned mainly with storing and retrieving rows from relational tables. Since both groups are quite independent, we separate the persistence layer in a data access layer and a data storage layer.

The access layer provides services to the business entity layer for change management and the creation, retrieval, saving and deletion of entity domain components. It needs to perform both an explicit creation (on a request from the process domain layer) and an implicit creation (when resolving references) of entity domain components.

The storage layer encapsulates the access to a specific data base. It hides the design of the data base, as well as the specifics of the data base access and retrieval language (for example, if dynamical SQL, prepared statements, stored procedures, or, e.g. CICS, transactions are used to access the database), and the transaction management (which, typically, maps its responsibilities to the transaction management of the database management system or of the DC-system).

The data access layer and a data storage layer may perform their responsibilities either interpretatively, by having few central objects that use mapping information stored in tables for all entity domain components, or by creating and compiling classes for each of the entity domain components, or in a mixed approach, interpretatively for simple cases and with compiled classes for non-standard or complex mappings.

3.2 Constituent Components of Business Components

The layers of a business component should themselves be strict components whenever possible, in order to minimize the programming and to maximize the composability of business components and the exchangeability and reusability of the layered objects within them. Consider for example an Employee business component. If its presentation layer is formed by a view component that contains no application and business logic, you can use a GUI editor or a component editor to build the view component without requiring any programming. If the view of the Employee is to be changed, or to be replaced by a different view for another group of endusers, you may exchange the view component, without programming, with a modified or a new one that has the same (both incoming and outgoing) interface. You may integrate the view component in the business component without programming.

A similar consideration applies to the data storage layer. Suppose you have an Employee data storage component for access to a certain database. When you need to access another database with different characteristics, you may exchange the data storage component without programming by one that has the same interface, but accesses a different database.

If one would include the objects on each layer each in a separate component, a business component would consist of four constituent components: a view component, a domain component, a data access component, and a data storage component. However, the data access layer and the domain layer collaborate very closely, in particular, when the data access layer performs the attribute change management. Also, a domain object is often derived from a persistent object on the data access layer. Therefore, it does not seem to be appropriate to integrate each of the two layers in a different component. When we include the objects of the data access layer and the domain layer in one component, a business component is composed of three constituent components:

- a view component,
- a domain and data access component (abbreviated: domain component), and
- a data storage component.

A constituent component should be a strict component if possible.

4 Business Entities and Business Processes

Business objects are classified into business entities and business processes. A business entity, like an Employee, represents the static state of the enterprise" [Casa95]. A business entity is passive: it may not change its state by itself. In contrast, a business process, like paying an Employee's salary, „represents the flow of work" and „acts on the business entities to cause the business to function" [Casa95]. A business process is active: it represents the active flow of control and accesses business entities; it may change their state by invoking state-changing operations.

Business entities and business processes have very little in common, except for the taxonomical classification (both represent things from the business domain) and the structuring in a view, domain and access, and a storage layer. Therefore, we propose a strict distinction.

4.1 Differences between Business Entities and Processes

Computer science has learned in its infancy or early childhood to partition a program strictly in two different parts: the state component (i.e. the data) of a program and its process component (i.e. the executable instructions). When we mix state and process, we can play much nicer tricks (remember self-modifying program code), but the consequences are disastrous. Why should the case be different for business objects?

However, the distinction between business entities and processes is more complicated than that of program data and program code, since a business entity has also behavior. The operations (of a domain-component) of a business entity embody business rules. The rules characterize the business entity and its possible (i.e. consistent) states, independently on the business process by which the operations are invoked. For example, the domain-component of a business entity „banking account" provides an operation „remove amount", which checks if the given amount can be subtracted from the balance, under the rules governing this type of account. An operation of a business entity may even use other business entity components and invoke their operations. That means the behavior of a business entity component may sometimes look very similar to, or be confused with an activity of a business process.

A business process is a processing sequence that is, with the exception of batch business processes, partially or completely controlled by user input. Business procedures and activities are more elementary parts of business processes (see [SS99]). For example, „withdraw money from an account with teller assistance" is a business procedure that is interactively controlled, and not an operation of account. It (i.e. its process domain component) invokes the operation remove amount of the (entity domain component of the) banking account.

The most important differences between business entities and business processes are:

1. A business entity has typically a permanent lifetime, and a permanent state that may be changed only by the execution of a business process. A business process has no permanent lifetime and, once its execution is completed, no permanent state.

2. The sharing of business entities involves elaborate transaction mechanisms to prevent that parallel invocation of state changing operations leads to wrong results. A (reentrant) business process may be executed multiple times in parallel without any problems.

3. A business process (domain component) is interacting with an end-user. Its flow is partially or completely controlled by user input, except for a batch business process. An operation of a business entity (domain component) is not interacting with an end-user; instead, it embodies business rules that are valid for all business procedures or processes in which the entity is involved. (If an operation of a business entity domain component might involve user interaction, the entity would not be usable in a batch business process.)

4. An operation of a business entity component performs, after its invocation, the (non-interactive) processing in one flow of control, and returns, possibly with a result. An activity of a business process is usually user-event driven (i.e. non-modal). It is not possible (or only under special, very restricted conditions) to embody such an activity within an operation, which is invoked to start the activity and which returns (possibly with a result), when the activity is terminated.

5. A business process invokes operations from business entities. But a business entity cannot invoke operations from a business process.

The conclusion is that business entities and business processes have completely different responsibilities; consequently, business entity components and business process components should be distinguished clearly and treated differently.

4.2 Alternative Viewpoint

Eeles and Sims [ES98] propose, in contrast, that there is a fluent transition from data-centric to process-centric business components, based on the argument that „a business entity component has not only structure, but also behavior“. This is certainly true; but the behavior of a business entity is nothing else than an abstraction of its state. Consider an abstract data type, which has also behavior and not only state. Its behavior abstracts from a concrete state, same as the behavior of a business entity does. Since abstract data types are better understood than business entities, one would not state, applying the same argument, that there is a fluent transition from abstract data types to processes in a program. With a strict distinction between state and process, no fluent transition from data-centric to process-centric business components is possible.

Let us demonstrate our viewpoint by the „standard“ activity „browse“. It consists of a fixed sequence of steps (i.e. more elementary activities):

1. End-user defines and enters a search criterion over a set of business entity components;

2. Search is performed and result displayed (end-user interaction may return to 1.);

3. End-user selects one or several entries from search result.

The activity has as a result a temporary business entity (i.e. state): the set of selected business entity components. The business activity browse can be reused with any set of business entity components.

In contrast, Eeles and Sims consider a customer browser as a data centric business component. Probably they do this since the browser returns a temporary result set; however, a function also returns a result without being considered as a state (i.e. data-centric). They use a data centric business component to implement an activity of the business process component (which is surprising from our viewpoint). Two severe problems originate from this approach:

- No reuse of the business activity browse is possible, though browsing is done for all different business entities in the same way!
- The result of the browsing activity must be transferred by hand by the end-user (e.g., by drag and drop) to the subsequent business activity.

5 Business Process Components and Business Entity Components

Both business entity components and business process components consist of layered constituent components (see Figure 6). We describe the constituent components shortly and sketch their cooperation.

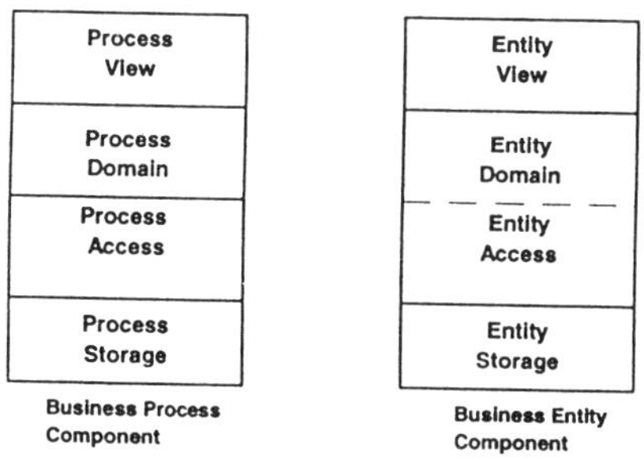

Figure 6 Business entity components and business process components

5.1 Constituent Components

A business entity component consists of three constituent components:

- An entity view component is used for the presentation of the business entity in different business procedures and activities. It should be a component in the strict sense such that it can be constructed by use of a GUI-editor without programming. This implies that it cannot collaborate directly with the entity domain component. An entity view component presents the attributes of an entity domain component in widgets for display or input. It may contain also buttons or similar widgets that are related to the business entity. They are used to indicate, for example, that the input to a group of related attribute fields is completed. The view component reacts on these widget events and generates entity-view specific events.
- An entity domain component provides the domain-specific operations of a business entity (by its domain layer), and maps (by its access layer) its attributes to the rows of, usually, relational tables. It collaborates with the entity storage component to retrieve, or store when required, or delete the table rows in the data base. An entity domain component should be a strict component, since it should be reusable without reprogramming and recompiling it in different business processes, procedures and activities. Therefore, it generates events if attribute values are changed.
- An entity storage component embodies the responsibilities described in section 3.1.

A business process component consists of four constituent components:

- A process view component provides for a screen space, in which the process domain component can display everything required, in particular the entity view components of visible business entities. Thus, a process view component is quite simple; it is, both a from a logical and a screen related viewpoint, a container for other view components and widgets. It is, to a large degree, standardized: it usually contains some buttons or similar widgets that are related to the business process, like an ok, commit, or cancel button. It reacts on the button generated events and generates process-specific events, like commitDone.
- A process domain component embodies the business process. Very often, it is composed hierarchically. For example, a business procedures may be composed of business activities and subactivities (compare [SS99]). The working of a business activity is described in the following section.
- A process access component. is not closely coupled to the process domain component. It is small and unimportant, since business processes have no permanent state, except possibly for break points at which they can be suspended and resumed. It is separated from the process domain component mainly for distribution purposes (see next section).
- An process storage component is also small and unimportant.

5.2 Collaborations of a Process Domain Component

When an activity of a business process (i.e, process domain component) is started, it sets up the screen and accesses and displays the business entities used. First, the activity makes its process view component visible. Second, it accesses the entity domain components of the used business entities and adds the entity view components to its process view component for display. In a third step, it transfers the attribute data from entity domain components to (the corresponding) entity view components and makes them visible.

After this initial set up, an activity waits both for events generated by entity view components or process view components, which trigger actions of the activity. Entity view component events are usually generated after input or editing of data displayed by the entity view. On such an event, an activity usually gets the input or edited data from the view, and invokes (with them as parameters) domain-specific operations of the corresponding entity domain components. On an event of a process view component like „commit“, an activity eventually may terminate itself and return.

5.3 Consequences on Layer Structure

As we have seen, the responsibilities of a process domain component are

- to create, access and delete or save entity domain components
- to invoke their operations
- to create and delete process view and entity view components and make them visible
- to react on user events generated by process and entity view components.

These responsibilities cannot be allocated to any other constituent component of a business process component or business entity component. They can be allocated neither to an entity view component nor to a process view component (a process view component should not terminate itself and create another process view component to be displayed next), nor to an entity domain component.

This allocation of responsibilities has consequences on the layer structure, in which the constituent components of business entity components and business process components collaborate. There is no question that both the entity view and process view components are allocated to the same layer, the presentation layer.

Typically, the next lower layer is the business object layer. It is usually subdivided in a higher business process layer and a lower business entity layer. However, an object on a given layer can create and/or access objects only if they are on the same layer or on a lower layer. Since a process domain component creates and accesses process view and entity view components, it must be on the same layer as the presentation layer or on a higher layer. We put the process domain layer, abbreviated: process layer, on top of the presentation layer, since it would not be appropriate to provide a combined layer. Below the presentation layer is the entity domain layer, abbreviated: entity layer. Below this layer is the data storage layer that contains both entity storage components and process storage components (see Figure 7).

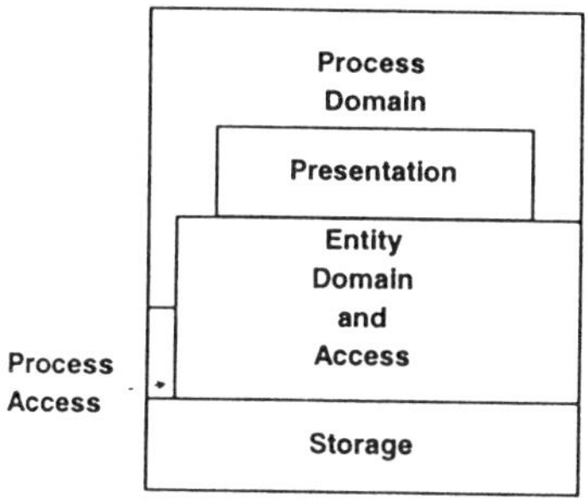

Figure 7 Layered component architecture

In special cases, the presentation layer can be the topmost layer, and the proposed layer structure is not required. For example, consider the production in a manufacturing cell which is visualized in one or several windows. The business process „production“ has one or a few windows associated, which are not exchanged and display all the time the same business entities (namely the machines etc. of the manufacturing cell). The only change is that business entities change their state and modify their view. Then, there is no need that a process domain component

- has a process view component (the context window is the process view!)
- creates and accesses the entity view components (which are Observers of the entity domain components). The reason is that the initialization of the entity domain components and of the screen with the entity view components may be done separately in an initialization step before the process is started.

6 Distribution Aspects

The presented architecture provides two suitable distribution boundaries. One distribution boundary may be put between the presentation layer and the entity domain layer, the other one between the entity domain layer and the data storage layer.

Ideally, layer boundaries are identical to distribution boundaries, if object, respectively component, distribution middleware is used. This is possible (except for distribution middleware generated stubs, which belong logically to the server layer, but must be shipped to the client tier); but Schmid [S99] shows that distribution boundaries that are identical with layer boundaries have considerable drawbacks with regard to ease of (i.e. too detailed distribution skills required for) client programming, performance and restricted distributed functionality.

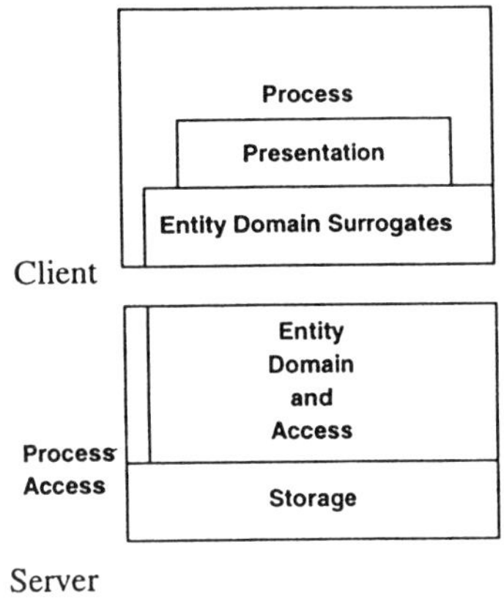

Figure 8 Client-server distribution of layered compnent architecture

It is advantageous to provide on the client node surrogates of the objects that form the layer boundary on the server side. The consequence is to add to the client as the lowest layer a thin entity domain surrogate component layer, which collaborates very closely, like a bracket over the network, with the entity domain component layer on the server (see Figure 8). However, this approach is not without some complexities (see [S99]).

In [ES98], the use of Workspace Distributed Objects is proposed that seem to have a similar responsibility as entity domain surrogate components. But it is not described how Workspace Distributed Objects are implemented.

If also a separate database server with the data storage component layer is introduced below the second distribution boundary, a thin data storage surrogate component layer would be added as the lowest layer to the application server.

7 Conclusions

We have shown that business components integrate business objects both horizontally and vertically. Horizontally, a kernel object is included together with dependent objects that collaborate very closely with it. Vertically, a business component integrates three layered constituent components, each of which has a different kind of responsibilities. An important result is that business entity components and business process components need to be distinguished clearly. They have different responsibilities: a process domain component collaborates with process view components, entity view components and entity domain components in very specific ways.

The presented architecture has been refined and evaluated in several Java client-server prototype implementations in cooperation with an insurance company and software houses with very good results.

8 Acknowledgments

My thanks are due to
- to the Ministerium fuer Wissenschaft und Forschung (Department of Science and Research) of Baden-Wuerttemberg that supported, in part, the project.
- to the Continentale Versicherungs AG, Dortmund, that supported, in part, the project; in particular to Messieurs Boylshausen, Bruenemayer, and Rittinghaus
- to the Argentinian-German Bilateral Cooperation in Computer Science and Technologysupported by the BMBF (Department of Science and Education of Germany).
- Ramiro Gonzalez Maciel, LIFIA, UNLP, La Plata, Argentina who gave important comments, and to Angela Barth-Kuepper who participated in the project and supported the preparation of this paper.

This paper would not have been written without many meetings and long discussions with the working group on frameworks of the GI (Society for Computer Science), Germany, with particular input from Achim Bechtel, Wolfgang Beneke, Arif Chughtai, Roland Hefter, Rolf Knoll, Martin Lefering, and Matthias Riebisch. My thanks are due to them.

9 References

[AF98] P.Allen, S.Frost: Component-Based Development for Enterprise Systems, Cambridge University Press, Cambridge, GreatBritain, 1998

[Burt 95] C.Burt (ed.): OMG BOMSIG survey with published definition of a business object. OMG document 95-02-04. See www.omg.org

[Casa95] C.Casanave: Business-Object Architectures and Standards; in [SPCHM97]

[ES98] P.Eeles, O.Sims: Building Business Objects; John Wiley & Sons, Chicester, UK, 1998

[GHJV95] E.Gamma, R.Helm, R.Johnson, J.Vlissides: Design Patterns: Elements of Reusable Object-Oriented Software; Addison-Wesley, 1994

[OMG97] Object Management Group OMG: Business Object DTF, Common Business Objects; 1997

[R98] G. Reese: Database Programming with JDBC and Java; O'Reilly, 1998

[Sz98] C.Szyperski: Component Software, Beyond Object-Oriented Programming; Addison-Wesley, 1997

[SPCHM97] J.Sutherland, D.Patel, C.Casanave, G.Hollowell, J.Miller (eds.): Business Object Design and Implementation; Springer, Berlin, 1997

[SS99] H.A.Schmid, F. Simonazzi: Business Processes are not Represented Adequately in Business Applications and Frameworks!; accepted for publication in: Business Object Component Design and Implementation, Springer, Berlin, 1999

[S99] H.A.Schmid: An Alternative Paradigm for Object and Component Distribution; submitted for publication

A Generic Object Oriented Enterprise Modelling Process and an Abstraction Mechanism

[1]Islam Choudhury, [2]Dilip Patel

[1]London Guildhall University, Department of Computing, Information Systems and Maths, 100 Minories, London EC3N 1JY. email: iarchoud@lgu.ac.uk
[2]South Bank University, School of Computing, Information Systems and Maths, 103 Borough Rd., London SE1 0AA. email: dilip@sbu.ac.uk

---

ABSTRACT: *A Generic Object Oriented Enterprise Modelling Process (GOOEMP) is a set of partially ordered steps intended to reach the objective of building a fully integrated, dynamic, object oriented model of the enterprise. An Abstraction Mechanism is proposed to enable this process. The process is generic because it applies to most types of enterprises. Enterprise models are the products developed from the process and these can be used by various stakeholders in an organisation to: a), give them an understanding of the enterprise; b), design integrated information systems; c), respond to business changes by evolving their enterprise models and information systems in a co-ordinated and coherent manner; and d), enable the enterprise models built within a particular industry to be reused and applied to many other industries.*
Keywords: Enterprise Modelling Process (EMP), Generic Business Object Models, Enterprise Integration, Object Oriented Business Engineering, Abstraction Mechanism.

---

1. Introduction

High level competition in a global market requires organisations to deliver high quality customised and short life span products and services at a low cost, low lead time, and provide full customer satisfaction at all times. This involves products and services being developed at a higher rate and in reduced time. Enterprises need to be agile, respond rapidly to changes and new ideas. This requires the enterprise to adopt an effective information systems strategy that maps the business needs accurately. The business processes, functions, data and systems must be fully understood, stored, made accessible, integrated and supported by a well designed information infrastructure. At present most of the information within an enterprise has been developed in a piecemeal manner. Information is stored in disorganised, disintegrated, incomplete company wide databases. Also the information models that were developed separated out the processes, functions, data, and systems. It is very difficult to access accurate and useful information as and when required quickly and efficiently. Computer aided modelling of the enterprise is a powerful tool for analysing business structures and the associated information infrastructures. Enterprise wide computer models represent the business structure, process, functions and information of an enterprise and can be used to develop a suitable information systems infrastructure (Graefe and Chan, 1993).

Enterprise models can be developed using object orientation which is a powerful concept that can be applied to almost all aspects of the life-cycle of a product from analysis, design, implementation and maintenance. The main benefit gained from using one paradigm throughout a life-cycle is that the difficulties of conceptual transformation from one level to other levels of the life-cycle is reduced. Object orientation modelling constructs help in understanding, abstracting and representing different levels of knowledge within the enterprise and encapsulating that knowledge within object components. Componentizing the enterprise helps to: a), reduce and mange the complexity within an enterprise; b), provides better understanding of the enterprise; c), helps to develop and represent an enterprise in a model; and d), help in integration, reuse and evolution of the enterprise model. This paper describes the development of an object oriented enterprise modelling process by synthesising, adapting and enhancing previous work in enterprise modelling.

There have been a variety of research approaches, methodologies, and frameworks in enterprise modelling including the following:

- the Information Engineering (IE) approach developed by Martin (1989)
- the Enterprise Integration methodologies developed by various researchers such as 'PERA' (Vallespir *et al.* 1991), 'GRAI integrated methodologies' (Williams, 1993), 'CIM-OSA' (Vernadat, 1992), and 'TOVE' (Fox, 1992)
- generic enterprise architectures, frameworks and methodologies such as the 'Generic Reusable Business Object Modelling' (Choudhury *et al.* 1997), the 'Generic Enterprise Reference Architecture and Methodology' (Bernus and Nemes, 1996) and 'Information Systems Architecture' (Zachman, 1992)
- object oriented business engineering and enterprise modelling such as 'Reengineering with Object Technology' (Jacobson *et al.* 1995), 'Business Engineering with Object Technology' (Taylor, 1995), Object Oriented Business Engineering (Shelton, 1994), and Object Oriented Enterprise Modelling (Gale and Eldred, 1996).

All the above research has one goal in common that is to help build enterprise models that can serve as a basis to understand the business and integrate all the appropriate aspects of the enterprise including the strategy, operations, people, processes, information, applications, systems and technology. Some of the main problems with enterprise modelling are: a), managing the complexity inherent in enterprises; b), abstracting the appropriate level of knowledge; c), representing that knowledge in an appropriate manner that is understandable by various stakeholders of the enterprise; d), time and cost overheads; e), reusing and evolving the models over time and as the business changes; f), capturing reusable elements within an industry that is applicable to various other industries; g), evaluating and usefully applying the enterprise models; and h), describing a process to develop enterprise models that would be generic and reusable.

To address the above issues, a comprehensive enterprise modelling process using the object oriented paradigm was developed. Such a modelling process is very useful as it provides steps for business to follow which will allow them to develop an integrated set of enterprise models. The object oriented paradigm, and especially the concept of business objects, contains modelling constructs which allow for the knowledge within the enterprise to be fully captured and represented in a form that is meaningful both to the business and information systems people. The object oriented paradigm also allows for the modelling of the data, functions, processes and systems within the company. These can be encapsulated into different types of components which can be effectively developed, stored, used and reused. The enterprise models that are built are integrated and co-ordinated within the company in such a way that the models can easily respond to changes. This will allow companies, safe in the understanding that their information systems can cope and evolve with business changes, to concentrate on improving their business by responding positively to change.

This paper describes an enterprise modelling process which concentrates and develops on, as well as integrating the work of the following researchers: Bernus and Nemes (1996), Choudhury *et al.* (1997) and Gale and Eldred (1996). Bernus and Nemes (1996) have developed a framework to define a generic enterprise reference architecture and methodology unifying and developing on the basis of 'PERA' (Vallespir *et al.* 1991), 'GRAI integrated methodologies' (Williams, 1992), 'CIM-OSA' (Vernadat, 1992), and 'TOVE' (Fox, 1992). Choudhury *et al.* have developed a Generic Reusable Business Object Modelling Framework based on the work of Jacobson *et al.* (1995), Taylor (1995), and the idea of business objects (Arrow *et al.* 1995). Gale and Eldred (1996) have developed the 'future strategy business planning' methodology to build object oriented enterprise models which are comprehensive and formal descriptions of the enterprise. They develop their model from general systems theory, conceptual modelling, information theory, and business theory.

Section 2 provides an overall description of the GROOEMP. Sections 3, 4 and 5 explain each of the three levels, conceptual, representational and instance level in detail and with examples. Finally, section 6 presents some conclusions.

2. An Overall description of the GOOEMP

To understand the modelling process a description of a model is first provided. Essentially, there are three types of models: The conceptual model, the representational model, and the instance model (Burkhart, *et. al.*, 1992). These models have two main functions:

- Filter out irrelevant detail and thereby display only information that is essential to the task (this involves abstraction)
- To represent that information in a useful and appropriate way to address the goal of modelling.

Burkhart, *et. al.* (1992) define a model as:

' ...the explicit interpretation of one's understanding of a situation, or merely one's ideas about that situation. It can be expressed in mathematics, symbols or words, but essentially a description of entities, processes or attributes and relationships between them. It may be prescriptive or illustrative, but above all, it must be useful.'

The goal of the GOOEMP in the context of this paper is to represent the enterprise in a model, taking into account ideas from the business as well as the information systems. It enables the stakeholders to gain knowledge about the business and to integrate the business components including processes, functions, data areas and their relations to one another. The business object models built from the GOOEMP can also be used as a reference point or starting point for design and implementation of information systems and for the analysis of change. The stakeholders of the models could be a number of people such as business processes designers, business developers, business managers, systems analysts and software engineers. A generic enterprise model is one that is sufficiently general to be used in several contexts (e.g. by different industries). The generality of the model must be optimised because if it is too general it would be of little use as the conceptual difficulty to convert the general to the specific would be too high. GOOEMP makes use of an abstraction technique, using the genericity dimension see Choudhury *et al.* (1997) to abstract appropriate industrial sectors and business domains that are to be modelled. Once a domain has been identified, the model of that domain is built according to the abstraction mechanism explained in Figure 2. This shows the abstraction levels for modelling, mapping and optimising the enterprise model. It explains the relationships between the business domain and the information systems domain to define an optimum generic level to enable effective reuse of the model. This takes into consideration conceptual difficulty to implementation, flexibility and ease with which the model can cope with change.

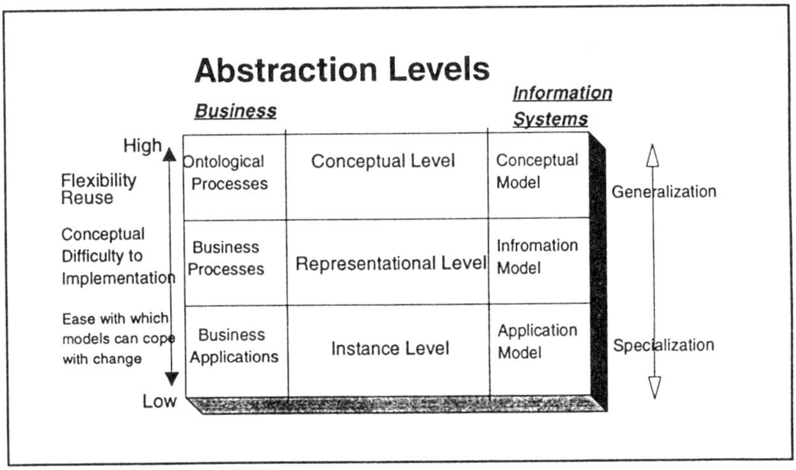

Figure 1. Abstraction Levels for modelling, mapping and optimising the enterprise model.

The object-oriented paradigm provides the appropriate modelling constructs and symbols to enable the effective capture and representation of information and knowledge within an enterprise at the conceptual, representational and instance levels. The object oriented modelling constructs that are useful for enterprise modelling include objects, abstraction, encapsulation, instantiation, inheritance, specialisation, polymorphism, composition, containment and association. The abstraction, encapsulation and representation of things meaningful to a business are referred to as business objects (Arrow *et al.* 1995). A business object model is an object oriented representation of a business domain, and is both methodology and language independent. Business object models can be developed at the three levels as described in Figure 1. The three levels correspond with the concept of abstract class, derived class and object in an object-oriented approach. The business object models are refined by either specialising or generalising the models as required by the designer of the business object model to an appropriate optimum level to enable reuse in different contexts. The different contexts of reuse are: reuse within the same organisation which built the model; reuse across vertical industries (i.e. companies within the same industrial sector e.g. Financial, Telecommunications, Health, etc.); or reuse across all industries. The final enterprise model would be a collection of all the business object models built and would be referred to as a generic object oriented enterprise model (GOOEM).

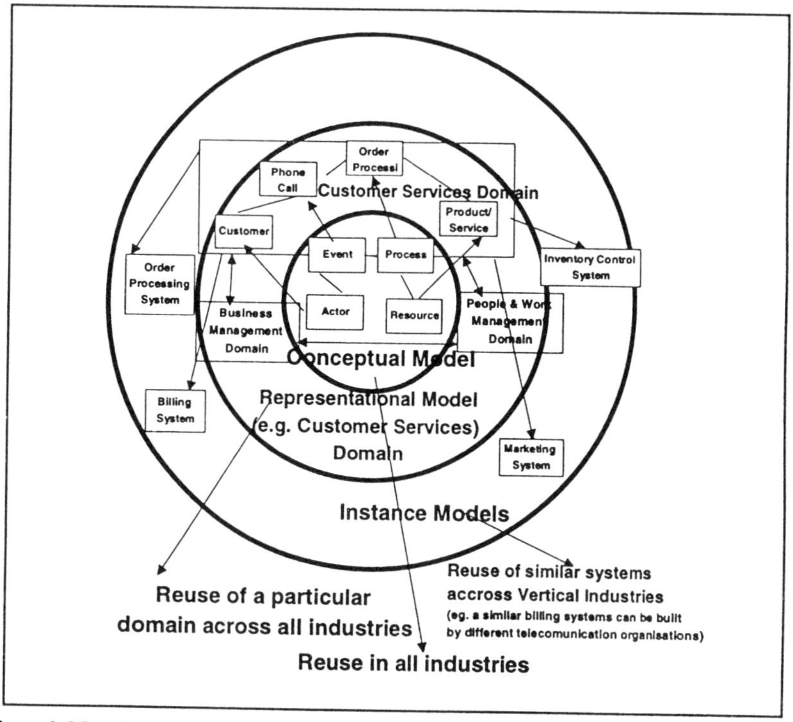

Figure 2. Mapping and Reuse Potential of the business object models at different Abstraction Levels

The following sections explain the conceptual level, representation level and instance levels in detail. These sections also explains through examples the steps required to build models at each level and the mappings between each level.

3. Conceptual Level of the GOOEMP

This refers to the generic concept objects within an enterprise such as Actor, Event, Process, Resource, etc. and their inter-relations. These terms are based on and developed from the enterprise ontology (Fox *et al.* 1992). These are the most basic terms that exist in all enterprises and can be the starting point to identifying the generic business domains and generic processes in an enterprise. Figure 3 shows part of a conceptual business object model containing the conceptual business objects and their interrelations.

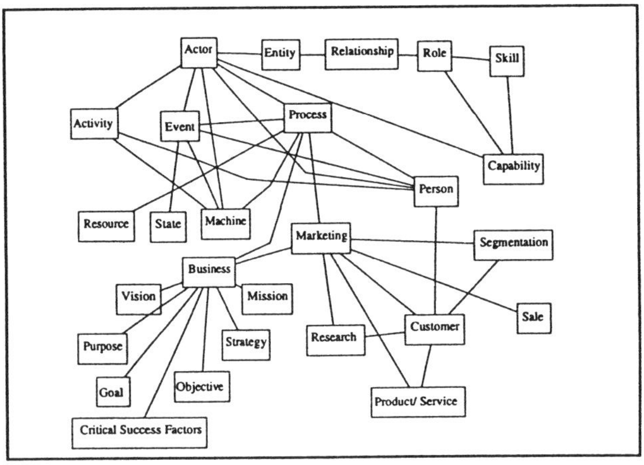

Figure 3. An Example Part of a conceptual model of an enterprise
(For simplicity the details of each link is omitted from this diagram)

4. Representational Level of the GOOEMP

The business domain can be divided up into various functional domains and the representational level refers to particular industrial domains being modelled, e.g. the customer services domain, business management domain or people and work management domain. The representational domain is built with the Generic Reusable Business Object Modelling (GRBOM) Framework (Choudhury *et. al.* 1997). The interactions of the conceptual business objects allows model developers to identify patterns with which to represent particular business processes and these business processes can be generalised to generic business processes. An example of one pattern, that could be extracted from the conceptual model, is the Actor - Event - Process - Resource (AEPR) pattern. The AEPR pattern can be found in several domains within an enterprise such as the customer services domain and can be generalised to the core, generic business processes of a domain. Figure 2, section 2 shows an example of mapping from the conceptual level to the representational level: Actor (Customer) is responsible for an Event (Phone Call) to a Process (Order Processing) to place an order for a Resource (Product/ Service). This pattern can be generalised to the Increase Business Generic Business Process of the Customer Service Domain. Many business patterns and generic business processes of the Customer Services Domain of the Telecommunications Industry have been identified (Choudhury *et al.* 1997).

Another important pattern that can be identified is the Process, Role, Actor, Capability (PRAC) pattern. This pattern is extremely important to the next stage of building an object oriented representational model. Figure 4 shows the transformation from generic business processes to business objects with attributes and methods. The tool used to develop the objects and subsequently the overall object oriented business object models was Rational Rose using the Unified Modelling Language (UML). The core generic business processes are identified for the industry. The core generic business processes in the telecommunication customer services domain have been represented in a core business model and is made up of five core generic business processes: Increase Business, Develop Product/ Service, Invoice and Collect Payment, Maintain Product/ Service, Initiate & Withdraw Product/ Service (Choudhury *et al.* 1997). Further studies into the customer services of the retail banking and fashion retail industries have shown similar core generic business processes. PRAC matrixes can be developed for each core Generic Business Process.

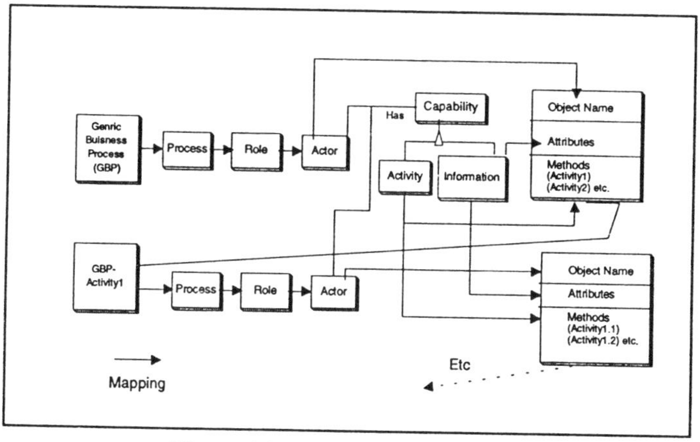

Figure 4. Transformation of Process to Objects

Table 1 is a Process-Role-Activity-Capability Matrix for the core generic business process, Increase Business. It is not in the scope of this paper to present all the results but a representative sample of the results is reproduced. The Generic Business Processes can be translated into roles played by actors with particular capabilities that allow them to carry out the process. The roles played by actors can be easily converted to objects with attributes and behaviour.

Type \ Pattern	Process	Role	Actor	Capability	
				Activity	Information
Generic Business Process (GBP)	Increase Business	Increase Business	Business Increaser	1.Handle Customer Contact (in)	Customers, Customer Events
				2.Handle Marketing	Product and Services Portfolio, Orders, Marketing Plan
				3.Manage Sales/ Lead and Prospects	Customers, Customer Events, P&S Portfolio, Sales Leads and Prospects
				4.Manage Sales Account	Customers, Customer Events, P&S Portfolio, Sales Leads and Prospects
GBP - Activity1 to Process	Handle Customer Contact (in)	Handling Customer Contact (in)	Customer Contact Handler	1.1 Manage Customer Dialogue	Customers, Customer Events
				1.2 Identify Reason for Contact	Customers, Customer Events
				1.3 Capture Customer Information	Customers, Customer Events
				1.4 Co-ordinate Customer Contacts	Customers, Customer Events
				1.5 Close Customer Contact (in)	Customers, Customer Events
GBP- Activity2 to Process	Handle Marketing	Handle Marketing	Marketing Handler	2.1 Develop Marketing Programme	P&S Portfolio, Orders, Marketing Plan
				2.2 Establish Monitoring Mechanism	Orders, Marketing Plan
				2.3 Run Marketing Program	Orders, Marketing Plan

Table 1. Part of a Process Role Activity Capability Matrix For Generic Business Process Increase Business found in telecommunications, retail banking and fashion retail industries.

As an example it can be seen that the Increase Business Generic Business Process can be converted to Increase Business Role which has to be carried out by a Business Increaser Actor object. The capability of that actor can be mapped to the responsibility of that object. The capability of an actor object is the total of all the business activities required to fulfil the responsibility of increasing business and is mapped to the operations of the business increaser actor object. The information required to fulfil the business increasing role is mapped to the attributes of the business increaser actor object. The attributes and operations are abstract at this stage. The activities of increase business can be further viewed as processes and the PRAC pattern can be repeated for each activity. This process is repeated until the discrete tasks carried out by each actor and the data areas required to fulfil these tasks are identified and represented in an object oriented model. The generic business processes can then be represented in an object collaboration diagram and an object interaction diagram. Once all the objects are identified the object collaboration diagram is developed to represent these processes. Figure 5 is a screen shot from the rational rose UML case tool, for part of the Increase Business collaboration diagram.

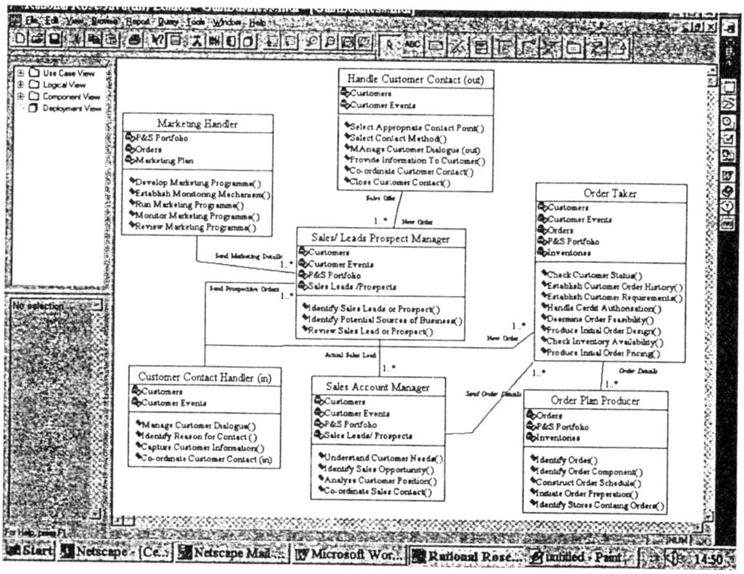

Figure 5. Screen Shot from a rational rose Object Collaboration Diagram - For part of Increase Business

The final result of this representational level modelling is a set of PRAC matrixes for all the generic business processes. A large static reference diagram of all the objects with their attributes and operations and links between all the objects is also developed. Finally, Object collaboration diagrams for all the generic business processes are developed. All these models are stored within the rational rose repository, for easy access of all the models, generic business concept objects, business process objects, business actor objects and business information objects.

5. Instance Level

The representational model can be used as a starting reference model to identify the systems that need to be built within a particular domain such as the Customer Services Domain. The instance model refers to actual instances of systems being built within the domain of interest. Jacobson's Use Case Engineering (Jacobson *et al.* 1995) approach was used to develop such systems. Each process is a use case containing an appropriate interaction of business interface objects, business control objects and business entity objects. Firstly it is important to identify the main areas of systems development. It was found that in the customer services domain of the telecommunications, retail banking and fashion retail industry, that four major areas were identified. These were Customer Handling Systems, Order and Product Management Systems, Billing Systems and Marketing Systems. Within each system various integrated applications need to be built. It is left to each industry to develop these systems and applications that suit the requirements of their particular organisation. The representational model would aid them in this task.

The instance model is developed from the repository of objects that have been built so far. Figure 6 shows how the various business objects could be used as building blocks and the subsequent interactions would be a solution to a particular business problem. A number of solutions could be proposed. These solution models are referred to as instance level models. These models would be provided to the systems, applications and technology experts to design actual systems for the organisation. Figure 6 shows the transformation from the Modelling level to the Physical Level via the Instance Level Model. Application developers and technology experts would have access to all the business object models built so far and they could adopt the most appropriate solution by discussing with the business experts and manipulating the business object models in such a way that the integrity of all the systems within the organisation would be maintained. As the business is represented as business objects, business people can communicate their needs with the systems and technology people in a language that everyone can understand.

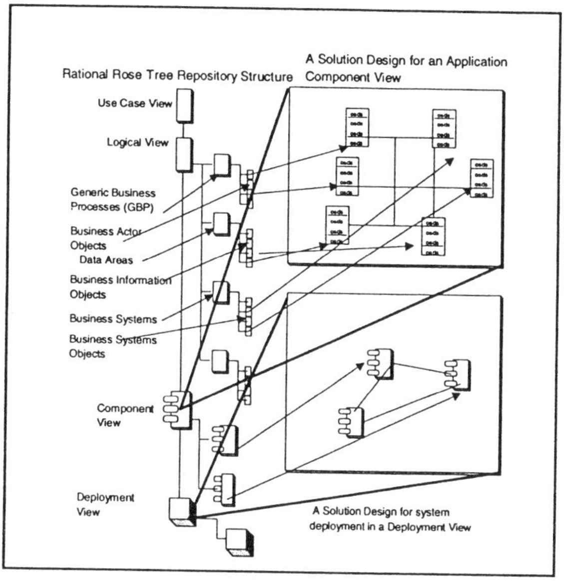

Figure 6 Business object component composition for solution designs using the Rational Rose Repository of models and objects - Instance Level Model

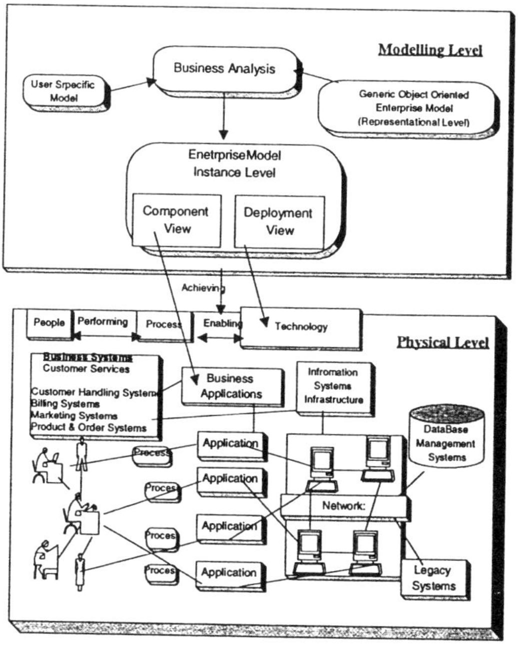

Figure 7 Modelling to Implementation

6. Conclusion

In this paper we have proposed a generic object oriented enterprise modelling process referred to as 'GOOEMP' for describing the steps required to build an integrated set of business object models within an organisation. Object oriented modelling constructs and the concept of business objects were invaluable for representing the various enterprise components at three different abstraction levels, which are conceptual, representational and instance levels. The rational rose case tool using UML was used to develop, store and manipulate these business object models.

Case studies carried out in British Telecommunications showed that the GOOEMP can be usefully applied in a real environment and some of the results were presented. It was important to evaluate the various issues addressed in figure 1 and figure 2, section 2. To enable this, two further case studies were carried out, one in the retail banking industry and the other in the fashion retail industry.

The issues that were addressed, for evaluation purposes include the reuse potential of various models at conceptual, representational and instance level. Also, reuse of various other components, models and objects. Further, flexibility; conceptual difficulty of implementing a solution to a problem starting from models at each of the three abstraction level, and the correctness, consistency, and usefulness of the information in the model.

From figure 1 and figure 2, it can be seen that reuse and flexibility is very high at the conceptual level. This is because the very general ontological concept objects can be found in all industries and this model can be adapted and reused easily in all industries. At the instance level, the models are too specific, and usually apply to one organisation. It is possible, if the model is built using the GOOEMP that some of the systems built would be similar to systems required in other organisations in the same industrial domain, e.g. if a billing system is built in a company within the telecommunications industry, a similar billing system could apply to another telecommunications company. However, the systems would be proprietary and very inflexible to change.

It was found that the most important issue being addressed is that of the conceptual difficulty to implementation. At the conceptual level, it is very difficult to map all the various concept objects on to an application, system or solution design, even though the reuse potential was high. At the instance level, it is quite easy to map on to an implementation but the reuse potential was low. It was found that the most appropriate and useful level for model reuse across industries is at the representational level. At this level generic domains are identified that are common across all industries, e.g. 'customer services domain', 'business management domain', 'people and work management domain' etc. The models built in these domains can be usefully mapped on to an implementation model and the models can also be usefully reused by different companies across several industrial sectors.

The main problem with obtaining information from an organisation and reusing it, is that this information is usually confidential, it represents a company's knowledge and expertise so the company will be reluctant to share their model. However we can foresee more of this knowledge becoming public over time especially if we can identify the right level of abstraction, generality and granularity. The most useful information that is required is that at the representational level for reasons identified earlier. The Massachusetts Institute of Technology (MIT) is developing a handbook of organisational processes (Malone, *et. al.*, 1997). When the book is published it will provide useful information required to help build more generic business object models at the representational level of abstraction.

Further work is underway to analyse, handle and evaluate the effects of change on these models and the impact it has on reuse using the change dimension of the GRBOM framework (Choudhury *et al.*). Further work is also underway to carry out a quantitative evaluation of reuse of the 'telecommunications industry customer services representation model', to measure the reuse potential of that model in the retail banking and fashion retail industry. This would be done by doing a statistical analysis of totalling up all the generic business processes objects, business activities, business information objects, business systems objects, business application objects, etc. discovered and developed from British Telecommunications. One-to-one mappings of each of the objects on to retail banking and fashion retail companies would be attempted. Correlation results will be a measure of the reuse potential.

7. References

Arrow, L., Barnwell, R., Burt, C. and Anderson, M.(eds.), 1995. OMG Business Object Survey. OMG Document 95-6-4. 25 May 1995

Bernus, P. and Nemes, L., 1996. A framework to define a generic enterprise reference architecture and methodology. *Computer Integrated Manufacturing Systems* **9(3)**, 1996, pp 179-191

Burkhart, R, Fulton, J., Gielingh, W., Marshall, C., Menzel, C., Petrie, C., and Zoutekouw, D., (1992). The Notion of a Model. *Proceedings of the First International Conference on Enterprise Integration.* Petrie, C. J., (ed.), pp 17-22.

Choudhury, I., Sun, Y., and Patel, D. (1997). Generic Reusable Business Object Model - A Framework and its Application in British Telecommunication plc. *OOIS97 Proceedings, 4th International Conference on Object-Oriented Information Systems.* Springer-Verlag, London.

Gale, T. and Eldred, J., (1996). Getting Results with the Object-Oriented Enterprise Model. *SIGS Publications,* New York.

Graefe, U., and Chan, W., (1993). An Enterprise Model as a design tool for information infrastructure. *Information Infrastructure Systems for Manufacturing (B-14), IFIP Transactions. Yoshikawa, H., and Goossenaerts (eds.)* Elsevier Science B. V., Holland., pp 183-192

Jacobson, I., Ericson, M. and Jacobson, A. (1995). The Object Advantage. Business Process Reengineering with Object Technology. *ACM Press.*

Malone, T.W., Crowston, K., Lee, J., Pentland, B., Dellarocas, C., Wyner, G., Quimby, J., Osborne, C., and Bernstein, A. (1997). Toward a handbook of organisational processes, *Centre for Co-ordination Science,* Massachusetts Institute of Technology, (http://ccs.mit.edu/CCSWP198).

Martin, J., (1989). Information Engineering, Book 1: Introduction, *Prentice Hall,* Englewood Cliffs, NJ.

Shelton, R.E.A. (1994). Object-oriented business engineering: delivering the distributed enterprise, *Proceeding of OOP'94,* London, 1994, SIGS Publications, New York.

Taylor, D. A. 1995. Business Engineering with Object Technology. *John Wiley and Sons, Inc.*

Vallespir, B., Chen, D., Zanettin, M. and Doumeingts, G., (1991). Definition of a CIM Architecture within the ESPIRIT Projects 'IMPACS', *Computer Applications in Production Engineering: Integration Aspects,* Elsevier, Amsterdam (1991) pp 731-738

Vernadat, F.B. 1992. CIMOSA - A European Development for Enterprise Integration. Part2: Enterprise Modelling. ESPIRIT Consortium AMICE. *Proceedings of the First International Conference on Enterprise Integration.* Petrie, C .J. 1992, pp 179-188

Williams, T.J. 1993. The Purdue Enterprise Reference Architecture *Information Infrastructure Systems for Manufacturing (B-14),* Yoshikawa, H. and Goosenaerts (eds.), Elsevier Science B. V., North Holland, pp 43-64

Zachman, J.A. A framework for information systems architecture, *IBM Systems Journal,* **26(3)**, 1987, pp276-292.

Class Identification in Business Information Systems

[1]Francesco Capozza, [2]Sergio deCesare, [3]Maria Carmina di Canillo

[1,3]Univeristy of Bari, Department of Statistical Sciences, Via Camillo, Rosalba, 53 - 70124 Bari
[2]South Bank University, School of Computing, Information Systems and Maths, 103 Borough Road, London, SE1 0AA

Email: [1] capozza@dss.uniba.it; [2] decesasa@sbu.ac.uk; [3]dicanillo@dss.uniba.it;

ABSTRACT: Many object-oriented methodologies have been proposed and presented as being suitable even for the analysis and design of business information systems (BIS). However, these methodologies lack in providing guidelines for the identification of the sequence with which subsystems and classes should be analysed. When modelling complex BIS, composed of many interrelated and interacting subsystems and objects, it would be opportune to define guidelines for determining the sequence with which classes are studied within an iterative and incremental analysis process. The objectives of such an approach are to handle complexity step by step, increase the quality of the final model, and augment efficiency and productivity.
This research study faces the issue of managing complexity in BIS analysis and proposes an object-oriented analysis process based on a preliminary decomposition of the BIS in different types of submodels and subsystems. The basic assumption of the process proposed in this paper is that the dynamic behavioural model, which defines states, transitions, and object interactions, is the most critical part of a BIS. The iterative and incremental process begins by analysing the most dynamic class (central class) and proceeds by identifying other classes which will be analysed one at a time on the basis of their class type and degree of coupling with other classes already analysed. The process proposed has been applied to analyse a case study of a transport enterprise BIS.
KEY WORDS: Business information systems, object-orientation, analysis process, submodel, subsystem, coupling, class type.

---

1. Introduction

Many object-oriented methodologies for software systems analysis have been proposed in recent years, e.g. (Booch, 1994), (Rumbaugh et al., 1991), (Shlaer and Mellor, 1988), (Coad and Youdon, 1990) (Jacobson et al., 1992). The main effort of methodologists has been to generalise these methodologies and make them suitable for modelling any software-based system, including business information systems (BIS) (Wang et al., 1998). For this purpose many methods and techniques based on the database paradigm and defined before the advent of object-oriented modelling, such as the entity-relationship model, data flow diagrams, etc., have been incorporated into object-oriented methodologies

All methodologies assume that classes can be identified from an initial set of formal or informal specifications. In many cases however specifications do not exist. For example, when a pre-existing BIS undergoes object-oriented reengineering as to add on new functionalities imposed by structural changes, or when re-organising operational procedures, the problem is normally defined by the modifications and additional requirements with respect to the pre-existing system. Even when specifications have been defined beforehand, they would be so voluminous as to not allow an easy identification of the many classes and relationships.

Furthermore, the development of a BIS requires enormous effort and a lot of time (generally years). As a consequence, new and different requirements normally arise during development, implying changes to the initial specifications and reorganisation of the development process. In order to reduce total project time, the classical waterfall model cannot be practically applied, but each phase should begin as soon as possible, i.e. design before analysis is completed, and implementation before design is terminated.

Therefore, complex BIS require a general process defining guidelines for the identification of all concepts relevant to the BIS model, i.e. classes, attributes, methods, relationships, constraints, states, events, etc.

2. Submodels and Subsystems

Business information system modelling should be capable of handling the intrinsic complexity of the business organisation. A way to tackle complexity is to pass from the real world business system to its corresponding information system through a series of coherent models. This enforces the iterative and incremental nature of the modelling process.

The BIS model can be decomposed into different submodels which represent complementary aspects of the system. The following submodels can be identified:

- **Simulation model**: simulates BIS structure and behaviour;
- **Information model**: represents queries and information retrieval;
- **Functional support model**: models tools for handling and avoiding anomalous situations, e.g. data recovery, reconstruction of secondary data, consistency checking of redundant data, fault tolerance, object deletion (preserving relationships), testing tools, on-line help, documentation, etc.

2.1 Simulation model

The simulation model is aimed at simulating the evolution of the modelled information system, by storing a sequence of events and related data (insertion, generation, etc.). The simulation model is composed of the structural and behavioural submodels.

Structural Model

The structural model represents system structure from a static viewpoint and is composed of:

- **Class Model**: represents system classes and objects along with the definition of their attributes, methods, constraints, and relationships. Class diagrams are used to represent this model;
- **External Interface Model**: defines and represents those systems that interact with the BIS.

Behavioural Model

The behavioural model defines system dynamics and is composed of the following submodels:

- **Object Behavioural Model**: represents the behaviour of objects. Object behaviour can be graphically represented by state and activity diagrams;
- **Object Interaction Model**: represents interactions among objects through message passing. The object interaction model can be represented by object interaction diagrams;
- **External Functional Model**: represents the system as an object that interacts with other objects, external to the system itself, determining how the system behaves globally, how it is viewed externally, and how it interacts with the outside world in terms of its inputs and outputs.

Another submodel, which can be called **inverse** or **complementary behavioural submodel** (with respect to the base model), should even include operations that do not correspond to normal real-world procedures, but which are generated instead by human error, failures or exceptional conditions even caused by the hardware and software system. If an operation produces its effects and is not correct or does not terminate correctly, operations for cancelling or correcting these effects must be defined.

Therefore, the inverse behavioural model represents those situations requiring business transactions to:

- rollback their effects passing from a present state to a past state;
- correct anomalous situations;
- execute operations that do not correspond to real-world procedures, but are caused by the information system itself.

2.2 Information Model

The Information Model concerns the modalities with which information needs are satisfied, i.e. collect and process data, related with the behavioural model, in different forms and compositions useful to the wide range of information needs. The behavioural model determines what happens, whereas the information model retrieves information on what has happened in the past (or on what can be predicted to happen in the future). It is obvious that a correct simulation model facilitates information retrieval. On the other hand, a simulation model which is incomplete or does not respond to the real-world system determines greater difficulty in retrieving information and in following the evolution of information requirements. Figure 1 illustrates the relationships between the different BIS models using the UML (Unified Modelling Language) Notation (UML, 1997).

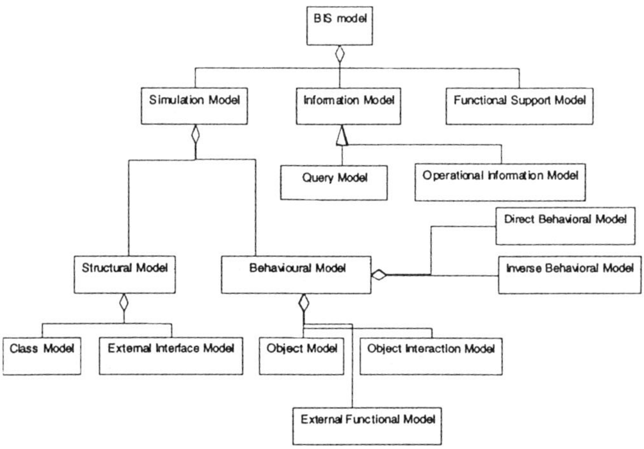

Figure 1 – General BIS Model

2.3 Simulation Modelling

The simulation model represents the core model (Figure 2) of the whole BIS model. Thus, in the initial phase of analysis, attention should be concentrated on the simulation model, in which real-world events are represented from a relevant information point of view. The behavioural model is the most important and most critical, because dynamics is more difficult to model and an error in this model is most likely to heavily propagate its effects onto the other submodels.

Simulation modelling is not complete until coherence with the requirements of other submodels (the information model especially) is verified. Concentrating on the simulation model means proceeding bottom-up. Many details are at first ignored. These relate with information querying, anomaly management, etc., i.e. operations that can be modelled relatively easily if the simulation model corresponds to the structure and behaviour of the real business system.

It is known that a complex system can be decomposed into subsystems, but even in this case the subsystems resulting from the decomposition must correspond to the structure of the problem. An object is in itself an elementary subsystem, since it can be considered as an aggregation of attributes and methods.

In a complex BIS a first way of decomposing the system is from a functional-organisational point of view (Taylor, 1995). Organisational units are identified along with their related operations and information needs. A criterion for identifying subsystems is to verify whether a set of operations can be automated independently from the rest of the system. For example, automation of customer and supplier accounting could be logically self-contained even if the rest of the accounts are not automated.

A preliminary decomposition into subsystems, carried out on the basis of a functional-organisational analysis and considering past experience or information acquired from the literature, is opportune as to divide the system into parts whose complexity can be managed more easily. As to reduce complexity a usual and logical approach would be to analyse one subsystem at a time.

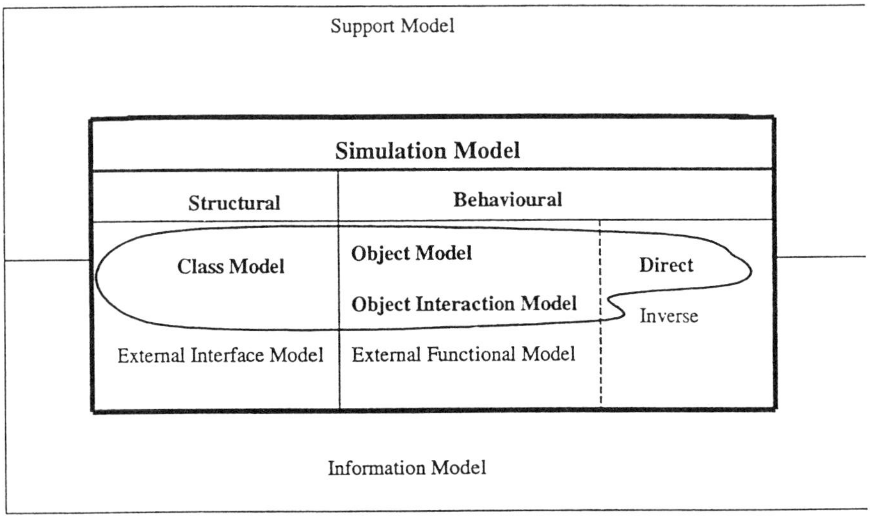

Figure 2 – Simulation Model as the BIS Core Model

3. BIS Objects Classification

Most BIS objects (or business objects) can be classified according to their degree of dynamics. The most dynamic objects evolve through a sequence of events and state transitions: For each state, possible events and corresponding transitions should be defined. These objects can be defined as **process objects**[1], in the sense that they evolve through a process.

The main purpose of some objects, essentially static in nature, is to provide information to other objects and can be classified as **service objects**.

Some objects represent BIS results and, thus, be called **result objects**. Result objects can be terminal objects or may evolve on the basis of new processes. For example, an invoice can be the result of a process, but at the same time it can evolve through new processes.

Process, service, and result classes can be defined as subclasses of the general modelling concept class.

An eventual reorganisation or reengineering or extension of BIS requirements have an impact on the processes of dynamic objects as when to execute operations or whether to execute them at all. For example, whether to print the bill of lading after generating a shipment or before the departure of the vehicle. Processes can be reorganised and parameterised. Service objects are in general less dependent on the process, because they correspond to automated information requirements (a significant example is a table coding different possible cases). Whether the services provided by these objects are automated or not, does not influence the behaviour of the information system as a whole. The absence of a service object (e.g. VAT table), only changes the degree of automation, control, and data input, in other words the user interface (i.e. input the VAT percentage each time) and does not heavily condition dynamic processes. Service objects are essentially tools utilised by processes to produce results. Hence, their definition is logically subordinated to processes.

Result objects can be viewed as terminal objects of processes. Their impact is determined by the fact that processes should be able to produce the results. Terminal result objects do not have further impact on the behavioural model. Instead, result objects become dynamically relevant if they become part of subsequent processes.

4. Subsystem Coupling

Two subsystems sharing the same process objects are strongly coupled, up to the point that there may be doubts on whether they should be defined as two separate subsystems or only one. Coupling is weaker if the final states of one process and the initial states of another are defined (sequential coupling) or when the processes are parallel. Coupling is even weaker if a dynamic object of one subsystem is a service object in another subsystem. Service coupling between subsystems is even weaker. The weakest form of coupling is between subsystems that generate result objects of the same class.

A scale of the degree of coupling, in descending order, could be the following:

- **Process coupling**: two subsystems share process objects;
- **Parallel coupling**: two subsystems process an object contemporarily, from different perspectives (it is equivalent to offices handling copies of the same document);
- **Sequential coupling**: two subsystems process the same object in sequence;

---

[1] Note that in this paper the term process object does not refer to a process modelled as an object.

- **Generation coupling**: result objects of a subsystem are processed by another;
- **Service coupling**: objects of a subsystem represent service objects for another subsystem.
- **Result coupling**: two subsystems generate result objects of the same class;

5. Scheme of a Business Information System Analysis Process

As to manage BIS complexity during analysis, the following steps (Figure 3) can be followed:

1. Decompose the system into subsystems in a preliminary phase;
2. Define the simulation model of a subsystem, taking into account the requirements of the information model;
3. Verify that the simulation model is coherent with the requirements of other submodels;
4. Complete the model by analysing the remaining submodels one at a time, and complete and modify, if necessary, the submodels previously analysed.

The following sections, describing the analysis process proposed in this work, refer to the simulation model. Analysis conducted with this process is consistent with the objectives and criteria of subsequent phases (design and implementation), such as iterative and incremental development, rapid prototyping, decomposition of work activities, resource management and project scheduling. A preliminary definition of the simulation model allows flexible organisation of the work that follows.

A process defining ways of analysing and identifying classes is useful for decomposing work into a series of steps. Each step is focused on a smaller and less complex part of the problem. Consistency control is a fundamental part of every step, i.e. verify that the submodel is consistent with submodels defined previously. An analysis process is effective when it reduces initial errors. The presence of errors implies costly corrections and the risk of introducing inconsistencies. This is why analysis should follow a consistent incremental scheme.

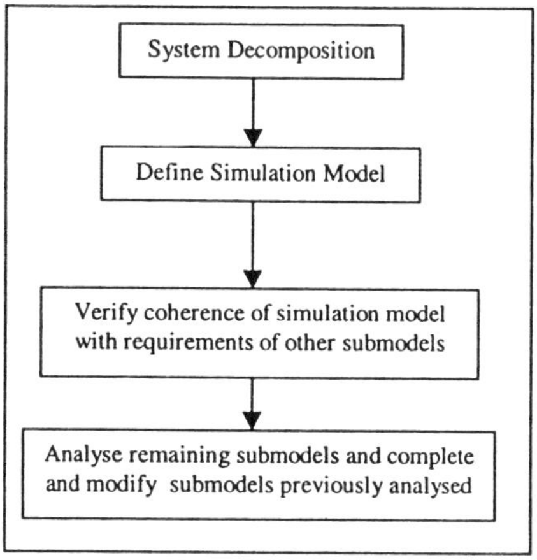

Figure 3 – BIS Analysis Process Macrophases

6. Central Class and Central Subsystems

When a BIS is decomposed into subsystems, there normally is a class whose behavioural model is extremely articulated and relevant to the system, and a few subsystems (often just one) representing processes of objects of that class. This class and these subsystems can be called **central class** and **central subsystems**, respectively. Central subsystems are generally highly related and can be considered as a single subsystem. Decomposition is nevertheless useful for complexity management.

The central class usually corresponds to dynamic objects whose treatment represents the BIS's main objective, e.g. products in a manufacturing enterprise, merchandise items (dynamically viewed) in a commercial enterprise, shipments in a transport enterprise, banking transaction in a bank, a journal entry in an accounting system, etc. The central class generally possesses the following characteristics:

- A very articulated inheritance hierarchy;
- Many attributes and methods;
- Many state transitions and events, i.e. complex state diagrams;
- Used by many subsystems;
- Related to many other classes (process, service, and result classes);
- Many information queries;

- Many associated business processes and exceptions.

Input operations related to central class objects are usually particularly complex and articulated because of the many relationships with other objects. As a first step it is therefore opportune to identify and analyse the central class.

7. Process

As with major object-oriented methodologies, the phases of the process proposed in this paper are aimed at identifying all concepts relevant to the BIS model (classes, relationships, states, events, etc.). Unlike other processes, however, the initial step is the identification of a central class which to build upon.

The BIS model is developed iteratively and incrementally. A generic process iteration is composed of the following phases (Figure 4):

1. Choose a class or a subsystem (the central class is the first class to be identified and selected);
2. Identify relationships (associations and inheritance hierarchies) and attributes;
3. Identify states and events for dynamic objects (state diagrams);
4. Identify methods;
5. Identify object interaction (object interaction diagram);
6. On the basis of the state diagram identify other concepts;
7. Verify the coherence of the concepts identified with BIS output requirements and consistency with previous steps;
8. Classify the classes identified during the iteration (process, service, result);
9. Iterate the previous steps until the analysis is complete.

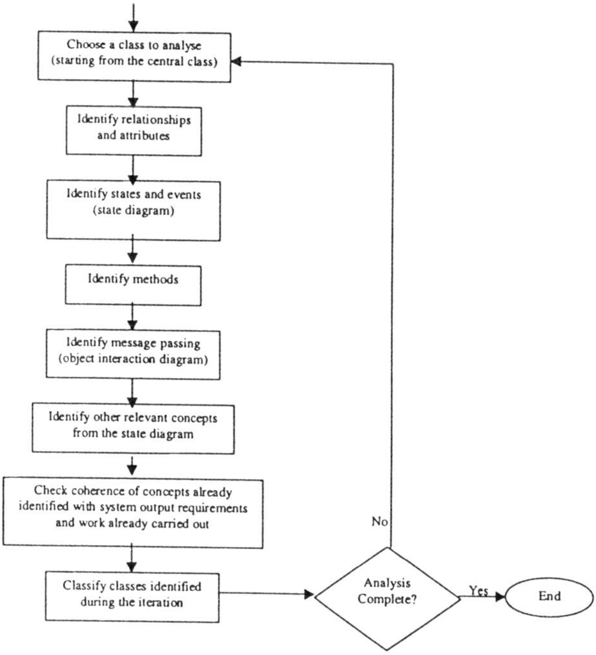

Figure 4 – Simulation Modelling Microphases

The first iteration is dedicated to identifying the BIS central class and defining its initial structure and dynamics. Further iterations are finalised at analysing other classes which have emerged previously and refining the model defined up to that moment.

As modelling proceeds from one process iteration to the other, one must decide which class to analyse next. A possible criterion is to first analyse process classes, and then service and result classes. This sequence responds to a logical principle: support and result handling can only be modelled after knowing the nature of the classes to service or send information from. Since process classes are normally more complex to model than others, this criterion is also justified by another principle, i.e. face complex issues first. Complex classes are more difficult to analyse, require more time, and, most importantly, affect the model of other associated classes. Therefore, if classes with minor complexity were to be studied first, this would most probably result in having to make major modifications afterwards. In an iterative and incremental process change is intrinsic, but since productivity is important as well, modellers should be able to take decisions which at every iteration bring the model a step closer to being complete, rather than making it more distant from reality. Each iteration should, in other words, bring the model one step further from the initial entropy it originated from.

Most object-oriented methodologies do not exclude this way of analysing the system. Nevertheless, the processes suggested by methodologists tend to initially identify classes and not the class. Furthermore, present methodologies do not classify classes according to their characteristics and importance. Identifying many classes implies dealing with many subsystems in the very first stage, because all of the classes identified would most likely belong to different subsystems.

8. Process Phases

The first iteration of simulation modelling is aimed at identifying the BIS central class and central subsystem. The BIS central class can be identified by starting from a brief description of the business' main activity. This description is generally sufficient in identifying the business core activity and therefore its most relevant concept.

Once the central class has been identified the next step is to identify its attributes and relationships. A general principle of the modelling process is not to force the identification of concepts, but wait until they naturally emerge. This could happen at any time and in any iteration. Thus, although only a few attributes and relationships could emerge initially, they are generally sufficient as to give clues as to what other concepts can be identified. During each phase any concept can emerge and when this happens the model should be incremented with its representation. This means that if the phase is dedicated to identifying attributes and relationships, for example, and relevant states and events eventually emerge, then these states or events should not be ignored and annotated for future reference. Attributes and relationships can be identified by analysing documents which accompany process objects during their lifetime and represent their information manifestation.

Any useful technique can be utilised in identifying concepts: classical approach (Coad and Yourdon 1991), behavioural analysis (Rubin and Goldberg, 1992), use case analysis (Jacobson et al., 1992), Linguistic-Based Information Analysis (Coad and Argila, 1996), etc. These approaches are generally considered as being aimed at identifying classes, nevertheless they can be deployed for the identification of any modelling concept. This shows how structural and behavioural aspects are closely inter-linked, especially in BIS, confirming that structure and behaviour should not be modelled separately, but in parallel.

The identification of states and events is modelled by analysing a description of the business process involving objects of the central class or, more in general, of the class being analysed. The result of this phase is a state diagram, which will be used to identify new concepts or refine the model. The state diagram represents the basis for identifying class methods: state diagrams model behaviour as a process and methods model behaviour through the definition of operations.

Process, service, and result classes are identified. A table (Figure 5) summarises this step. This table can summarise the following aspects:

- Subsystem in which the class is defined;
- Class type: process, service, or result;
- Degree of coupling with the class analysed in the iteration (class coupling is the same as the degree of coupling between the subsystems the classes belong to).
- Events generating objects of that class. This is necessary as to define degree of coupling;
- Precedences: objects that must pre-exist before creating a new object (e.g. a client must generally exist before executing an operation involving a client);
- Subjective relevance representing an evaluation of the importance of a class in the system with respect to classes of the same type.

In order to choose the next class to analyse, classes should be ranked according to their importance in the system. Possible ranking criteria follow:

1. Analyse process classes first, followed by service and result classes, respectively;
2. Analyse classes with highest degree of coupling, from process to result coupling (Section 4);
3. Precedence, preference is given to objects of classes which temporally precede other objects;
4. Class relevance.

Class	Source Subsystem	Class Type	Coupling	Object Generating Events	Relevance	Precedence

Figure 5 – Structure of a summary table

In each iteration, previously defined models must be controlled and eventually completed or modified. A recurrent situation is the identification of similar concepts, e.g. similar classes. This implies a process of generalisation and the definition of a superclass which modifies the inheritance hierarchy.

9. Case Study

9.1 Context and Basic Assumptions

The object-oriented process for BIS proposed in this paper has been applied to model a transport enterprise BIS. The transportation domain is a significant example of a specific business domain, since it is centred on a service requiring complex data handling and behavioural modelling. Many concepts are common to all, or many, types of businesses.

A transport enterprise is typically organised into the following subsystems: Shipment Management, Invoicing, Payments, Accounting, Internal Accounting, Correspondent-Distributor Accounting, Analytical Accounting, and Statistics. These subsystems coincide with functional units (e.g. offices) that handle these activities in a transport enterprise.

The central class is shipment and the central subsystem is the Shipment Management subsystem. This subsystem can be decomposed as follows: Collection, Departures, Deliveries, Receipt of Payments, Held Shipment Management, Damaged Shipment Management, Warehousing, Contracts (commercial office), and Communications (contacts with clients, correspondents, and distributors). By observing an existing BIS, other subsystems can be identified, e.g. Locations, Persons, and Conveyance.

In the initial phases of analysis useful information can be extracted from documents handled by the system: bill of lading, manifests, invoices, held shipment and documentation related to damaged shipments.

Two main functional units are competent for shipment management: the departure and delivery offices. The Departure subsystem handles shipments transported from the shipper to the destination branch, whereas the Delivery subsystem handles shipments transported from the destination branch to the final consignee.

Another shipment management function is collection, i.e. phase in which a short distance vehicle collects shipments from the shippers' premises. Collection is not a candidate for being central, because it refers to grouped unidentified shipments, which will be identified later on.

9.2 Central Class and Central Subsystems

At first it is not clear which subsystem (Departure or Delivery) is more relevant. As to manage complexity, it would be preferable to analyse them separately and eventually merge them afterwards, if they result being tightly coupled. From a temporal viewpoint, the departure of a shipment precedes its delivery, thus it would be logical to start analysing the departure subsystem first. This is how automation in transport enterprises has historically evolved: departures have been generally automated before deliveries. This decision most probably does not influence the final result of analysis significantly.

The following classes emerge from the analysis of the departure subsystem: Bill of Lading, Label, Shipment Manifest, Master, Branch, Client, Consignee, Transport Contract, Correspondent, Item, Supplier Contract, Package, Shipper, Vehicle, and Waypoint. All classes are associated to shipment. Table 1 summarises the classes identified during the first iteration along with their characteristics. Item and package simply compose a shipment and therefore cannot be considered process, service, or result classes.

From the analysis of the Departure subsystem two process classes emerge: COD and invoice. These classes belong to the Receipts of Payment and Invoicing subsystems, respectively, which have already been identified previously on the basis of the business' organisational structure. Both subsystems are coupled to Departure subsystem by process coupling.

Analysis of the shipment class should be completed by analysing shipment management in the Delivery subsystem. Table 2 documents the classes that emerge during this analysis. The only process classes that emerge are Held Shipment and Damaged Shipment. Held Shipment is process coupled with both the Departure and the Delivery subsystems, because it concerns shipments that may be sent back to the shipper or redelivered, respectively. Other bonds between the Departure and Delivery subsystems also emerge. When analysing the process a shipment undergoes, variations of normal shipping emerge. These variations, direct and local shipping, show how departures and deliveries are strongly coupled and could be merged.

During this phase the Distribution Vehicle subclass emerges, implying that a generalised Vehicle class should be defined, whereas the Vehicle class defined in Table 1 should be more appropriately renamed Long Distance Vehicle. Even the Contract class can be similarly refined (a new Distribution Contract subclass is defined).

Class	**Source Subsystem**	**Class Type**	**Coupling**
COD	Receipt of Payments	P	Process
Invoice	Invoicing	P	Process
Bill of Lading	--------	R	--------
Label	--------	R	--------
Manifest	--------	R	--------
Master	--------	R	--------
Branch	--------	S	--------
Client	Persons	S	Service
Consignee	Persons	S	Service
Transport Contract	Contracts	S	Service
Correspondent	Persons	S	Service
Item	--------	C	--------
Supplier Contract	Contracts	S	Service
Package	--------	C	--------
Shipper	Persons	S	Service
Vehicle	Conveyance	S	Service
Waypoint	Locations	S	Service

Table 1 – Shipment analysis summary table (Departure Subsystem)

Legend: P-Process, S-Service, R-Result, C-Component, ---- Subsystem not yet identified

Class	Source Subsystem	Class Type	Coupling
Held Shipment	Held Shipment Management	P	Process
Damaged Shipment	Anomaly Management	P	Generation/ Process
Deficit	--------	P	--------
Surplus	--------	P	--------
Journal Entry	Accounting	P	Generation/ Process
Distribution Master	--------	R	--------
Distributor	Persons	S	Service
Distribution Zone	--------	S	--------
Distribution Contract	Contracts	S	Service
Distribution Vehicle	Conveyance	S	Service

Table 2 - Shipment analysis summary table (Delivery Subsystem)

Legend: P-Process, S-Service, R-Result, ------ Subsystem not yet identified

The decision on which class to analyse during the third iteration should be taken on the basis of the criteria explained in section 8 applied to Table 1 and Table 2. Process classes which can be candidates for the next iteration are: COD, Invoice, Held Shipment, Damaged Shipment, Deficit, Surplus, and Journal Entry. Only COD, invoice, and held shipment are process coupled with the Departure and Delivery subsystems. Hence, one of these three classes will be chosen (Table 3).

Class	Object Generation Events	Precedes
COD	Generation of a shipment with COD	Invoice Held Shipment
Invoice	(Many different events and cases)	Not relevant In this case
Held Shipment	Undelivered shipment	Invoice

Table 3 – Decision Table

9.3 Second Iteration: COD

Candidate classes for the second iteration are: COD, invoice, and held shipment. COD and held shipment precede invoice from a temporal point of view. The decision lies between COD and held shipment. COD is selected, because in a shipping process a COD is generated before a held shipment.

Subsequent iterations follow the process defined above, i.e. process classes, such as held shipment, invoice, etc., first, followed by service and result classes, respectively. The most important service classes that will emerge during analysis are person, contract, vehicle, etc. Their importance is determined by the number of subclasses, precedence, and relevance.

An intuitive sequence based on the importance of subsystems perceived by the people working in the organisation could have lead to analysing the Departure subsystem first, followed by Invoicing, COD, Held Shipment, Delivery, etc. Since important dynamic aspects of Delivery, COD, and Held Shipments subsystems would have been initially ignored, the model would have been heavily perturbed in later phases when considering new dynamic aspects. On the contrary, it is very important that process classes are identified and modelled in the initial phases.

Almost all classes and most of the modelling concepts (about 80%) have been identified during the analysis of the departure and delivery subsystems.

In the case study, as analysis proceeded, the model has been gradually refined and several specialisations have been identified. Many of these specialisations were related to service classes. Hence, at least in this case, analysing service classes after process classes has been appropriate, because the inheritance hierarchies have been defined with a broader knowledge of the problem.

10. Conclusions and Related Topics

The process proposed in this paper provides guidelines for the analysis of a complex BIS, like the transport BIS modelled as a case study in this work. In each step the analyst's attention is concentrated on a limited part of the whole system. The system is studied starting from the most relevant aspects and the model is progressively completed. Every phase is concluded by checking the coherence of the results obtained with results of previous phases and overall requirements.

Bibliography

Booch G. (1994), Object-Oriented Analysis and Design With Applications, Benjamin/Cummings, Redwood City, California.

Coad P., Yourdon E. (1990), OOA -- Object-Oriented Analysis, 2nd Edition, Prentice Hall, Englewood Cliffs, New Jersey.

Jacobson, I., Christerson, M., Jonsonn, P., Overgaard, G., (1992). Object-Oriented Software Engineering, Addison-Wesley.

Rubin, K., Goldberg, A., September 1992. Object Behavior Analysis. Communications of the ACM, vol. 35(9), p.48.

Rumbaugh J., Blaha M., Premerlani W., Eddy F., Lorensen W., (1991) Object-Oriented Modeling and Design, Prentice Hall, Englewood Cliffs, New Jersey.

Shlaer S., Mellor S.J., (1988). Object-Oriented Systems Analysis: Modeling the World in Data, Yourdon Press: Prentice Hall, Englewood Cliffs, New Jersey,

Taylor, D.A., (1995). Business Engineering with Object Technology, John Wiley & Sons.

UML Notation Guide, Version 1.1, September 1997.

Yourdon, E., Argila, C., (1996). Case Studies in Object Oriented Analysis and Design, Yourdon Press Computing Series.

Wang, Y., Choudhury, I., Patel, D., Patel, S., Dorling, A., Wickberg, H., (1998). *A Perspective on Foundations of Object-Oriented Information Systems*, in Proceedings of the 1998 International Conference on Object Oriented Information Systems, Springer.

Author Index